73958

8t Groms cleys
for VGL

SPC   1921   +18

Best wishes

Peter Brunn

6. Dec. 1983.

Economic images

Current economic controversies

Peter Browning

Longman
London and New York

Longman Group Limited
Longman House, Burnt Mill, Harlow
Essex CM20 2JE, England
Associated companies throughout the world

*Published in the United States of America
by Longman Inc., New York*

First published 1983

British Library Cataloguing in Publication Data
Browning, Peter
  Economic images.
  1. Economics
  330.1   HB171

  ISBN 0-582-29630-7

Library of Congress Cataloging in Publication Data
Browning, Peter, 1920–
  Economic images.

  Bibliography: p. 214
  Includes index.
  1. Economics. 2. Monetary policy — Great Britain. I. Title.
HB71.B779   1983   338.941   82-13086
ISBN 0-582-29630-7

Set in 10/11pt Linotron 202 Plantin
Printed in Hong Kong by
Wilture Printing Co. Ltd

Contents

Part four

Preface

'I think I should understand that better,' Alice said very politely, 'if I had it written down: but I'm afraid I can't quite follow it as you say it.'

Lewis Carroll, Alice's Adventures in Wonderland

The preface is where the author pays his thanks and makes his excuses for inflicting upon the public 'another damned, thick, square book'.

My first thanks are to all those authors upon whose shoulders I have stood and who have allowed me to use their insights and their words. A full acknowledgement of copyright is made elsewhere; but I must acknowledge a special debt to Professor Hutchison for his books on Keynes and the Keynesians, and on economics and economic policy. In the matter of books generally, Joe Wormald eased my task considerably by his kindness in making available to me, beyond the call of librarianship, a number of key sources.

I thank George and Heather Rowe, and Bernie Sluman for reading an early typescript, and for their comments and encouragement.

For help in converting my raw material into a finished product I am indebted to Liz Peyton, Jane Thompson, Susan Smallwood and Di Westbeech; and I am very grateful to Longman's anonymous reader for his constructive criticism.

All the opinions and remaining errors are mine. The book was written between the end of 1980 and March 1982, and it will bear the marks of that period. By the time it appears in print, events will have moved on. It would be foolish of me to suppose that what I have to say is of permanent interest, although I do hope it will survive and be relevant for the span of a year or two. But, alas, some parts of the story, notably those concerned with the early British monetarist experiment, will date. For these parts I ask the tolerance of the reader who comes to the book when they are history.

Keynes opened the Preface to the *General Theory of Employment, Interest and Money**** with these words: 'This book is chiefly addressed to my fellow economists. I hope that it will be intelligible to others.' I could almost turn that round and say that this book is chiefly addressed to 'others' but I hope it will be intelligible to my fellow economists. Almost, but not quite: I am sure it will be intelligible to economists; whether they will also find it agreeable, in both senses of that word, is another matter.

Anyone who has ever tried to present a rather abstract scientific subject in a popular manner knows the great difficulties of such an attempt. Either he succeeds in being intelligible by concealing the core of the problem and by offering the reader only superficial aspects or vague allusions, thus deceiving the reader by arousing in him the deceptive illusion of comprehension; or else he gives an expert account of the problems; but in such a fashion that the untrained reader is unable to follow the exposition and becomes discouraged from reading any further.

The words in that paragraph are not mine, but Albert Einstein's[†] and they express my difficulty precisely (over-precisely at one point, for I cannot conceive of an illusion that is other than deceptive).

Whether I have succeeded only the reader can say. For me, I plead that, like Alice, I thought I might understand it better if I had it written down; and I did. I hope you do too.

Peter Browning

---

[*] Through the text this title will occasionally be abbreviated as GT.
[†] *The Universe and Dr Einstein*, Lincoln Barnett. Gollancz 1949.

Acknowledgements

We are grateful to the following for permission to reproduce copyright material:

George Allen and Unwin for extracts from *Economics and Economic Policy in Britain 1946–66* by T. W. Hutchinson; the author's agent for the poem 'In Broken Images' by Robert Graves; Macmillan, London and Basingstoke, The Royal Economic Society and Harcourt Brace Jovanovich Inc for extracts from *The General Theory of Employment, Interest and Money* by John Maynard Keynes; Times Newspapers Ltd for extracts from 'The Problems of the Steady Level' *The Times* 12.1.37, an extract from 'Dear Money' *The Times* 13.1.37 and extracts from 'Borrowing for Defense: Is It Inflation' *The Times* 11.3.37.

He is quick, thinking in clear images;
I am slow, thinking in broken images.

He becomes dull, trusting to his clear images;
I become sharp, mistrusting my broken images.

Trusting his images, he assumes their relevance;
Mistrusting my images, I question their relevance.

Assuming their relevance, he assumes the fact;
Questioning their relevance, I question the fact.

When the fact fails him, he questions his senses;
When the fact fails me, I approve my senses.

He continues quick and dull in his clear images;
I continue slow and sharp in my broken images.

He in a new confusion of his understanding;
I in a new understanding of my confusion.

Robert Graves, 'In Broken Images'

Part one

Particulars are not to be examined till the whole has been surveyed.

Dr Samuel Johnson

Chapter one
Introduction

And we are here as on a darkling plain
Swept with confused claims of struggle and flight
Where ignorant armies clash by night.

Matthew Arnold

Over the last decade an economic doctrine known as monetarism has come increasingly into favour. So much so that we now have the unusual spectacle of a Government identified with this doctrine; indeed, to the dismay of some of its supporters, identified with little else; dismay because the main short-term result of the application of monetarist doctrine seems to have been a depressed economy and a considerable increase in unemployment. In the longer term, we are assured, benefits will accrue, and that may well be so.

The feature of monetarism which is, not unnaturally, most prominent is the commitment to the control of the money supply. But there is more to monetarism than that. Monetarism requires a faith in the efficiency of markets and part of its purpose is to extend the area of economic life subject to the discipline of the market. In this it bears a marked resemblance to the system of economics understood and taught by the so-called classical economics; monetarism has been styled 'the new classicism'.

The classical system of economics was extensively modified, some would say undermined, by John Maynard Keynes because it appeared to be incapable of coping with the problem of chronic unemployment. We now, so it seems, are again experiencing a combination of classical economics and unemployment. We appear to have come full circle.

This poses a number of questions; is new monetarism old classicism writ anew? If so, and if Keynes was right in his criticism of the old classicism and if his theories and proposals made it possible to eliminate unemployment, why cannot his remedies be applied today to the new classicism? Or was Keynes wrong anyway?

These are the major questions which this book sets out to investigate; and the plan, if that is not too strong a word, of the book flows from the questions. In Chapter 2 we look at the economic orthodoxy which Keynes inherited and found wanting. Chapter 3 introduces Keynes and the climate of his times, and in Chapter 4 we conclude Part I with a consideration of his new economic theory – the General Theory.

Just as we cannot understand Keynes without an appreciation of the times in which his theories were developed, so we cannot understand monetarism without some appreciation of the circumstances which gave it life. So, in Part II we move from the theories of the 1930s to the policies of the United Kingdom in the post-war years and we consider in Chapter 5 how far the failure of these policies could be fairly attributed to Keynes. In Chapter 6 we take a first look at the new monetarism; we consider, in Chapter 7, certain similarities and suggest that the new monetarism is perhaps less old classicism than an extension, in an important respect, of Keynes. Keynesianism attracts those of the political left and centre and monetarism those of the political right. In Chapter 8 we consider why this should be so.

Parts I and II have been concerned with the unfolding of theories in the context of their times. In Part III we come closer to the events of today and to the problems and policies of today. We begin with the money supply. There may be more to monetarism than the control of the money supply, but that, nevertheless, remains central to the doctrine. So in Chapter 9 we consider whether there is something called the money supply, the control of which would be beneficial; and how it might be controlled. In Chapter 10 we look at recent British experience in applying monetarist theory; and an Appendix analyses the medium-term financial strategy.

The popularity, if that is the word, of monetarism in the late 1970s and 1980s, stemmed from its claim that to control the money supply was the only way permanently to cure inflation. On the other hand, Keynesianism was held, by some, largely to blame for inflation. Inflation therefore, is a testing ground for the theories and their related policies. Moreover, the problem of inflation has been with us for a long time and it is worth trying to understand the issues for their own sake, apart from their relevance to the debate between monetarists and Keynesians. The next two chapters of Part III are therefore devoted to inflation and its control. Chapter 12 contains an analysis of the nature of wage bargaining, a matter central to an understanding of incomes policies. Chapter 13 and its Appendix investigates the important matter of the relationship between employment, real wages and the money supply.

All the analysis up to this point has been conducted largely in terms of a closed economy, that is to say an economy without foreign trade. This helped to focus on the essentials of the arguments; but clearly we *do* have foreign trade, including flows of capital. Chapter 14 introduces the foreign sector and its related problems; and there is an Appendix on a neglected matter – the terms of trade.

In Part IV Chapter 15 summarises the main features of the alternative 'models' we have been looking at. Finally, there is a summing up.

To summarise, Part I begins with the Classical system of economics and outlines Keynes's theory and its origins. Part II shows how this theory was applied, or misapplied, and introduces monetarism in both its economic and its political clothing. Part III focuses on some of the prominent issues of the day: the money supply, inflation and its control, the nature of wage bargaining and the relationship between these things. Part IV compares the different economic models, and sums up.

To those who come to the book with a curiosity about current economic controversy but without any formal economic education and without much background knowledge of the development of economic doctrine, the book is perhaps best read in the order presented. Others, that is to say those familiar with Keynes's work and with monetarism, may find Parts I and II tedious – although I would hope that even here they would find something of interest – and may care to move on to Parts III and IV where matters of more contemporary concern are discussed.

The book does not include a discussion of the scope and method of economics, interesting though that might be: I want to get straight on with the business of untangling present economic controversies. But to get the most out of a book it always helps if one approaches it with certain specific questions in mind, and this is perhaps particularly so with economics, because the ramifications of the subject are so many, and the scenery along the way sometimes so fascinating, that one can forget where one is going. Accordingly, it will be useful to have at the back of our minds the major questions that economists studying this branch of economics are trying to answer. They are:

1. What determines the level of output and employment?
2. What determines the price level?
3. What are the causes of inflation?
4. How much does money matter?

Questions 2 and 3 are closely related and could be put together into 'What determines the price level and its rate of change?'

To help them answer these questions economists develop 'models'. At first sight the idea of an economic model may seem rather daunting, and indeed some models do daunt. But it need not be so. Economic models can be very rudimentary affairs, and everybody with an economic opinion has one, although he may not realise it. If, for example, one believes in the slogan that inflation is 'too much money chasing too few goods', that implies an economic model of the way the economy works.

A model does two things. It describes the way the economy is believed to work, the way, that is, that the main 'variables' – such as the money supply, government spending, interest rates, the exchange rate, wages, prices and employment – react with one another. Secondly, it strips this scheme of things down to its essentials, so as to display its properties.

We may take an analogy from the motor car. We know what a motor car is, and we know what a scale model car is – it is the same thing only smaller. An economic model is not that sort of model. An 'economic model' of a car would not be a physical thing, but would be a description written down, and it might run something like this: A motor car is a device for carrying up to five people in a seated position, with a wheel at each corner, and an in-built source of energy conversion that transmits power to the wheels to drive the vehicle forward. It has a steering device and simple controls to regulate speed and bring it to a stop.

Simple economic models give us just enough information to envisage the essential structure of the beast. Economic models are very useful as a pedagogic aid and to enable us to carry in our minds and manipulate all the major aspects of a structure that is, in reality, highly detailed and complex. But, by definition, a model of the kind we are talking about can be constructed only by a process of heroic abstraction. And we must never forget that our model *is* an abstraction and not a real economy. It can be dangerous to try to translate directly to the real world theories derived from simple models. (It may be even more dangerous to translate complex models under the delusion that a model with 500 equations is 50 times closer to reality than one with 10.)

I have tried throughout to make the argument accessible to the non-economist. But economics is a complex subject and it is difficult, even for economists, to fit all the pieces together; and there may be places where the non-economist gets lost. If that happens, I apologise. But whilst I will readily admit that more patience or more care or more understanding or more clarity on my part might have made the road to understanding easier, I would also plead that there *is* no easy road to economic understanding. Economics *is* a difficult subject, and it would be as well to be suspicious of anybody who pretends that it is not. With economics we are in a position akin to that of the man who held that 'anyone who isn't confused here doesn't really know what's going on'.

I would suggest that those who do meet a difficulty should look it squarely in the face, pass on to the next section and come back to it later. One of the problems with economics is that everything depends on everything else and there is no linear presentation which will clear all of the conundrums out of the way in neat order; it may well happen that something said later will illuminate an earlier obscurity. In short, I would ask the reader for a certain amount of patience and a measure of goodwill. Keynes makes the plea with characteristic eloquence:

It is, I think, of the essential nature of economic exposition that it gives not a complex statement which even if it were possible, would be prolix and complicated to the point of obscurity, but a sample statement so to speak, out of all the things which could be said, intended to suggest to the reader, the whole bundle of associated ideas, so that, if he catches the bundle, he will not in the least be confused or impeded by the technical incompleteness of the mere words which the author had written down, taken by themselves.

This means, on the one hand, that an economics writer requires from his reader much goodwill and intelligence and a large measure of co-operation; and, on the other hand, that there are a thousand futile, yet verbally legitimate, objections which an objector can raise.[1]

Notes

1. *Collected writings* Vol. xiii, pp. 469–70 (quoted by D. E. Moggridge in 'Keynes: The Economist', in *Keynes: Aspects of the Man and his work*.)

Chapter two
Orthodoxy

The difficulty lies not in the new ideas, but in escaping from the old ones, which ramify, for those brought up as most of us have been, into every corner of our minds.

Keynes[1]

What was this orthodoxy that held Keynes, no puny spirit, in such a Jesuitical hold?

The search for order and understanding

The early study of economics had its roots in moral philosophy and the concept of natural law. Adam Smith's ' . . . whole approach developed out of the natural law foundation'. 'The Wealth of Nations was in fact the first fully systematic quasi-natural law treatment of economics'.[2,3]

A system of natural law supposes that there is an underlying order to material phenomena, and that the 'laws' of this system may be discovered. If these laws are immutable it follows that there is little point in disputing them; and whether they work to the benefit of mankind or not is really beside the point, since they cannot be repealed. What is required is a society free of artificial constraint so that the laws may work; and a degree of belief that 'nature', who made the laws, is not an idiot and that all will work out reasonably well in the end. The natural lawyers would not have agreed with Voltaire that 'the secret of the arts is to correct nature'. It is not, I think, too fanciful to suggest that some such faith in 'natural law' forms the philosophical basis of the modern monetarist school; and leads to the suggestion that modern monetarism is old classicism revisited.

The body of classical economic knowledge and economic theory was built up through the search for these natural laws, for an understanding of how the system worked; how it came about that, without any central direction, goods were in shops and warehouses for people and merchants to buy, that factories were built, food grown, the labourer, the entrepeneur and the rentier rewarded.

The answer lay, and, for capitalists, lies, in three things: self-interest, competition and the price system. Self-interest will lead, or drive, a man to work to produce those goods and services which others are willing to pay for. The operation of the price system, in a competitive environment, will signal those things that are required. Competition, operating on prices, will allocate resources to where they are most needed.

The system thus established is self-regulating, self-correcting, always tending towards some sort of equilibrium, albeit a moving equilibrium because the economy never stands still.

Supply and demand

The laws of supply and demand establish, together, the price and the quantity of goods bought and sold. It is common experience that if a commodity becomes cheaper more will be bought. It is also sensible to believe that as prices are bid up, more of a commodity will be supplied. The proposition that more can be supplied only at a higher price does depend on an assumption that production has already passed the point where unit costs are falling. However, it does no great violence to experience to assume that, at least in the very short run, more can be supplied only at greater cost, for example because overtime has to be paid or because inferior land or machinery has to be brought into use.

We may therefore draw up two schedules, one relating the quantity demanded to price (the demand schedule); and the other relating the quantity supplied to price (the supply schedule). (The schedules are also called 'functions', quantities both demanded and supplied being said to be, in mathematical terminology, 'functions of price'.)

It is possible of course that the two schedules so drawn up would not match, or meet, the lowest supply price being higher than the highest demand price. For goods in common trade, however, there would be a correspondence, so that the schedules matched, at least roughly and at least in part. If we make the assumption that the two schedules are made up of very small gradations of price and quantity – are 'continuous functions' – then there will be an exact correspondence of price and quantity at some point. Since this price and this quantity satisfies both buyer and seller, trade will take place. Price is determined not by demand, not by supply but by the two operating together, rather like the two blades of a pair of scissors. The

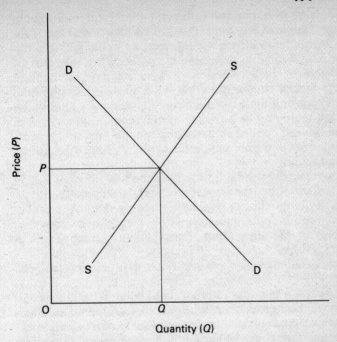

Fig. 2.1

concept, probably the best known and most powerful in economics, is illustrated by the well-known diagram shown in Fig. 2.1

The demand schedule slopes downwards from left to right, indicating that greater quantities are demanded as prices fall; and the supply schedule slopes upwards from left to right, indicating that greater quantities are forthcoming only at higher prices. Trade takes place at price P when quantity Q is traded. Of course, this is all highly schematic. In practice it is not as simple as that: for example, if traders do not have perfect knowledge of the market, (as customarily they will not have) trade will take place at 'false' prices, i.e. prices other than P. So economic theory assumes either perfect knowledge or a system of auction and re-contract; both quite unrealistic assumptions and an example of the dangers of translating economic theory directly into real life. Nevertheless, the theory and the diagram are extremely fruitful. We can see, for example, how necessary is the assumption of competition. (Not necessarily 'perfect competition' which itself, as already suggested, requires a number of assumptions.) If there was only one (monopoly) supplier, or a few

9

suppliers acting in combination, then the supply curve (a straight line can be a curve in this context) would be a horizontal line if the supplier wanted to decide the *price* at which he would sell; or a vertical line if he wanted to determine the *quantity*. But note that he cannot determine both (unless he picks a point on the demand schedule). Similar arguments apply to a single (monopsonistic) buyer. Of course, if there is a monopoly supplier and a monopsony buyer, then there may be no solution: price and quantity could be indeterminate and decided by bargaining. So, for their proper functioning, the laws of supply and demand require competition among buyers and sellers.

The diagram may also be used to illustrate how the price system allocates resources, i.e. the resources of land, labour, skill and capital available for production, which are always, limited *and* have alternative uses. Indeed, 'the economic problem' may be defined as 'the problem of allocating scarce resources with alternative uses to competing ends'.

The schedules of demand and supply are, as it were, photographs of the situation at a point in time. They assume all influences fixed; incomes, tastes, techniques of production, political conditions and so on. If these change, then the schedules move. Suppose for example that the demand curve is the demand schedule for ostrich feathers just before they go out of fashion. When this happens the curve drops sharply towards the origin 'O'. The resources devoted to growing ostrich feathers must be diverted to some other use. The point need not be laboured. With or without the use of the apparatus of supply and demand curves, we can see that changes in income, in the distribution of income, and in tastes are reflected in what consumers will pay for goods and these changes in the *relative* price of things induce producers and entrepreneurs to shift resources to where they will yield the greatest return. Or, to be more precise, to where they think they will yield the greatest return: miscalculations can be made, leading to a misallocation of resources.

No value or political judgements are made in this method of resource allocation. It is not necessarily the 'best', in some sense, or the most just allocation. It is merely the way in which a competitive market, reflecting self-interest on the part of both buyers and sellers and operating through the price system allocates resources. It can of course be overridden; by taxes, subsidies, controls, rationing or, more subtly, by a redistribution of income. It can also be influenced by advertising.

We have talked so far of the demand for and supply of goods. Similar principles can be applied to labour and to money.

Wages

Real wages, that is to say the real value of what wages will buy after adjustment for the price level, are governed by real output, that is, the physical product of labour. This is easily seen if we consider a total real output, O, produced solely by a number of workers, N. The average real output (wage) per worker must be neither more nor less than $\dfrac{O}{N}$. That is only the average: it may be that some workers, one way or another, are able to obtain more than the average – but then others must take less, since the total to be divided is fixed. It may be argued that real wages could be increased by taking a share of profits. That is possible; but that is really only an extension of the principle; it is either an argument about how much wages and profit *did* actually and separately contribute to real output; or, if that is not in dispute, it is one party taking more than his earned share and another less. The sum of the real output of the separate factors of production cannot exceed, or fall short of, total real output.

The theory of wage determination is unsatisfactory in both 'classical' and present day economics. Wages are taken to be a price and determined by supply and demand, just as is the price of goods. But while a can of beans is a can of beans, a worker may be any one of a thousand different sorts. Workers are not a homogeneous product. Nor does a worker have a cost of production – and it is cost of production which underlies supply price. Labour is perishable: the labourer does not have the option of withholding his labour indefinitely, (unemployment pay and supplementary benefit notwithstanding) should he consider the offer price too low. Labour is not, as we have remarked, homogeneous: there is an almost infinite variety of jobs; workers even within one class of job have different training, experience, skills, aptitude, energy and application. Labour is not always, perhaps not usually, sold in a competitive market: on the one side, there are unions and on the other there may be only one, or few employers. (The market for television news readers, for example, is limited.)

It is thus extremely difficult to squeeze the demand for and supply of labour, and thus its price and the quantity employed, into the straightjacket of supply and demand analysis.

Nevertheless, this is what economic theory does. There is, after all, a supply of and a demand for labour, and however complex and untidy the factors underlying this supply and demand, the two must meet. So, for the purposes of general equilibrium theory, it is assumed that the wage level (price) and the level of employment (quantity) are jointly determined by the conditions of supply and demand for labour. It is also evident that each firm's demand for labour schedule must be based on what that labour is worth to the firm, i.e. what it produces. In economic language, a firm will find it sensible to employ (and therefore to demand) labour up to the point where the cost of one additional worker is equal to the additional revenue which that worker produces (his marginal revenue product).

We have said that supply and demand determine not only the wage but the number employed, i.e. the level of employment. We have also seen that the real wage cannot overall and for very long differ from real output. From this it followed, for the pre-Keynesian orthodoxy, that if there was unemployment it was because the real wage was too high. The cure for unemployment was to lower the real wage.

In terms of Fig. 2.1 the supply curve was too high and thus cut the demand curve at a point to the left of Q, assuming Q to represent full employment. It might be argued that instead of lowering the supply curve (reducing real wages) full employment could be restored by raising the demand curve (shifting it to the right). But to do that would imply (since demand was being increased) that there was a deficiency of demand. And the pre-Keynesian orthodoxy held that a deficiency of demand was impossible because, according to **Say's Law,** supply created its own demand.

Say's law was derived essentially from a non-monetary economy, that is, a barter economy, and it is surprising that it survived so long, unquestioned, into the economics of monetary economies, which are rather different. But survive it did. One reason for its survival was that money was not accorded an active role in the working of the economy: it was little more than a lubricant, or, to change the analogy, a sort of veil beneath which a 'real' economy worked. In a barter economy it is true that supply does constitute demand: if I come to market with *supplies* of commodity A, I cannot do business without *demanding* commodities B, C . . . etc. Say's law can be true in a money economy but it is not self-evidently as true as it is in barter.

Interest

We have dealt with the price of goods and the price of labour, and must now deal with the determination of the rate of interest. In the pre-Keynesian orthodoxy interest was a 'real' not a monetary phenomenon, although it was expressed, like everything else, in the money of the day. The rate of interest brought into equilibrium the demand for and the supply of savings.

In saving, consumers abstained from consumption *now* in the expectation of consumption in the future. Present pleasures have a premium over future (and therefore uncertain) pleasures, and therefore the act of abstention has to be paid for.

The higher the reward for abstaining (saving), the more will be saved. It is thus easy to conceive a supply curve of saving which (with the rate of interest in the vertical axis and the quantity saved on the horizontal axis) slopes upwards from left to right.

To earn interest, savers have to lend to someone. (No interest is paid on hoarding, whether of notes, specie or goods.) Borrowers will borrow only if the money borrowed will earn its keep, i.e. pay the rate of interest. The real rate of interest paid, or willing to be paid, by borrowers depends on the return to be obtained from whatever use the borrowed money is put to. Suppose a new piece of machinery costing £1,000 can produce additional revenue of £150 a year. Then it is, just, worth borrowing at 15 per cent. If there are some projects which will yield a return of 15 per cent then it is probable that there are fewer projects which will yield 25 per cent and more projects which will yield a modest 10 per cent or 5 per cent. Bringing all such projects together in an aggregate demand schedule for savings, we can draw a schedule of demand for savings which slopes downwards from left to right, the demand being smaller at high rates of interest and greater at lower rates.

Again, the intersection of the supply curve of savings with the demand curve for investment determines the rate of interest and the amount saved/borrowed.

It is perhaps worth noting that we are talking here of *new* savings and *new* investment or, in economic terms, of flows of saving and investment. But saving and investment both have a 'life' and there will also exist *stocks* of saving and investment. The distinction between stocks and flows is an important one in economics and its ready recognition perhaps one of the marks distinguishing the experienced economist from the tyro. (There will also be stocks and flows in a pure barter exchange: there is nothing to say, unless the theorist specifies it, that the parties to barter have to barter all their supplies in any period. A barterer may hold some back. But this could be categorised as 'demand for own product' and added to the demand schedule).

Money

Having settled the determinants of the major aggregates in the real economy – output, prices, wages, employment, investment and the rate of interest – we now turn to the role of money.

Money's major function – apart from its usefulness as a means of exchange, of transacting business – was to determine the price level (but see below).

The basic proposition of the Quantity Theory of Money had been recognised since the beginning of the classical period at the end of the eighteenth century but its definitive formulation came from Irving Fisher in his now famous equation of exchange

$$MV = PT$$

where M is the quantity of money, V is its velocity of circulation (the number of times each piece of money changes hands within a period) P is average prices and T is the number of transactions. The two sides of the equation are by definition equal, indeed it is not an equation but an identity.[4] As an identity it has no analytical content, but as an equation certain assumptions can be made to illustrate certain truisms.

The velocity of circulation V is believed to be fairly constant, as it derives from custom and institutions. If we for argument assume that T, the number of transactions in a period, is also fairly constant (at the full output level, as the orthodoxy would suggest) then the moveable parts are M and P; the money supply determines average prices. (The alternative proposition that average prices determine the money supply was not usually considered, possibly because the money supply was assumed to be specie, or specie-based, and therefore outside voluntary control by the authorities.) Even without assuming anything about the relative stability of V and T we can see that

$$\frac{MV}{T} = P$$

We can also deduce that if prices and transactions are fixed or given then, with a fixed and given quantity of money, velocity must increase until the equation be satisfied. Equally, if changes in the money supply M are necessarily to affect P and T, then V *must* be stable. (Otherwise changes in M could be absorbed by an inverse movement in V.)[5]

Although the early economists regarded money as important mainly for its effects upon the price level, they did nevertheless recognise that it could have a significant effect upon output (and through demand and output, on prices). An initial inflow of gold and silver (the basis of the money supply) was seen as gradually working its way through the economy as the original receivers of the additional money sought to employ it or spend it. The initial expenditure had the usual ripple effects spreading outwards through the whole economy (what we would now call multiplier effects) raising demand, output and, after a lag, prices. Once a new level of wages and prices was established, the effect ceased. Some of the increased output came from the more efficient or intensive use of resources (higher productivity) but it is interesting that, (despite Say's law) some initial unemployment, or at least underemployment, seems to have been implicitly assumed. A contraction in the money stock would have opposite effects.

The system

We can now bring together the elements of the economic orthodoxy as it existed when Keynes wrote his GT.

Equilibrium in the market for goods and services was established by the laws of supply and demand operating through a flexible system of prices, reflecting individual preferences and the (flexible) responses of supply to changing demand. Although there might be temporary disturbances; e.g. crop failure, causing economic depression and unemployment, in the longer run there could be no shortage of demand because the act of supply created its own demand.

Wages and the level of employment were also determined by the laws of supply and demand applied to labour. If real wages were higher than the equilibrium price, employment would be lower. Employment could always be increased by lowering the real wage, and there could, therefore, be no such thing as involuntary unemployment.

The amount of investment in production goods (and thus, in the longer-term growth of the economy) was dependent upon the technical conditions of production, new invention and the rate of interest. More opportunities for investment would raise the demand for capital, raise the rate of interest and thus call forth more savings. A dearth of investment opportunities would lower the rate of interest and reduce the incentive to save. An autonomous increase in saving would lower the rate of interest and thus bring more investment within the range of profitability.

The *relative* prices of goods, services and labour were determined by supply and demand in the appropriate markets. The *absolute* price, the price level, was determined by the quantity of money. If

15

prices were 'too high' then domestic goods became relatively more expensive than foreign goods, the balance of trade deteriorated, gold flowed out and (gold being the basis of the money stock) the quantity of money fell, prices fell and the foreign balance was, in time, corrected. Conversely, if internal prices were lower than the foreign competition, gold flowed in, credit expanded and (in the process sketched in above) the ripples of expenditure spread throughout the economy, raising output and, after a lag, prices. (The main lever affecting the balance of trade was seen to be the *relative price* of domestic and foreign goods but some earlier economists, foreshadowing Keynes, saw *incomes* as a factor.)

That, in very broad outline, was the system. The essential assumption underlying it was that it was a *natural* system, obeying certain natural laws (mainly the pursuit of enlightened self-interest) which always and necessarily operated in such a way as to bring the system back into equilibrium, should it depart from that state. It followed from this, or at least it was thought to follow, that any intervention to 'correct' the system, could only make matters worse.[6] Much of the fervour of the present-day monetarists flows from a passionate belief in, free enterprise and the self-correcting nature of a free-market economy.

Notes

1. Closing words of the Preface to *General Theory of Employment, Interest and Money* (Macmillan 1954).

2. D. P. O'Brien, *The Classical Economists*, Clarendon Press, Oxford 1975.

3. If moral philosophy went off into economics in one direction, it went off into religion in another. In Chapter I of Book V, Smith devotes 65 pages to 'the expenses of institutions of instruction' in the course of which he deplores the degeneration of the teaching of moral philosophy into a sub-branch of a joyless theology so that 'Casuistry, and an ascetic morality, made up, in most cases, the greater part of the moral philosophy of the schools'.

   Two pages further on (and this had little to do with moral philosophy) he deplores the English practice of sending young people to travel abroad instead of to university, a practice engendered by 'the discredit' into which the universities had fallen. The unfortunate young person: 'at a distance from the inspection and control of his parents . . . commonly returns home more conceited, more unprincipled, more dissipated, and more incapable of any serious application, either to study or to business, than he could well have become in so short a time had he lived at home'.

   Latter-day fathers whose sons and daughters have left the dole queue

to make the pilgrimage to Sri Lanka, Kathmandu or wherever can reflect on Smith's parting shot:
'By sending his son abroad, a father delivers himself, at least for some time, from so disagreeable an object as that of a son unemployed, neglected, and going to ruin before his eyes.'

Smith's long – and delightful – discourse on education does not, however, lead him to any firm conclusion on who should pay:
'The expense of the institutions for education and religious instruction is likewise, no doubt, beneficial to the whole society, and may, therefore, without injustice, be defrayed by the general contribution of the whole society. This expense, however, might, perhaps, with equal propriety, and even with some advantage, be defrayed altogether by those who receive the immediate benefit of such education and instruction, or by the voluntary contribution of those who think they have occasion for either the one or the other.'

(Compare Milton and Rose Friedman 'What's wrong with our schools?' in *Free to Choose* (Secker and Warburg 1980). The Friedmans strongly criticise the American educational system and make proposals, including a voucher system, for giving parents a wider choice and relief to the taxpayer.)

There seems very little, from the distressing proclivities of the young to the moral superiority of the Romans over the Greeks, that Adam Smith did not feel able to bring under the umbrella of economics. Modern textbooks are more to the point, but with some loss of entertainment value.

All quotations are from *Inquiry into the Nature and Causes of the Wealth of Nations*, Vols I and II. (Henry Frowde, Oxford University Press 1904; first published in 1776.)

4. A distinction may be drawn between the *identity* $MV \equiv PT$ and the equation $M\overline{V} = P\overline{T}$ in which V and T are assumed constant, or stable, and a causal relationship is assumed running from M to P. (The bar over the V and T signifies that they are constants).

5. V, velocity, is money on the wing; but at any time, all the money in existence must be held by someone somewhere. We can therefore develop a formulation which expresses this. In the Fisher equation it becomes

$$M = \frac{PT}{V}$$

$$= \frac{1}{V}(PT)$$

which says that people hold a fraction $\frac{1}{V}$ of the value of all transactions in the form of money.

From here we can move to a more modern formulation of the Quantity Theory, known as the Cambridge equation.

The Fisher formulation is in terms of *all* transactions, not all of which will be for goods and services, and *income* is a measure only of the value of goods and services produced in a period. If we exclude transactions not included in income, we can write Y (= income) for PT to yield

$$MV = Y$$

$$M = \frac{1}{V}Y$$

But this is not quite correct because $\frac{1}{V}$ is the reciprocal of the *transactions* velocity (relevant to PT) and we want the reciprocal of the *income* velocity, appropriate to Y. Call this K. The Cambridge equation then becomes

$$M = KY$$

which says that K is the proportion of Y that people want to hold in cash (money). Again, we can see that the effect that changes in M will have on Y depend upon the stability of K. If K is volatile, the effect on Y is unpredictable. We can now see why it is so important for modern monetarists to establish, one way or another, that 'the demand for money' is stable.

The Cambridge formulation is important because it focuses attention on reasons for holding money. It was the basis upon which Keynes (a Cambridge economist) developed his theory of liquidity preference. It also underlies modern monetarist theory.

6. Some flavour of the neo-classical school and its vitality at the London School of Economics *c.* 1930 may be gained from the following extract from Sir John Hicks's *The Formation of an Economist* (Banca Nazionale del Lavoro, Sept. 1979)

'What we economists thought we were doing was not only to bring to life the inheritance of the British Classical Economist, but also to widen the horizons of the British economists of our own time by bringing in a refreshment from what was being done, and had been done, in other countries.'

'. . . . I was readily seduced by the great 'neo-classical synthesis' . . . according to which a competitive system, free of monopoly elements, which would only grow if they were buttressed by state 'interference', would easily find an 'equilibrium'. I was willing to apply this doctrine, even to the labour market; though there I had some reservation . . .'

Compare Friedman *et al* today.

Chapter three

A distinguished heretic

The reason of the new doctrines recommended them to some, their novelty to many; the hatred and contempt of the established clergy to a still greater number; but the zealous, passionate, and fanatical, though frequently coarse and rustic eloquence, with which they were almost everywhere inculcated, recommended them to by far the greatest number.

Adam Smith[1]

The climate of heresy

Between January 1931 and May 1933 in the United Kingdom the percentage of insured workers unemployed never fell below 20 per cent. In August 1932 and January 1933 it reached 23 per cent, its highest point. In the 19 years from January 1921 to January 1939 the January count never fell below 10 per cent. It was scarcely the picture of an economy self-equilibrating at the full employment level.

The social history of the period has been well documented – the hopelessness of the unemployed, the hunger marches, the General Strike of 1926 which carried the fear of revolution. To those alive in the 1920s and 1930s chronic unemployment (and, incidentally, great inequalities of wealth, income and privilege), appeared as the natural – or, in another sense, the unnatural – state of affairs to which existing social and political arrangements provided no solution.

Abroad, notably in the United States after 1929 and in Germany, it was a similar story. In Germany, Hitler offered, and provided, a solution. Germany and Italy solved the unemployment problem by the imposition of authoritarian states and the regimentation of the people.

What alternative was offered by those economists, then, as ever, for the most part good, socially concerned and compassionate men,[2] who sought a solution within a liberal-democratic framework?

They offered varying and contradictory diagnoses of the problem. To some it stemmed from a saturation of wants, and the consequent stagnation of the economy. With between one-tenth and one-quarter of the population unemployed and their families living in poverty, this was scarcely plausible.

To others, and these were in the majority, the depression stemmed from under-consumption and a lack of demand. Their remedy was public works.[3] The state should 'prime the economic pump' by employing people to build roads and other useful things. The money thus spent (income generated, as we would now say) would, as well as providing direct employment, lead to the employment of others providing goods and services to those primarily employed. The economy would, as it were, lift itself by its own bootstraps. This remedy had the approval of many, perhaps most, of the leading economists of the day[4] (the most notable exceptions were Robbins and Hayek at the London School of Economics) and of politicians. The proposals foundered, in the United Kingdom, for two, related, reasons.

1. Practically, they were opposed by the Treasury, who did not believe in bootstrap economics but did believe in a balanced budget. Any money borrowed to pay for public works would be at the expense of industry. Thus public works could make no net addition to employment. This was the essence of the famous, or infamous, 'Treasury View' of 1929. By the mid 1930s the Treasury may have become more receptive of Keynes's ideas.[5] This 'crowding out' theory has re-emerged, in a new form, under the new monetarists.
2. The practical proposals of the economists could not be reconciled with their accepted theory. They were thus in a weak position in arguing (against the Treasury view) the theoretical, as distinct from the pragmatic, justification for their proposals.[6]

The heretic

It was to provide the theoretical underpinning for public works *in conditions of substantial and chronic unemployment* that Keynes wrote the *General Theory of Employment, Interest and Money*. It is worth noting the precise wording of the title: it is more than a theory of employment.

In order to understand the GT and the controversies which it has generated, and still generates, it is essential to understand not only the circumstances, the historical time, in which it was written – of which the briefest sketch has been given above – but also something of Keynes himself.

There is now a vast and still growing literature about Keynes, his life and his work, the writing of which constitutes a sort of Keynesian cottage industry. I do not propose to add to it. But it is important to understand two things about him: his philosophy and his power.

Keynes, the apostle of the philosopher G. E. Moore, believed above all in the individual, in the importance and value of the individual life. Life was for living. The most important time was now. The possibility of the good life should be open to all men. And when the time of 'economic bliss' came, as he was reasonably sure it would, 'We shall honour those who can teach us how to pluck the hour and the day virtuously and well, the delightful people who are capable of taking direct enjoyment in things, the lilies of the field who toil not, neither do they spin.'[7] The bourgeois capitalist society, purged, so far as may be, of its impurities, offered, in his view, the best prospect of the future he wanted and predicted.

Keynes concludes the GT with 'Notes on the Social Philosophy towards which the GT might lead'. He notes that there will be some '. . . central controls necessary to ensure full employment', but these apart 'there is no more reason to socialise economic life than there was before'. There will

. . . still remain a wide field for the exercise of private initiative and responsibility. Within this field the traditional advantages of individualism will still hold good.

Let us stop for a moment to remind ourselves what these advantages are. They are partly advantages of efficiency – the advantages of decentralisation and of the play of self-interest. The advantage to efficiency of the decentralisation of decisions and of individual reponsibility is even greater, perhaps, than the nineteenth century supposed; and the reaction against the appeal to self-interest may have gone too far. But, above all, individualism, if it can be purged of its defects and its abuses, is the best safeguard of personal liberty in the sense that, compared with any other system, it greatly widens the field for the exercise of personal choice. It is also the best safeguard of the variety of life, which emerges precisely from this extended field of personal choice, and the loss of which is the greatest of all the losses of the homogeneous or totalitarian state. For this variety preserves the traditions which embody the most secure and successful choices of former generations; it colours the present with the diversification of its fancy; and, being the handmaid of experiment as well as of tradition and of fancy, it is the most powerful instrument to better the future.

Thus, the state was to be responsible (for no one else was[8]) for ensuring that demand was kept at a sufficiently high level for all to be employed who wished to be employed. Beyond that, all was to be left to the market, the individual and the pursuit of self-interest. It is an irony which Keynes himself might have enjoyed that the man who believed so passionately in the benefits to the individual of the bourgeois capitalist society should be categorised, as he has been, as the economic father of socialism.

Keynes has been accused, with some truth, of being arrogant, of presenting his arguments in an unnecessarily combative and strident manner, of being cruel to those 'classical' economists whom he chose to ridicule or, as some would have it, whom he set up as straw men. But from this distance we have to remember that at the time he wrote, in the mid-thirties, capitalism and its economists were seen to be incapable of curing the all-pervading malaise of chronic unemployment; and the only remedy seen to work was fascism in its various forms. Keynes was desperate to provide *and to have accepted* a non-fascist solution and thus provide at least the possibility of preserving the sort of bourgeois democratic society which, for him, was the only society worth living in. Wild words he may have used, but with a purpose: 'Words ought to be a little wild' he said 'for they are the assault of thoughts upon the unthinking.'[9] Keynes sought to explain the world partly in order to shape it to his image of the sort of world that was desirable; and partly to provide a theory that accorded with observed phenomena.[10]

If Keynes was to succeed in his purpose he had not only to provide a restructuring of economic theory but to have it accepted by economists, civil servants and politicians and its policy implications put into affect. His success in the latter task was astonishing,[11] perhaps even to Keynes himself, who had written in the final paragraph of the GT:

But if the ideas are correct – an hypothesis on which the author himself must necessarily base what he writes – it would be a mistake, I predict, to dispute their potency over a period of time. At the present moment people are unusually expectant of a more fundamental diagnosis; more particularly ready to receive it; eager to try it out, if it should be even plausible.

He follows this with a much-quoted passage:

But apart from this contemporary mood, the ideas of economists and political philosophers, both when they are right and when they are wrong, are more powerful than is commonly understood. Indeed the world is ruled by little else. Practical men, who believe themselves to be quite

exempt from any intellectual influences, are usually the slaves of some
defunct economist. Madmen in authority, who hear voices in the air, are
distilling their frenzy, from some academic scribbler of a few years back.

It is fashionable now to cast Keynes himself in the role of a defunct
economist: just how defunct we shall try to discover. For the
moment we are concerned to identify the sources of his power.

Keynes was born into the ruling class of Great Britain, into the
class, that is, from which was almost exclusively drawn, in Victorian
and Edwardian Britain, the relatively small number of people who
effectively governed the country – the politicians and senior civil
servants.

It was a world in which a voter was allowed to choose between Herbert
Asquith, the Craven Scholar from Balliol College, Oxford, and Arthur
Balfour, the Etonian intellectual from Trinity College, Cambridge, as to
who should exercise responsibility for Sir Robert Chalmers or Sir John
Bradbury, who ruled the Treasury, and their Oxford and Cambridge
counterparts through every level of a civil service recruited on the best
principles of meritocracy by competitive examination in subjects which
only Oxford and Cambridge could teach.

Into this narrow world of a benevolent avuncular bureaucracy
administered by a conscientious but narrowly inbred élite and responding
to their intellectual valuations, Keynes had entered by the time-honoured
channel of success in competitive examination at the age of fourteen for
an Eton scholarship. From then on he was one of them...[12]

From Eton he went to Cambridge.

Cambridge was an important constituent of England. She trained a large
proportion of those destined to guide public opinion and to execute policy.
There were personal links between the University and those high in public
affairs; Mrs. Henry Sidgwick was herself the sister of Mr Balfour, who
became Prime Minister.[13]

From Cambridge he went into the Civil Service, but not, at that
time, to the Treasury.[14]

Keynes entered the Treasury early in 1915 'for the duration' and,
by the end of the war, when he was still only 35 years old, had
established for himself a considerable reputation. After the war he
went as Treasury representative to the Peace Conference.

Between 1919 and 1939 Keynes made his name and his fortune.
The former through a series of books and newspaper articles and
the latter largely through speculation in currencies and commodities,
although he also earned considerable sums from his books and his
journalism. He began currency speculation in 1919, was at first
highly successful, was wiped out in 1920, recovered, extended his

speculation to commodities and by 1937 had a fortune of over half a million pounds. King's College Cambridge, where he was First Bursar from the mid-1920s, also benefited considerably from his investment skills. From 1923 he was on the board of the Provincial Insurance Company.

His series of post-war books[15] began with *The Economic Consequences of the Peace* (1919) and continued with *Treatise on Probability* (1921), *A Revision of The Treaty* (1922), *A Tract on Monetary Reform* (1923), *The End of Laissez Faire* (1926). *A Treatise on Money* (1930), a collection, *Essays in Persuasion* (1931), and *Essays in Biography* (1933).

Throughout this period he was a Fellow of King's College, Cambridge, and in 1929 was made a Fellow of the British Academy. In the same year he was appointed a member of the Committee of Enquiry into Finance and Industry (the Macmillan Committee); and in 1930 became a member of the new Economic Advisory Council.

All this is the briefest possible suggestion of the range and influence of his activities even within the domain of politics and economics. It says nothing of his work and achievements in the arts. But it is enough to make it clear that when the GT appeared in 1936 it was not just a new economics textbook by any old economist – not even any old Cambridge economist. It was a new book by Keynes; and we had his own word for it that it was a very important book.[16]

But the books, the articles, the appointments to high places, the material success, could in themselves be no more – although in sum a great deal – than the mark, and the reward, of an exceptionally clever, dedicated, ambitious and industrious man. Such rare men are to be found. They do not all, however, cast their spell as Keynes cast his; and for an explanation of this aspect and source of his power we have to go not to his books but to the man.

He was, by the common consent of all who met him or had discourse with him, exceedingly clever. Bertrand Russell, for example, wrote that 'Keynes's intellect was the sharpest and clearest I have ever known. . . I was sometimes inclined to feel that so much cleverness must be incompatible with depth, but I do not think this feeling justified.'[17] But mere cleverness, powers of reasoning, the ability to assemble an argument into a logical and irresistible sequence, the gift of words, all of which Keynes possessed, are not all and are, in any case, subsumed in the catalogue of his output. For the rest we must turn to those who knew him and have written about him; and as these are many we must select. Let us listen to his biographer, R. F. Harrod, who knew him.

A little knowledge of him soon persuaded one that he was utterly unlike anyone else that existed or had ever existed. For his friends the sound 'Maynard' instantly conjured up an extraordinarily intense flavour, almost comparable to a sensible quality in its definiteness and precision – or should one compare it to a symphony long familiar? It was not the economist or the writer or the financier that the word evoked. One knew all about that, of course. It was a peculiar pattern of behaviour, physical and mental – the quick twinkle, the arching eyebrows, the whole face expressing his acute sense of the droll, the fun giving way to a period of lucid exposition in his soft mellow voice, which culminated in its turn in another burst of the ridiculous; his kindly expression, his beautiful steady eyes seeking agreement and testing your appreciation; the rapidity of the movement of ideas, yet always without strain; his enjoyment of the feast of reason, his comfortable companionship. No doubt all human beings have their own unique individuality for the seeing eye. In Keynes, perhaps, because all his qualities were raised to a high point, the individuality was more insistant. Yet it often expressed itself in the enunciation of what was purely and exquisitely reasonable, and reason is supposed to be a universal quality, the same for all. We may remind ourselves that the great masters, whose words or works have had a universal appeal in many lands and ages, were also most intensely individual, their signatures being plainly visible on all their products. So it was with Keynes.

As an economist he sought to bring about the well-being of mankind in the abstract; as a man he craved for the well-being of those with whom he had contact. Thus his work was infused with a spirit of warm feeling towards all whom he taught or strove to persuade. It was this quality of love which may entitle us to raise him above the status of wise man and rank him as a prophet in our modern age. He put his hand on your shoulder and opened the book of life before you; with his delicate finger he traced its story; his delight in it was infectious, and his vision became your vision.[18]

Harrod occupies a special position, as Keynes's biographer, and biographers are allowed some hyperbole, so it may be more persuasive to quote the words of a man who in the 1930s was not always in agreement with Keynes. Milo Keynes concludes his preface to *Essays on John Maynard Keynes* with an extract from the diary kept by Lord Robbins at the Bretton Woods negotiations of 1944:

Keynes was in his most persuasive mood; and the effect was irresistable. At such moments I often find myself thinking that Keynes must be one of the most remarkable men that has ever lived – the quick logic, the birdlike swoop of invention, the vivid fancy, the wide vision, above all the incomparable sense of the fitness of words, all combine to make something several degrees beyond the limit of ordinary human achievement.

From those who knew him there is much more in this vein, testifying to his personality, his voice, his charm, his powers of persuasion, his presence. I think it was H. G. Johnson who recorded that in post-1946 Cambridge, after Keynes's death, they still talked about 'Maynard' as if he might come into the room. It is a powerful legend.

Notes

1. *Wealth of Nations*. He is talking about the doctrines of the Reformation. The analogy with Keynes's reformation cannot be pushed very far. His eloquence was scarcely coarse and rustic. Nor would it seem entirely fair to suggest that Keynes and his apostles prevailed over the established economists because 'The austerity of their manners gave them authority with the common people, who contrasted the strict regularity of their conduct with the disorderly lives of the greater part of their own clergy'.

2. I hope that the myth of the classical economists (and their successors) as grim hard-faced men taking pleasure in providing a theoretical underpinning to justify the grinding of the faces of the poor has by now been dispelled. They were decent men led reluctantly and sometimes despairingly to the logical conclusions of their theories. Heilbroner (*The Great Economists*, Eyre and Spottiswoode 1955) quotes Sir James Mackintosh, the Scottish philosopher, as saying 'I have known Adam Smith slightly, Ricardo well and Malthus intimately. Is it not something to say for a science that its three greatest masters were about the three best men I ever knew?'

3. The 'unemployment problem' and the public works solution had existed before the First World War.

4. Including Pigou, whom Keynes later selected as the focus of much of his attack on classical economics; and Robertson, with whom Keynes had a long and sad disagreement.

5. For a discussion on this see G. C. Peden 'Keynes, the Treasury and unemployment in the later nineteen-thirties', *Oxford Economic Papers*, Vol. 32, No. 1. Mar, 1980.

6. Professor Robbins, as we have noted, was not a proponent of public works and, in a footnote to the GT Keynes notes 'It is the distinction of Prof. Robbins that he, almost alone, continues to maintain a consistent scheme of thought, his practical recommendations belonging to the same system as his theory.'

7. *Economic Possibilities for our Grandchildren* (1930). Reprinted in *Essays in Persuasion*, Macmillan 1931.

8. There is an argument that, *under a loose monetary regime*, the trade unions have assumed this 'responsibility' in the sense that, by their wage demands, supported by their power, they can frustrate a Government's desire to reduce demand by fiscal action.

9. 'National Self-Sufficiency' (Part 5) *New Statesman and Nation*, 15 July 1933. (Quoted by Elizabeth S. Johnson in *The Shadow of Keynes*.)

10. As G. L. S. Shackle has noted 'The initiative for theory-making is the

need to have one's mind at rest'. *Evolutions of thought in economics* Banca Nationale Del Lavoro, No. 132, 1980.

11. I think it is fair to say that this is the consensus. H. G. Johnson (*The Keynesian Revolution and the Monetarist Counterrevolution*, The University of Chicago Press 1975) for example refers to 'its rapid acceptance and propagation among professional economists'. Given the innate and inbred conservatism of British politicians and civil servants, especially those at the Treasury, it was remarkable that the new theories were so swiftly translated into policy, and became the conventional wisdom. However, it must be recorded that Robert Skidelsky takes the opposite view and asks rather why Keynes was so unpersuasive, and seeks an 'explanation of his failure to exert political influence', – Robert Skidelsky, 'The reception of the Keynesian revolution' in *Essays on John Maynard Keynes*, Milo Keynes (ed.), (Cambridge University Press 1975).

12. Austen Robinson, 'A personal view' in *Essays on John Maynard Keynes*, Cambridge University Press 1975

13. R. F. Harrod, *The Life of John Maynard Keynes*, Macmillan 1951. Henry Sidgwick was the author of *Principles of Political Economy*.

14. Keynes came second in the examination, and the one post in the Treasury was taken by the man who came first. In economics Keynes came eighth or ninth, a result that enraged him.

15. He had published *Indian Currency and Finance* in 1913.

16. He wrote to G. B. Shaw (1.1.1935) '. . . I believe myself to be writing a book on economic theory which will largely revolutionise. . . the way the world thinks about economic problems. . . . But for myself I don't merely hope what I say, – in my own mind I'm quite sure'.(Harrod op. cit., p. 462)

17. Quoted by Milo Keynes in 'Maynard and Lydia Keynes' in *Essays on John Maynard Keynes* (Cambridge University Press 1975).

18. R. F. Harrod, op. cit.

Chapter four

Another man's doxy

Orthodoxy is my doxy; heterodoxy is another man's doxy

Bishop Warburton

I said that Keynes wrote the GT to provide a theoretical underpinning for programmes of public works. That is true, and it makes the point that Keynes was essentially an economist who was in business to solve the economic problems of his day. At the theoretical level his aim can be expressed differently. Public works would be necessary only if the system was not self-adjusting to the full employment level and, as we have seen, it was the conclusion of orthodox economic theory that it was so self-adjusting. What Keynes had to show, therefore, was that there existed more than one point at which an economy might establish some sort of equilibrium. A working definition of economic equilibrium would be a state of affairs to which an economy has an inherent tendency to return. Of course the definition, and possibly the whole concept of equilibrium, is unsatisfactory, because no economy, except the most primitive, is ever in equilibrium: it is always moving from one equilibrium to the next.

Say's law, saving and investment

In positioning his pieces for his attack on the 'postulates of the classical economists' Keynes comes early, in his GT, to Say's law, about which we have already said a little. Keynes writes:[1]

From the time of Say and Ricardo the classical economists have taught that supply creates its own demand; – meaning by this in some significant, but not clearly defined, sense that the whole of the costs of production must necessarily be spent in the aggregate, directly or indirectly, on purchasing the product.

The conviction . . . that money makes no real difference except frictionally and that the theory of production and employment can be worked out as being based on 'real' exchanges with money introduced perfunctorily in a later chapter, is the modern version of the classical tradition.
Contemporary thought is still deeply steeped in the notion that if people do not spend their money in one way they will spend it in another.

With Say's law as a silent assumption it is natural to suppose that:

. . . an act of individual saving inevitably leads to a parallel act of investment.

Those who think this way are deceived, nevertheless, by an optical illusion, which makes two essentially different activities appear to be the same. They are fallaciously supposing that there is a nexus which unites decisions to abstain from present consumption with decisions to provide for future consumption; whereas the motives which determine the latter are not linked in any simple way with the motives which determine the former.

The observation that decisions to save and decisions to invest are quite separate and are, characteristically, taken by different sets of people, is, although seemingly obvious, of crucial importance and lies at the heart of Keynesian theory.

The circular flow of income

The concept of the circular flow of income is fairly readily understood: people realise that they receive money (income) from their employment and spend this money on buying goods and services; and this money goes to the firms who provide the goods and services and is paid out by these firms as income to their employees, who spend it on goods and services; and so on. (Of course, the process is simultaneous as well as sequential.)

If the economy consisted of firms who made goods for consump-

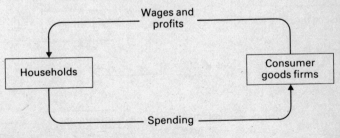

Fig. 4.1

tion and households who spent all their income there would be no problem (and few macroeconomists) (Fig. 4.1). (Transactions between firms are cancelled out within the 'firms' box.)

But people do not spend all their income: they save some (Fig. 4.2).[2] ('Wages and profits' has been relabelled 'Incomes'.)

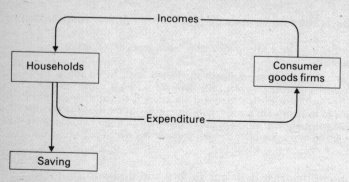

Fig. 4.2

There is now a leak in the system; not all the money paid out by firms in incomes comes back to them in expenditure. It is clear that without anything to offset the savings the system would run down, although not completely, since there will always be *some* consumption.

Let us now add to the system firms who make goods other than goods for immediate consumption, i.e. investment goods. The employees of these firms will receive incomes which they will spend in consumption, or save (Fig. 4.3).

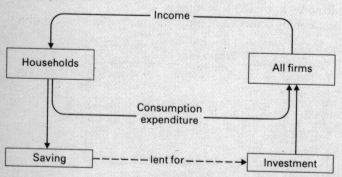

Fig. 4.3

Thus, the circular flow of incomes is complete again; and, if the amount of investment is equal to the 'original' leakage through savings, will be complete at its former level of income and expenditure. We may assume for the purpose of this very simple model that savings are lent directly to firms making investment goods. In practice the market for capital is more complicated than that.

What we have outlined above is an extremely simple model of an economy. It tells us that there is a circular flow of incomes and expenditure but it does not tell us at what level this circular flow will stabilise; specifically it does not tell us whether all the resources of the economy, in particular its manpower, will be fully employed. All it tells us is that the flows of income and expenditure will be in equilibrium when investment equals savings. The equality of investment and savings is a necessary condition for equilibrium but it is not a sufficient condition for full employment.

If the system is in equilibrium at a level of activity that does not employ all the resources of the economy (underemployment equilibrium) it can be raised to a higher level of activity by either a reduction in saving or an increase in investment, subject, of course, to the limitation that activity cannot be raised beyond the point at which all resources are fully (and optimally) employed. There is also a limit to the reduction in savings: they cannot generally speaking be reduced below zero for any length of time. For sustained expansion an increase in investment is the preferred solution.

Consumption

If it is the case that people spend less than their income it is likely to be true that they will also spend less than any *increase* in income. This was Keynes's assumption: 'The psychology of the community is such that when aggregate real income is increased aggregate consumption is increased, but not by so much as income'.[3] This apparently obvious statement forms the foundation upon which the Keynesian edifice is built.[4] If the community has a propensity to spend on consumption less than the whole of any increase in income, and if we know what this propensity is, we can say what increase in income will be the result of a given increase in investment; and what increase in investment is required to produce a given change in income. And since, with wages known, there is a direct relationship between total income and total employment we can, in principle, say what change in investment is required to produce a desired change in employment.

It is worthwhile, therefore, taking some trouble to understand what the *marginal propensity to consume* is and what its implications are. An understanding will, alas, require a slightly less relaxed attention than has been necessary so far, but it is worth it.

It is unfortunate that this illuminating concept has such an arcane name. The cynic may suspect that the arcanery is merely a device to endow an otherwise common-sense idea with a specious scientific aura: it is not unknown for scientists and scientists *manqué* to get up to such tricks. But it does emerge that 'marginal propensity to consume' is a correct description, and more or less inescapable.

Why marginal? Well, marginal in economics is used, not unreasonably, to designate changes which take place 'at the margin', that is to say at the edge or the limit of whatever is under discussion. For example, if my income is £100 a week then sums adjacent to £100, above or below, are 'marginal income'. The considerations which determine how I spend my one-hundred-and-first pound are clearly different from the considerations governing the disposal of my eleventh or twenty-fourth pound. Similarly, whether I work 40 or 41 hours a week is a decision subject to different desiderata from whether I work 10 or 20 hours. So, 'marginal' means related to small changes, and, in this context, the response of consumption to small changes in income.

Why propensity? Because we are concerned with subjective phenomena rather than observed facts. We cannot say that a man spends £180 out of an income of £200 if he has never had an income of £200. We simply do not know. But we can say, from experience, that he has a propensity so to consume. More confidently, we can apply the laws of large numbers and declare that a community or an economy has certain propensities.

The multiplier

It is becoming clear that investment plays a crucial role in determining the level of income. In building the skeleton of the Keynesian system, therefore, we need a relationship between changes in investment and changes in income. That relationship is provided by the multiplier; and the multiplier is derived from the marginal propensity to consume (MPC). 'The multiplier' sounds rather grand, but it is no more than the formalization of the simple idea that the more that people in general spend out of additions to their income provided by new investment the more income will that investment generate as the spending spreads.

The next few paragraphs are devoted to the elaboration of this idea and to a formal derivation of the multiplier from the marginal propensity to consume. Those who find this tedious should skip to the first paragraph following the equations.

Let us begin by returning to our simple model of the circular flow of income and assume that all increases in income are wholly spent; or, in our new jargon, that the marginal propensity to consume is one (unity).

Now suppose that in this situation there is injected into the economy £1 million of new investment on construction. This work will need the employment of architects, civil engineers – the whole range of construction workers. Machinery will be bought or hired. Vast quantities of materials will be bought. According to our assumption all the money paid out for these various purposes will be spent by the recipients, spent on eating, drinking, cars, holidays and so on. And *that* expenditure, received as income, will in turn be spent. And so it will go on. There is no end to it. If the economy was underemployed it will soon be fully employed, but still the spending will go on (but doing nothing but raise prices).

In practice, we know, it does not happen like that. And the reason it does not happen is that not all income is spent. Some of it is saved. And, in a world more complicated than our very simple model, some would go to pay taxes and some would be spent abroad on imports. Money leaks out of the circular flow into savings, taxes and imports. Let us concentrate on savings. Suppose people save one-fifth of any additional income. Their marginal propensity to save (MPS) is one-fifth and their marginal propensity to consume (MPC) is four-fifths. In successive rounds the amounts spent and saved would be as shown in Table 4.1. It is apparent that the two series are diminishing. The total amount spent on consumption after six rounds is not

Table 4.1

Expenditure round	Amount spent on consumption £ thousand	Amount saved £ thousand
1	1,000	
2	800	200
3	640	160
4	512	128
5	410	102
6	328	82
Total after 6 rounds	3,690	672
Total after n rounds	5,000	1,000

£6,000 but £3,690 (all figures are in thousands). More interestingly it can be shown mathematically[5] that the total will reach (will not exceed) £5,000 spent on consumption and £1,000 saved. More interestingly, because £5,000 is exactly five times the initial investment; and £1,000 is equal to the initial investment.

If we drew up a similar table for an MPC of two-thirds (MPS 1/3) we should find that the total of consumption after *n* periods was £3,000 and the total saved £1,000.

Let us define the multiplier as that factor which, if multiplied by the initial investment, gives the sum of the expenditure on consumption.

In the first example it is five and in the second it is three. And in the first example the MPS is one-fifth and in the second it is one-third. In each case the multiplier is the reciprocal (the 'upside down') of the MPS, i.e.

$$\frac{1}{1/5} = 5 \quad \text{and} \quad \frac{1}{1/3} = 3$$

We can generalise this result and say that the multiplier is the reciprocal of the MPS:

$$\text{Multiplier} = \frac{1}{\text{MPS}}$$

But, for reasons that will become apparent, it is more convenient to express the multiplier in terms of the marginal propensity to consume (MPC). And we know that the MPS is equal to one minus the MPC:

$$\text{MPS} = 1 - \text{MPC}$$

So, substituting this into the first expression, the

$$\text{Multiplier} = \frac{1}{1 - \text{MPC}}$$

We now know, in formal terms, what the multiplier is: it is one divided by one minus the marginal propensity to consume. If we apply this factor to the change in investment we arrive at the consequent change in income. This formulation makes it clear that the *larger* the MPC the *larger* will be the multiplier; which is what we would expect.

That, really, is all, or possibly more than, we need to know about the multiplier to give us an understanding of its nature. But we should note in passing that a single injection of investment, as in our example, does, as we have seen, fade away to nothing and does not permanently raise the level of incomes. To do that we should need successive injections, in each round, of further investment. What we would then have is, as it were, a series of geometric progressions laid one on top of the other, so that as one fades away another takes over. Using our figures, such a process would raise income by £5 million and generate £1 million of savings, sufficient to finance a continuing investment of £1 million.

The multiplier, which was discovered not by Keynes but by his Cambridge colleague R. F. Kahn[6] and adapted by Keynes, is important because it demonstrates three things. First that a programme of economic pump priming not only can be but will be eventually self-financing in terms of savings. (It also showed that provided the MPC was less than unity the process of expansion would not go on for ever). Secondly it demonstrated a process in economic adjustment which could lead *away* from full employment – for the multiplier works in a downward direction in response to a fall in investment – in sharp contradistinction to classical theory which assumed that all adjustment processes maintained or moved towards full employment. And thirdly it showed that saving and investment were brought into equilibrium not by the rate of interest but by changes in the level of income.

In essence the multiplier is simply a formalisation of the idea that spending power injected into the economy at any point is passed on by the original recipient to others, so that the total increase in expenditure is some multiple of the original injection. The propensity to consume tells us what this multiple will be and at the same time ensures that the process comes to an end. At the completion of the process the saving generated finances, exactly, the investment.

Finally, to bring us back to earth, we must remember that we do not live in a closed economy without foreign trade and without government. The other leakages from the income flow that we mentioned earlier – imports and taxes – will be present and will need to be taken into account in the calculation of the multiplier. Clearly, the more leakages there are the smaller will be the multiplier. In particular we might note, anticipating a matter we come to in Chapter 13, that if the propensity to import is high then a significant part of new expenditure will leak away abroad, doing little to stimulate domestic activity but much to push the balance of payments on current account into deficit.

The system so far

It is my desire and intention to keep the number of diagrams to a minimum, because some readers may find them off-putting. There is however one diagram that illustrates the income and expenditure approach to macroeconomics, along with the propensity to consume and the multiplier process, so powerfully that it cannot be omitted.

Let us first remind ourselves of the simple identities of the Keynesian system. In equilibrium, income equals expenditure. Part of income is spent on consumption and what is left is defined as saving, which means that income *minus* consumption equals saving. And consumption *plus* saving equals income. In equilibrium, saving equals investment. So income equals expenditure on consumption *plus* expenditure on investment.

For those who are not put off by symbols the matter may be clearly displayed as follows:

Let us call Income Y (everyone does – it is the convention).
Consumption = C Saving = S Investment = I
Then Income (Y) minus Consumption (C) equals Saving (S)

1. $Y - C = S$

2.   Therefore $Y = S + C$
                        $= C + S$

In equilibrium Saving equals Investment, so

3. $S = I$

Substituting I for S in equation 2 we have

4. $Y = C + I$

which says that income is equal to (generated by) expenditure on consumption and expenditure on investment. This is the seminal Keynesian equation, an equation which, in its day, did for economics what $E = mc^2$ did for physics.

By definition income will always equal consumption plus investment; but the *level* of income will depend on how much consumption and how much investment. So the first thing we are interested in in our diagram is to display all those possible positions where income equals expenditure. We draw the usual vertical and horizontal axes and we measure expenditure up the vertical axis and income along the horizontal axis (see Fig. 4.4). The two axes form a right angle. If we bisect this angle with a line drawn at 45° through the origin (the point where the axes meet) every point on that line will be an equal distance from each axis. At all points on the line income equals expenditure; and all points at which income equals expenditure lie on that line, and lie nowhere else.

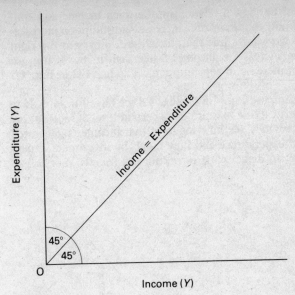

Fig. 4.4

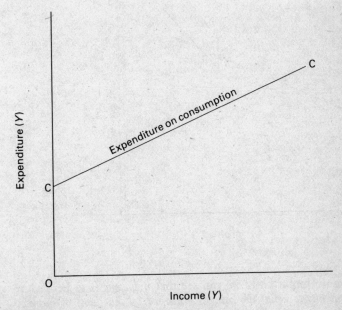

Fig. 4.5

Next we want to show a relationship between income and consumption. We know that as income increases consumption increases but by less. So we want a line that, as it were, moves to the right (representing an increase in income) faster than it moves upward (representing an increase in consumption). The line CC in Fig. 4.5 is such a line.

If we now superimpose Fig. 4.5 on Fig. 4.4 we have Fig. 4.6. If to that we add a vertical line to represent a certain level of income, say Y, we can immediately see how much of that income is generated by consumption expenditure and how much by investment expenditure. We have, in diagramatic form, our old friends $Y = C + S$ and $Y = C + I$.

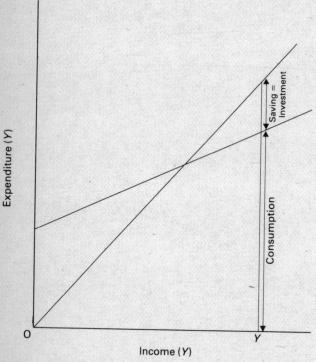

Fig. 4.6

But more importantly we can see that *if income is to be Y then investment has to equal the savings generated by that level of income.* For if investment is less than that a lower level of income will be generated, a level that could be represented by a vertical line drawn somewhere to the left of Y. At a lower level of income there will be lower savings, and equilibrium is restored when the lower savings equal the lower investment.

Conversely, if investment is greater than that required to sustain an income of Y then income will rise, represented in the diagram by a movement to the right of the vertical income line. At the higher level of income a higher level of savings will be generated until once more savings equal investment.

We have not got all we can out of this diagram. It can be used to illustrate the multiplier, which, as we have seen, is *derived* from the propensity to consume. Suppose (Fig. 4.7) income increases from Y_2 to Y_3 (this should be a small increase but is shown large to make the diagram readable). Then while income increases by the distance AB, consumption increases by the height DB. The marginal propensity to consume out of income is, therefore, $\dfrac{DB}{AB}$. And $\dfrac{DB}{AB}$ is the slope of the line CC (and since CC is a straight line is constant throughout). The slope of the consumption function CC therefore reflects the value of the multiplier: the steeper the slope the larger

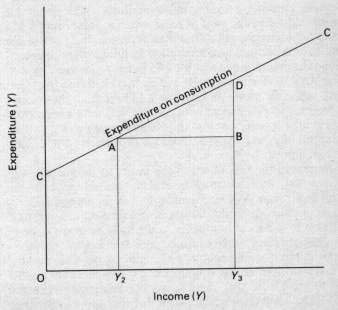

Fig. 4.7

the multiplier, as readily becomes apparent if, using a little imagination, we swivel the consumption function around the pivot of its intersection with the 45° line in Fig. 4.6. The steeper the consumption function becomes the *smaller* is the amount of investment required to move income between any two given levels. Or, to put it the other way round, the *larger* is the change in income induced by a given change in investment.

In the limiting case the line CC lies on the 45° line and income is sustained by consumption alone, no investment being required.

Thus our little diagram (Fig. 4.6) colloquially known as the Keynesian cross, shows the relationship between income, consumption and investment; and summarises[7] the real (as distinct from the monetary) side of the Keynesian theory of income determination. It should perhaps be noted that the diagram exhibits only a set of identities and equilibrium positions, and does not show the disequilibrium positions that obtain in the passage from one income level to another.

The scheme of things outlined above has assumed a closed economy, that is an economy with no foreign trade. Nor is there any mention of Government spending and taxation. These matters are not unimportant and indeed the elaboration of the model to incorporate these elements provides much harmless employment for economists and forms the stuff of most undergraduate courses and text books on macroeconomics. But their exclusion does not damage the validity of the central idea while their inclusion might unnecessarily cloud the perception of that idea. In passing, however, we may note that their treatment is largely symmetrical with the treatment of saving and investment. As saving is a leakage from the system, so are imports (because expenditure goes abroad) and taxation. And as investment is an injection into the income stream so are government expenditure and exports (because expenditure on exports comes from abroad).

The genesis of the GT, of which the theory of income determination is a part, was the desire to explain, and so cure, chronic unemployment. How does employment fit into the foregoing?

Income is paid out to the factors of production, and the total amount paid to factors of production is the measure of the value of output. Output is another face of income. Income equals output.

Output is produced by people, i.e. employed persons, working with a given stock of capital equipment. We may therefore assume with some confidence that there is a close relationship between income (output) and employment, such that they move in the same direction. It is true that income can increase without any increase in the numbers employed, e.g. by overtime working, better organisation; and in the longer term, with which we are not here concerned, we may expect a secular increase in productivity associated with more and better capital equipment and improved techniques. But in the short term we assume that changes in income mean changes in numbers employed in the same direction. The theory of income determination is therefore also the theory of employment determination. It follows that income in real (i.e. price adjusted) terms cannot increase beyond the full employment level – whatever that is. Thus, if in the diagram Y is the full employment level of income, income cannot move to the right of Y; and movement to the left will represent unemployment.

Interest and money

In the classical system, as we have seen, the rate of interest was determined by the supply of savings and the demand for investment; or, to put it another way, the supply of savings and the demand for investment were brought into equilibrium by the rate of interest. The rate of interest was determined by 'real' factors and had little to do with money.

In the system developed by Keynes saving and investment were, as we have just seen, brought into equilibrium by changes in *income*. What then, determined the rate of interest, which must be the price of something, and determined by the supply of and demand for something? Keynes decided that the 'something' was money: the rate of interest was the equilibrium price for the supply of and demand for money.

The demand for money is a very curious concept to non-economists, and we may as well meet this curiosity, and its associated difficulties, head on. The difficulties will be largely cleared away if we understand that the demand for money is not a demand for wealth or for income. For these, the demand is almost infinite.

We must think of the demand for money in the same way as we would think of the demand for eggs. All very well, but the concept of an egg is relatively unambiguous: everyone knows what an egg is. But what is money? Well, the truth is that we had better not say. For if we say, someone will disagree with us. We are fairly safe in saying that money is notes and coins and current account deposits at the bank. Beyond that, all is confusion and uncertainty. We can agree that a house is not money because although it is worth money its exact price is uncertain and its disposal would take some time.

The value of shares, (equities) is similarly uncertain over more than a very short period, although their disposal is quick. With deposits with a building society and investment accounts in the National Savings Bank the position is reversed: we know their value but their conversion into money (cash) takes time. What about deposit accounts at a clearing bank? An obliging bank manager will normally not deny funds if a substantial collateral is available in a deposit account at the same bank. So are deposit account balances money? The sad fact – sad from the viewpoint of economic theory – is that your answer is about as good as anyone else's.

And if money is no more than some readily accessible means universally acceptable for the purchase of goods, what about hire-purchase and credit generally? If my bank manager will allow me to overdraw by £500, as and when I need it for some worthy cause, like improvement of property, is that money?

Money is what you define money to be; and for present purposes we shall define it as a readily available and universally accepted means of payment that does not earn any monetary return. So, the demand for money is the demand to hold this sort of stuff.

Now it is immediately apparent that holding money has a cost, and the cost is the income foregone in investing it in something which *does* have a monetary return, in the form of interest, dividend or capital appreciation. If holding money has a cost we shall want to hold as little of it as is consistent with our needs.

While we may recognise that investing our money will yield us a return we may nevertheless believe that, say, present interest rates are too low and will rise, so that if we invest now we shall not only get a lower interest rate than we should later on – if our expectations are fulfilled – but shall in addition incur a capital loss.[8] So we prefer to hold money, even though it earns no interest. We may call this the speculative motive. (This will vary from individual to individual: some prefer large risks for large gains and others small risks for small gains).

We might like to hold money 'just in case' – in case the car blows up on the motorway, in case the water tank bursts. This is the precautionary motive. But most of all we hold money from the 'transaction motive' – simply because we need it to buy things and to be able to write cheques on our current account. The amount we hold will be determined within fairly narrow limits by our money income (and at what intervals we receive it) and by the general level of prices. This is common experience and needs no elaboration.

As we have suggested, money may be invested in many different ways to yield a return. For the purposes of exposition, to make the idea simple, let us suppose that the alternative to holding money is to invest it in Government securities yielding a fixed rate of interest. The more money we hold the more income we forego in the shape of the interest we might have earned.[9] As we noted, holding money has a cost. On a priori grounds we can argue that the greater the cost i.e. the higher the rate of interest foregone, the less money we shall try to hold. And the lower the rate of interest the lower will be our incentive to get rid of our ready money – we shall prefer to keep our options open and remain liquid. At high rates of interest our preference for liquidity will be low and at low rates it will be high. This relationship between our desire for liquidity (ready money) and the rate of interest may be depicted graphically, as in Fig. 4.8.

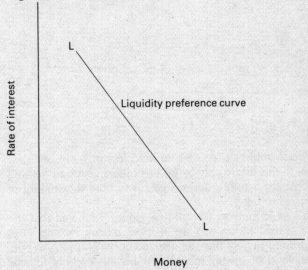

Fig. 4.8

This curve[10] may be generalised to represent the liquidity preference of the whole community. We now have a curve of the demand for money to hold in relation to the rate of interest. It is a subjective curve, representing preferences at any given time.

To determine the rate of interest we need a supply curve (S) for money, and as the amount of money is at any given moment fixed, this may be represented by a vertical line (see Fig. 4.9).

The rate of interest bringing the demand for money into equilibrium with the stock of money will be i. Note that at any one time the whole stock of money *must* be held by the community collec-

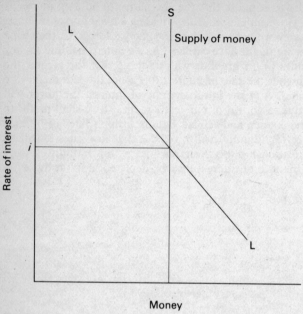

Fig. 4.9

tively. Individual holders may wish to hold less or more but they can give effect to this desire only by finding others who want to hold more or less. At the rate of interest *i* each will hold the amount of money he desires to hold.

In examining the motives for holding money we noted that the most weighty consideration was the level of money income. It is therefore important to note that the demand curve L applies to one, and only one, level of money income. At higher levels of income more liquidity would be demanded at every rate of interest, and the whole curve would shift to the right.

Given the L curve, the quantity of money and the rate of interest are mutually determined. From this is derived the well-known proposition that the authorities cannot determine at the same time *both* the quantity of money and the rate of interest. It is one or the other.

We can also see why attemps to control inflation by strict control of the money supply drive up interest rates: with inflation the L curve is shifting constantly further to the right while the money supply line is by definition either fixed or moving only slowly to the right.[11]

There are competent observers who hold that Keynes's concept of liquidity preference was his most original and most lasting contribution to economic theory.[12] Paradoxically, it is the basis of much of the new monetarium.

Investment

In discussing 'the inducement to invest', that is to say why and in what conditions and in what amounts new investment in capital equipment takes place, Keynes broke little new ground.

Investment depends upon the *marginal efficiency of capital* which Keynes defines as 'being equal to that rate of discount which would make the present value of the series of annuities given by the returns expected from the capital-asset during its life just equal to its supply price'.

He admits that his definition is 'fairly close' to Marshall's 'marginal net efficiency' and 'marginal utility of capital'; and identical to Fisher's 'rate of return over costs'.[13] Keynes has been accused of inventing fancy names for simple concepts – for example, the propensity to consume – just to make the whole theory appear more difficult, exciting, novel and esoteric than it really is. Overall the criticism has no justification because the new terms *do* describe new concepts; but in the case of the marginal efficiency of capital the critics have a point: it *was* a high-sounding new name used to describe a concept already to be found in the orthodox economics.

The value of Keynes's treatment is that it is lucid and emphasises – which some orthodox discussion did not – that investment is concerned not with the current yield of a capital asset but with its *expected* yield over its life. His emphasis on expectations is important because expectations concern the future, about which nothing is known, and consideration of which must involve uncertainty and guesswork.

It is a mistake to think of investment in static terms. Durable goods link the present with the future. 'The fact' notes Keynes, 'that the assumptions of the static state often underlie present-day economic theory, imports into it a large element of unreality'[14] In subsequent writings on the GT, Keynes placed great importance on expectations and uncertainty; and Shackle thought this one of his most significant contributions.[15]

For our purposes it is sufficient to understand that the marginal efficiency of capital provides a schedule which gives a relationship of investment to the rate of interest such that the lower the rate of interest the greater the investment. (But investment alone does not determine the rate of interest).

The General Theory

We are now in a position to fit the various pieces of the GT into a coherent whole.

A given liquidity preference schedule and a given quantity of money gives us a rate of interest for a given level of income. The rate of interest will determine the amount of investment which, through the multiplier derived from the marginal propensity to consume, will determine the level of income. Thus, the rate of interest and the level of income are mutually and simultaneously determined.[16] Given the real wage, the level of income (= output) gives the level of employment; but there is nothing in the system to ensure that this will be, or will move towards a full employment level.

How general is the GT? Well, it depends on what you mean by general. The GT claimed in its title to be only a general theory of employment, interest and money. It was couched in terms of a closed economy and so has nothing directly to say about the balance of payments. The discussion is conducted throughout in real terms, that is to say in pounds of constant value, so it is limited in its application to the theory of the general price level, or inflation, which is essentially about money of an unconstant value. More fundamentally, from the purely theoretical point of view, critics argue that the economic system cannot, as the GT purports to show, settle at any point below full employment because of what is known as the real balance effect. The argument runs thus: as the economy runs down prices will fall and with a given quantity of money people's holdings of money – all of which, remember, has to be held by someone – will increase in *real* value. If prices are allowed to fall far enough the increase in the *real* stock of money will stimulate spending of all sorts, and, at the new price level, restore full employment. Thus the conclusion of the GT that the economy can settle at a point below full employment is correct only if it is assumed that prices will not so fall. Thus the GT is not a general theory but only a special case of the orthodox theory, in which prices are not flexible downwards. From the point of view of abstract theory, the point is well taken. But in any real world prices would be unlikely to fall far enough for the real balance effect to be anything but very weak.

Ah! you may say, but why go to all the pain of allowing prices to fall and fall. Why not just increase the quantity of money? Well then we are back in the Keynesian world in which the quantity of money influences expenditure only through the rate of interest and the inducement to invest. And the inducement to invest is not necessarily strong enough to produce full employment – although it may do so.[17]

General theories of anything rarely last for ever: they are overtaken by new knowledge. That is the nature of science. If Keynes were alive today, he would write a different book. But, 'general theory' or not, every economic text book of the last 40 years has been a Keynesian text, full of the whole Keynesian bag of tricks and extensions and elaborations thereof. So far as undergraduates are concerned, 'Keynes' has been the general theory of economics. That, some will say, has been the trouble. But we shall come to that soon.

Keynes and the balance of payments

For expository reasons the GT was constructed in terms of a closed economy, an economy with no foreign trade. The apparatus is, however, easily extended to take account of at least the current account of the balance of payments; and it so happens that the model of an economy which it exhibits throws a flood of light on the problems of the British economy in the years from the end of the war up to the time when our balance of payments difficulties were solved, temporarily, at least, by North Sea Oil. This matter is examined in more detail when we come to the foreign sector (Chapter 14).

Keynes and inflation

As we have noted, the Keynesian analysis, being conducted throughout in money of constant value, is not best suited to handling the problem of inflation. Yet it does offer, and rather elegantly, an explanation of, and therefore a remedy for, inflation. Of course it is the mark of a good theory that it offers explanations of problems that it was not designed to cope with; and Keynesians were certainly gratified to find that their system could cope with inflation as well as with unemployment. The trouble is that the Keynesian analysis leads almost ineluctably to one particular diagnosis of inflation and in so doing obscures other possible diagnoses.

The Keynesian analysis tells us that to raise output to the full employment level we must increase demand. What happens if demand is increased beyond that point? By definition output cannot increase further, so if money expenditure and money income (output) are to be brought into equilibrium prices must rise. Keynes himself recognised this. 'When a further increase in the quantity of effective demand produces no further increase in output and entirely spends itself on an increase in the cost unit fully proportionate to the increase in effective demand, we have reached a condition which

47

might be appropriately designated as one of true inflation'.[18] Now this leads straight to the conclusion that inflation is caused by excess demand, is demand-determined: and the cure is to reduce demand. And certainly this analysis accorded with the experience of the post-war years, where creeping inflation was associated with high, some would say excessive, levels of demand.

From the idea that excess demand causes price rises we slip easily into the formulation that demand pulls up prices; and when we say 'prices' we mean the prices of goods rather than of factors of production. Thus the alternative interpretation that prices might be, as it were, pushed up from below by costs of production, and in particular, by the power of the unions, tends to be obscured. (Although Keynes, in the passage quoted, specifically refers to an 'increase in the cost-unit'). It is entirely possible that union action could raise costs (wages), costs would raise prices and then the higher wages would add to demand. We should not however necessarily conclude from this that 'unions cause or can cause inflation'; one monetarist view holds that a cost inflation of this nature is impossible *unless validated by an increase in the money supply*. But more of all this later.

Effective demand

The Keynesian theory of employment is a theory of effective demand, and it will be appropriate to conclude this section with a restatement of this theory. The difficulty of the concept stems from its simplicity, or its obviousness. Why should we need a new theory which styles itself the Theory of Effective Demand? Does this mean that the old theory was a Theory of Ineffective Demand? In a word, yes.

An understanding of the matter will be eased if we go back for a moment to the simple supply and demand cross (Fig. 4.10). Let this represent the supply of and the demand for anything, and assume that a price P_1, obtains. At that price there is an excess of supply over demand equal to the distance AB; and a deficiency of demand below supply of the same amount. Excess supply equals deficient demand. Both will be simultaneously and necessarily eliminated by a movement of price from P_1 to P_2.

Let us leave the diagram and consider conditions of supply and demand in the economy as a whole.

The income paid out to factors of production producing consumer goods/services and investment goods constitutes, in a closed economy, both the supply price of total output and the demand for

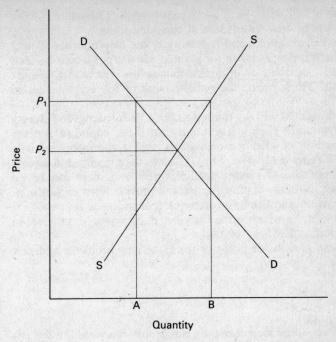

Fig. 4.10

total output. At full employment there will be a demand for the whole output of which the economy is capable.

At less than full employment:

1. The supply price of output will be less than the total value of demand at the full employment level – there is deficient demand for output;
2. More people are offering to supply labour than there will be offers of work – there is an excess supply of labour.

Orthodox equilibrium theory teaches that an excess supply and a deficient demand are eliminated by a fall in price. Thus there must be some system of prices that would bring the supply of and demand for total output into equilibrium. But the demand for the total output of the economy is a *notional* demand and it becomes *effective* demand only at full employment. Certainly the unemployed have an unsatisfied demand for goods but this cannot be communicated to those who might employ them to produce those goods.[19] The unemployed have no effective means of transmitting to the market those signals that will draw forth additional output. The failure of the market, left to itself, is a failure of communication.

Orthodox economics had no theory of the determinants of total output: it was simply taken for granted that output would be total output, give or take a bit of cyclical fluctuation. The hidden *assumption* of full employment allowed the *result* of full employment to emerge.

With hindsight we may think the GT an unduly large and clumsy hammer to crack such a fragile nut; but if the notion of and the understanding of effective demand is now a commonplace it is because Keynes made it so. The GT grew out of the need to explain the phenomenon of *chronic* unemployment and there can be no doubt that its theory of effective demand provided that explanation.

We have looked briefly at orthodox economics, at the problems of the 1930s, to which orthodox economics appeared to have no answer, and at Keynes' solution.

We turn now to the post-war world, to new problems and new solutions.

Notes

1. GT, p. 18.
2. They can spend more than their income, by borrowing. But this is a minor complication which can be ignored, since it does not affect the main issue.
3. GT, p. 27.
4. 'This psychological law was of the utmost importance in the development of my own thought, and it is, I think, absolutely fundamental to the theory of effective demand as set forth in my book.' Keynes, 'After The General Theory', *Quarterly Journal of Economics*, Feb. 1937 (*Collected Writings*, Vol. xiv).
5. The series is a geometrical progression, the formula for which (when r is less than unity) is

$$1 + r + r^2 + r^3 \ldots\ldots + r^n = \frac{1}{1-r}$$

So we have $1 + 4/5 + (4/5)^2 + (4/5)^3 \ldots + (4/5)^n = \frac{1}{1 - 4/5} = 5$

In units of a million equals 5 million.

Since 4/5 is the MPC, the multiplier, $\frac{1}{1 - \text{MPC}}$ is 5.

Strictly, the sum of the series never exceeds $\frac{1}{1-r}$ but continually approaches it and becomes indefinitely near it as *n* indefinitely increases.

6. 'The relation of home investment to unemployment', *Economic Journal*, June 1931.

7. It is interesting, and puzzling, that Keynes himself never used this diagram in presenting his GT. (Indeed, in the whole book he used only one diagram.) But it was invented long before his death and, so far as I am aware, he did not disapprove of it. The same cannot be said of other things done in his name.

8. If the interest rate is 5 per cent a return of £5 may be obtained from £100. But if the rate rises to 10 per cent it may be obtained from £50. As interest rates rise, capital values fall. In this example a fall of only one-twentieth in the capital value, from £100 to £95, would wipe out the whole of one year's interest.

9. This is the very useful concept of 'opportunity cost': the cost of anything may be equated with the loss arising from an opportunity foregone.

10. Straight lines are 'curves' in this context. Curves are also curves.

11. But from a monetarist viewpoint, this rather begs the question of why, or how, there should be continuing inflation when the money supply is fixed. An answer will have to wait until we come to discuss monetarist theory.

12. For example: 'The liquidity-preference theory itself, though intimately necessary to the General Theory, can be considered in isolation, and stands as Keyne's most inalienable piece of original economic thought.' (Shackle, *The Years of High Theory*, Cambridge University Press, 1967, p. 145)

13. '. . . that rate which, employed in computing the present worth of all costs and the present worth of all the returns, will make these two equal.' (GT, p. 140).

14. GT, p. 146.

15. 'But our ignorance of the future was the one big thing which the refinements of equilibrium economics had allowed to slide into oblivion.' (Shackle, op. cit., p. 136)

16. It may be helpful to think of the system as an interrelated set of simultaneous equations which are solved to give the rate of interest and the level of income.

17. In their attacks on Keynes the monetarists sometimes misrepresent him as saying that the economy would or must settle at an unemployment equilibrium. This is false: he demonstrated the possibility of an unemployment equilibrium but his analysis does not exclude a full employment equilibrium – but this would come about by luck rather than from any inherent forces at work in the economy.

18. GT, p. 303.

19. This is true in a money economy with division of labour. It would not be true if the worker consumed nothing but the actual article he produced.

Part two

Chapter five
The conventional unwisdom

It is also misleading, and historically unjustifiable, to take in vain the adjective 'Keynesian' or its opposite 'non-' or 'anti-Keynesian', as terms of approbation or denigration, for one side or the other, in policy disputes which are of a so vastly different nature from those on which Keynes himself pronounced in the inter-war years.

T.W. Hutchison[1]

There can be but few evils that have not been committed in the name of God; not because God is evil but because the faithful, having the word of God in their ear, always seem to hear the message they had thought of in the first place. Keynes was not God, although a certain deification did tend to set in, as it were, *ex-post*. Nor, to be fair, did his disciples claim any direct communication with him after 1946; but this did not prevent some of them expressing considerable certainty about what he would have wanted. Sir Roy Harrod, for example, in the *New Statesman* of 5 December 1969 wrote:

People sometimes say to me that what worried Keynes was the massive unemployment of pre-war days. Surely he would not object to raising unemployment from 1.5 to 2.5 per cent in this country or from 3.3 per cent to 4 per cent in the USA if, as so many are now urging, that cured the external deficits of those countries? . . . He certainly would object.[2]

Sir Roy Harrod – a distinguished and influential Keynesian – was, as we have noted, Keynes's biographer. Other leading economists who had worked with Keynes took a view similar to Sir Roy's. Let us be quite clear what that view is: it is that Keynes would certainly have opposed a level of unemployment as high as 2.5 per cent.

Other economists, that is to say those less closely associated with Keynes, may have enjoyed less direct guidance on what Keynes would and would not have approved of but they did not, in the majority, dissent from the view that 2.5 per cent unemployment, representing over half a million people out of work, was too high.

There were economists who argued that it was not sensible to try to run an economy so near to the limits of its capacity, but these were in a minority. The consensus among economists, including the younger economists in government, was that something like 2.5 per cent was the upper limit to unemployment; and that if this limit seemed in danger of being exceeded, action must be taken to prevent it.

That this consensus was extremely effective in influencing policy can be seen from a glance at the statistics: in the 20 years from 1948 to 1967 unemployment only twice reached 2.5 per cent and in 14 of those years it was below 2.0 per cent.[3] In eight of those years the number unemployed was exceeded by the number of unfilled vacancies. In the 20 years the value of money halved, there were recurrent balance of payments crises, and the period ended with the devaluation of sterling for the second time since the war.

For the next seven years the economy continued to be run at a high pressure of demand and in five of those years the unemployment percentage was still within a point either way of 2.5.

Those years, from 1948 up to the present time, were years of considerable prosperity for the British people, with the standard of living about doubling. There were those, however, who saw this prosperity as a dangerous illusion, an absolute improvement which masked a relative decline. This view was expressed by the Chancellor of the Exchequer, Sir Geoffrey Howe in the House of Commons on 22 May 1979 shortly after the election of the Conservative Government:

If we look back to 1950, we find that even at that time Britain was still one of the world's great commercial and industrial nations. We accounted at that time for one-quarter of the world's trade. Our standard of living then was almost the highest in the world – almost twice as high as that in Germany or in France.

It is during the last 15 years that the deterioration has become serious. Our share of world trade has fallen to less than 10 per cent. This has been accompanied by a steady decline of some of our major industries. We produced no more iron and steel last year than in 1957. Last year we produced no more cars than we did in 1960. In the past 15 years, our share of world markets for cars, ships and steel has been halved. Over the same period, more than 1 million jobs have been lost in manufacturing.

Those trends have been made much worse by the developments of the last five years. The general decline of our manufacturing industry has accelerated in those five years.

Only the advent of North Sea oil has prevented the deterioration in our industrial performance being translated forthwith into sharply falling living standards and a seriously adverse balance of payments.

The Chancellor returned to this theme in a speech to a *Financial Times* conference at the Dorchester Hotel on 23 July 1979:

. . . the roots of today's problems are much more than five years old. This is why we need to understand the nature and extent of the relative decline of the British economy.

. . . if we are to reverse our relative economic decline . . .

without a substantial improvement in our own economic performance, there is a real danger that our relative economic decline may turn into an absolute decline.

. . . our condition could easily become incurable.

The budget is the first step in a long-term strategy to arrest and reverse our economic decline. . . . our strategy for reversing our long-term decline.

We have now reached the point where we are perilously close to destroying the economy's capacity to generate any economic growth whatsoever.

Now whether or not we go all the way with Sir Geoffrey in his diagnosis of the inefficient, rigid, unenterprising and generally moribund state of British industry, it is undeniable that some decline in our prosperity relative to other leading industrial nations has taken place over the last 20 years. And this relative worsening of our position has been accompanied by a much faster rate of decline in the value of money then other comparable economies have experienced.

Sir Geoffrey and the Conservative Government intended to reverse this decline. And it was well known that the central point of their strategy was the control of the money supply, not only as a sufficient condition for the conquest of inflation but as a necessary condition for the regeneration of British industry and to 'create conditions conducive to growth'.[4] There was much more to monetarism, it was emphasised, than the control of inflation; monetarism was about restoring the efficiency of markets.

And monetarism was contrasted to Keynesianism which, it was suggested, had been, at bottom, the cause of all the trouble. Well, perhaps not *all* the trouble, but certainly the Keynesians shunted us into a nasty little economic siding while the non-Keynesian economies sped by on the main line. In his speech to the *Financial Times* conference referred to above, Sir Geoffrey identified three 'lessons of decline.' The third of these was:

We need to change our fundamental approach to macroeconomic management. The analysis which was bequeathed to us by John Maynard Keynes – and which, sadly, he did not survive to re-examine – argued that

> Government's major concern should be with the management of
> aggregate demand. The theory was that this would assure a steady,
> upward climb of employment and income. That has not turned out to be
> the case.

I am not sure that that is quite what the theory was. But that is not the
point. The point – to which this preamble has been leading – is
this:

*If we accept the Conservative diagnosis of economic decline; and if
we recognise, as we must, our failure (both absolute and relative to other
countries) to control inflation; and if we accept that our failure properly
to manage demand has been an important causative factor in these fail-
ures, how far is it fair to blame Keynes?*

Keynes was above all a policy-orientated economist. For him the
purpose of economics was to improve the quality of life. All his life,
in books, pamphlets, newspaper articles, broadcasts, speeches, he
argued for practical solutions to the economic problems of the day.
The greatest of these problems, in the central part of his life, was
the problem of chronic unemployment. His major work, the *General
Theory*, was written to provide the intellectual underpinning for a
solution. The solution was to maintain an adequate level of aggregate
demand. The instrument was public works, to fill any shortfall left
by private works. He sought, in short, to provide a theoretical refu-
tation of 'the orthodox Treasury doctrine which has steadfastly held
that . . . very little additional employment can in fact and as a general rule be created by State borrowing and expenditure.'[5]

Keynes was lucky: he published the GT in 1936, and shortly
afterwards Britain began to re-arm and he was thus, quite fortui-
tously, accorded what few economists can hope for – a full-scale test
of his theory. As he said in a broadcast in May 1939:

> I began by saying that the grand experiment has begun. If it works, if
> expenditure in armaments really does cure unemployment, I predict that
> we shall never go all the way back to the old state of affairs. If we can cure
> unemployment for the purpose of armaments, we can cure it for the
> productive purpose of peace. Good may come out of evil. We may learn a
> trick or two which will come in useful when the day of peace comes, as in
> the fullness of time it must.

It can scarcely have come as a surprise to Keynes that his experiment should be conducted in the context of preparation for a possible war. For he had noted in the GT (p. 130) that ' . . . wars have
been the only form of large-scale loan expenditure which statesmen
have thought justifiable . . . ' But no matter: 'Pyramid-building,

earthquakes, even wars may serve to increase wealth, if the education of our statesmen on the principles of the classical economics stands in the way of anything better'. (p. 129). Or if the Treasury were to fill old bottles with banknotes, bury them in disused coal mines and leave it to private enterprise to dig them up again.

Keynes himself did not survive into the day of peace, and for his views on how his theories might be applied to a peacetime economy we have to rest on three articles he wrote for *The Times* in January 1937, and one of March 1937. At this time unemployment was around 12 per cent. In his first article of 12 January 1937 'The Problem of the Steady Level', he wrote (my italics):

It is natural to interject that it is premature to abate our efforts to increase employment so long as the figures of unemployment remain so large. In a sense this must be true. But I believe that we are approaching, or have reached, the point where there is not much advantage in applying *a further general stimulus at the centre.* So long a surplus resources were widely diffused between industries and localities, it was no great matter at what point in the economic structure the impulse of an increased demand was applied. But the evidence grows that – for several reasons into which there is no space to enter here – the economic structure is unfortunately rigid and that (for example) building activity in the home counties is less effective than one might have hoped in decreasing unemployment in the distressed areas. It follows that the later stages of recovery require *a different technique...* We are in more need today of *a rightly distributed demand than of a greater aggregate demand ...*

This echoes Chapter 21 of the *General Theory*:

If there is a perfect balance in the respective quantities of specialised unemployed resources, the point of full employment will be reached for all of them simultaneously. But, in general, the demand for some services and commodities will reach a level beyond which their supply is, for the time being, perfectly inelastic whilst in other directions there is still a substantial surplus of resources without employment. Thus as output increases, a series of 'bottle-necks' will be successively reached, where the supply of particular commodities ceases to be elastic ... .

In his 12 January article he pointed to the great difficulty of arriving, by 'planning' at the correct level of investment and continued:

The best we can hope to achieve is to use those kinds of investment which it is relatively easy to plan as a makeweight, bringing them in so as to preserve as much stability of aggregate investment as we can manage at the right and appropriate level. Three years ago it was important to use public policy to increase investment. It may soon be equally important to retard certain types of investment ...

In his next article ' "Dear" Money' he wrote:

Nevertheless a phase of recovery may be at hand when it will be desirable to find other methods temporarily to damp down aggregate demand . . .

Just as it was advisable for the Government to incur debt during the slump, so for the same reasons it is now advisable that they should incline to the opposite policy. Aggregate demand is increased by loan-expenditure and decreased when loans are discharged out of taxation. In view of the high cost of the armaments, which we cannot postpone, it would put too much strain on our fiscal system actually to discharge debt, but the Chancellor of the Exchequer should, I suggest, meet the main part of the cost of armaments out of taxation, raising taxes and withholding all reliefs for the present as something in hand for 1938 or 1939, or whenever there are signs of recession. The boom, not the slump, is the right time for austerity at the Treasury.

Just as it was advisable for local authorities to press on with capital expenditure during the slump, so it is now advisable that they should postpone whatever new enterprises can reasonably be held back.

Keynes was writing when the rearmament programme was under way and he, not knowing, of course, that war was to come, was concerned to avoid the next slump. Nevertheless, with unemployment at 12 per cent, he argues against any further increase in aggregate demand and for a balanced budget. It is clear too that he regards any attempt to plan total investment as too ambitious, and wants only to use 'makeweight' public works. But these should not be called into play now: local authorities should hold back postponable expenditure. His whole approach is modest and cautious in the extreme.

In his *Times* article of 11 March 1937 Keynes asked whether the Chancellor of the Exchequer's plan to borrow £80 m. a year for rearmament was likely to be inflationary. He concluded that it *need* not be, although it might be 'rather near the limit'; and this even though 'The number of insured persons who are still unemployed is, indeed as high as $12\frac{1}{2}$ per cent'.

He returned again to the point that it was the *distribution* of demand that was all important. Some relief could be expected from increased imports.

But it remains particularly advisable to do anything possible to stimulate our staple exports. For it is here that our reserves of surplus labour are chiefly to be found.

Thirdly, measures to ensure that all possible orders are placed in the special areas where surplus resources are available will greatly help . . . whether demand is or is not inflationary depends on whether it is directed towards trades and localities, which have no surplus capacity. To organise output in the special areas is a means of claiming rearmament without inflation.

It is clear from this, and from his earlier emphasis on the need for a rightly distributed demand that Keynes was far from thinking in the simplistic aggregative terms that later became the stock-in-trade of any self-styled 'Keynesian.' Keynes concluded:

It is easy to employ 80 to 90 per cent of the national resources without taking much thought as to how to fit things in. For there is a margin to play with, almost all round. But to employ 95 to 100 per cent of the national resources is a different task altogether. It cannot be done without care and management; and the attempt to do so might lead to an inflation . . .

It cannot be inferred from any of this that Keynes regarded $12\frac{1}{2}$ per cent or 10 per cent or 5 per cent or any other per cent as the 'natural' rate of unemployment. What can be inferred is that he viewed any stimulation of demand beyond the point where the economy was employing around 90 per cent of its resources, as a matter to be undertaken only with great caution and with a care for directing the increased demand to areas where surplus capacity existed. It can also be inferred that Keynes did not regard the reduction – let alone the elimination – of unemployment as an absolute objective, to be pursued at the expense of other objectives: he was much concerned to avoid inflation.

The answer to the question posed at the beginning of this section is that it is not fair at all: Keynes is blameless. The charge fails to distinguish between Keynes and 'the Keynesians', or, as it has become fashionable to call them, 'the pseudo-Keynesians'.

How did it come about that policies committed in the name of Keynes were so far from the policies he himself had advocated? That is to say, to spell it out, why was the attempt made, for more than 20 years, to run the British economy close to its absolute production-possibility-frontier by maintaining a very high pressure of demand, when Keynes himself was so cautious in advancing much beyond the 90 per cent frontier?

The short, and question-begging answer, is 'because that is what politicians decided'. But politicians are not, usually, economists. They do not operate in an intellectual vacuum, and in economic matters they do take advice from economists. Indeed, they customarily have more economic advice than they need. One of the major fringe benefits of economics as a profession is the opportunities it gives for offering advice, often at quite uneconomic prices. It may be protested that we cannot blame economists for decisions that are ultimately political, but I think we can. If advice from economic 'experts' is overwhelmingly of the same character, politicians cannot reasonably be expected to ignore it and follow some other course of action which economists tell them will be disastrous or, at best, sub-optimal. Economics, after all, claims to be, a 'science' and science enjoys great prestige. It is in any case doubtful whether economists would strenuously disclaim any responsibility for *successful* policies carried out by politicians on their advice.

Even so, even if it is agreed that it is economists' blood we are after, the question is not susceptible to a simple or definitive answer. Because what we are asked to do is to display the advice, competence, motivation of countless economists, often anonymous, over a period of nearly a quarter of a century. The task can be done, should be done, and has, in part, already been done,[1] but I do not propose to essay it anew here. All I propose to do is to offer some lines of thought on the reasons for economists' failure.

Ignorance

It is entirely possible that many economists were unaware of the *policy* advice tendered by Keynes in peacetime. They may also have misunderstood his overall purpose, which was *not* to provide a blueprint guaranteeing complete full employment for ever, but to solve the problem of severe unemployment lasting for a long period of time – in short, the problem of chronic unemployment.

In his *Economics and Economic Policy* Professor Hutchison contrasted the situation in post-war Britain with that faced by Keynes:

It is the pressing claims of a wide range of competing policy objectives, or the fact that throughout much of the post-war period the British economy has been on, or pretty near, a kind of policy-possibility-frontier . . . which constitutes such a complete contrast with the policy situations which confronted Keynes in the inter-war years. Keynes made the point that when one moves from conditions of unemployment to those of full employment a number of theoretical and policy propositions which held in the one case, cease to hold in the other. . . . Policy problems certainly take on a very different and more complex form when one moves from an economy averaging 14 per cent unemployment . . . to one averaging $1\frac{1}{2}$ to $2\frac{1}{2}$ per cent.

With unemployment at 10, 15 and 22 per cent for years and decades on end, there was one starkly simple, overriding policy objective on which to concentrate, . . . which conflicted hardly at all with any, or most, other substantial objectives . . . such a stark situation introduced and permitted an immense simplification of economic policy issues...Certainly there were conflicts ... The fight against these was hard enough, but, in waging it, Keynes was largely justified...in disregarding as negligible the interests and objectives conflicting with his overriding employment objective, and in advocating it as 'the one thing necessary'.

No economist, for most of the two decades following the war, was justified in treating the interests and objectives threatened by his particular policy nostrum in the same cavalier fashion, though many did so. The uniqueness of the policy situation confronted and attacked by Keynes has not been sufficiently recognised in the two decades after his death, and this has obscured the need to define and choose policy objectives much more precisely, and to make explicit estimates of the cost of attaining a higher level in any one particular objective, in terms of the probable losses in terms of others.

The long-drawn-out unemployment of the inter-war years was a terrible, destroying thing. The lives of two generations were needlessly impoverished by it. The residue was a bitterness, a fear and loathing of unemployment and a fierce resolve that it must never happen again. The word became a curse, an abstraction, a devil's incantation, an anathema; and in the process it lost all content: unemployment was unemployment. The emotive force of the mere word was such that it forbad analysis and obscured distinctions, such as the distinction between a million and more people unemployed for 20 years and a few hundred thousand (a third of whom were probably unemployable) moving between jobs. (And cushioned, in the process, by an adequate system of unemployment and social security benefit). Thus, *any* increase in unemployment, from whatever level, triggered a Pavlovian response. It was immoral, it was claimed, to use unemployment as an instrument of economic policy[6] and no doubt it was. The trouble was that the moralists in their fervour were unable to make the distinction between unemployment as an *instrument* and unemployment as a *consequence* of other policies honourable in their own right.

Arrogance

The Keynesian analysis was so intellectually exciting and beguiling that economists came to believe that at last they had a truly scientific tool to use. This attitude was supported by the good fortune that the Keynesian apparatus was readily expressible in mathematical terms. There is nothing to compare with mathematics for adding credence and apparent simplicity to an otherwise complex argument: so much can be subsumed in the symbols.

To be fair, the economists had good cause to be cock-a-hoop: the

25 years following the war *were* a period of great and growing prosperity, in marked contrast to the 25 or more years before the war; and there can be no doubt that at least part of this economic success stemmed directly from Keynes' ideas.

Possessed of an intellectually satisfying theory and apparent evidence of its successful application to policy, economists became unstoppable, especially as they had at their disposal increasingly better statistics and computers. The economy *could*, under their guidance, be forecast and managed in a scientific way. If the management of demand could reduce unemployment to 3 per cent, then why not 2 per cent, 1 per cent, even zero?

It is likely that Keynes, who could be as arrogant as the next man, would have had none of this. 'If economists' he wrote, 'could manage to get themselves thought of as humble, competent people, on a level with dentists, that would be splendid!'[7]

Bias and wishful thinking

One would find it unusual to see a reference to a 'left-wing chemist' or a 'right-wing geologist', yet the adjectives applied to economists pass without comment. This is not surprising: it acknowledges that economics is a social science and that the matters which are of interest to economists – such as the level of unemployment, wages and prices – are also of pressing concern to politicians. Nor is political bias in these matters anything to be ashamed of. What is to be deplored is political bias passed off as objective economics. As T. W. Hutchison[1] has observed:

> It is not cultivating economics as a serious subject to use it for rationalising what party leaders or groups want to hear, or for dressing up particular preconceptions and prejudices as fashionable 'expertise' or for covering over inevitable ignorance with ideologically biased dogmatism.[8]

That a good deal of dressing up of essentially political ideas in economic clothing does go on is undeniable. Nor is this reprehensible *if it is what the economist is being paid to do*. Government economists are required, like other civil servants, to provide ammunition and argument for the policies of the government of the day. There is nothing wrong in that: in that capacity an economist's role is analogous to that of the barrister retained to present a case.

What is less easily defended is the practice of presenting economic analysis and advice as objective when in truth it derives as much from the author's political values as from his economics. Fortunately, the political standpoint of the more prolific commentators

Roy Harrod? Wyml?

soon becomes apparent, or may be explicitly declared, so that an appropriate discounting can be made.

If we drew a line to represent the political spectrum, with the state collectivists on the extreme left and the anarchists on the right-hand end, and placed representative economists along it we would find, say, Dr. Balogh towards the left-hand end, Kenneth Galbraith somewhere in the middle and Keynes and Friedman fairly close together up towards the right-hand end. Yet Keynesian economics has always attracted economists and politicians of a broadly leftward orientation. (This is not to say that right-wing economists cannot work within Keynes's framework: they can and have. Marxists, however, do not find Keynes congenial).

This attraction of Keynesianism for the political left has several roots. First is Keynesianism's origin in the problem of unemployment, a problem, rightly, of passionate concern to labour movements. The problem, however, has been transformed from one of providing employment for most of the people most of the time into one of ensuring employment for all of the people all of the time. Secondly, Keynesianism implies the need for state intervention 'to make capitalism work.' Keynes himself envisaged such intervention as minimal and acknowledged its necessity somewhat reluctantly; but intervention is much more congenial to those in the middle and left of the spectrum, with the result that minimal and necessary intervention of a makeweight character is transmuted into economic planning and the purposive management of the economy. Thirdly, Keynesianism implies the need for budget deficits, when appropriate, and for public expenditure. Public expenditure occupies a very special place in the socialist pantheon, to the extent that it sometimes seems to possess a virtue which is inherent and independent of the purpose of the expenditure. In a contrary sense it also has a special place in the demonology of the right.

No one would argue that the mismanagement of the British economy in the post-war years, if mismanagement there was, was entirely or largely attributable to politically coloured advice from left-wing economists. But it does seem to have been the case, until quite recently, that what, for want of a better term, we might call the British economic establishment has been dominated by economists of an orientation that has led them to believe, and to advise, that the economy can be run at a much higher pressure of demand than in fact it can. They believed either that an extremely low level of unemployment was compatible with the achievement of other objectives; or they gave other objectives – price stability, for example – much lower priority.

Professor Harry Johnson put these matters, rather more robustly, thus:[9]

Finally, the Keynesian revolution, and more specifically its policy residue in the form of the assumption that the capitalist system ought to be capable of delivering at all times a politically determined minimum percentage of unemployment within an equally politically determined tolerable maximum rate of inflation, usually equated with zero, was widely interpreted as setting the seal of scientific legitimacy on a standard of performance impossible for any economic system to fulfill. (It also sanctified two much longer-standing tenets of radical belief: that the self-seeking activities of monopolies of labour have a social legitimacy denied with loathing to monopolies based on capital or industrial knowledge, and that society possesses vast reservoirs of resources that only the stupidity or self-seeking of the capitalists prevents from being used for noble social purposes.)

Superficialities of this kind are remarkable only for their capacity to seduce self-respecting and otherwise reasonable and educated people, and perhaps as demonstrating that P. T. Barnum's dictum that 'there's a sucker born every minute' is a masterpiece of understatement.

. . . the pre-eminence of Cambridge, England, in economics achieved at the end of the 1930s, largely due to Keynes's General Theory, both enabled Keynes's successors to exploit Cambridge's prestige for the propagation of their own political beliefs (which were vastly different from Keynes's own), and attracted to Cambridge a continuing stream of able students who became 'devoted proselytisers for the true faith among the heathen from whose ranks they sprang'.

. . . at every point of crucial economic policy decision British economics has reacted either with political dogma or with political opportunism.

Economics is far from an exact science, if, indeed, it is a science at all.[12] To be sure, the economist works with axioms, hypotheses, logical deduction and empirical evidence. But while the logic may be sound the axioms are few, the hypotheses many and the empirical evidence rarely conclusive and often conflicting. These rather meagre ingredients of the economic pudding have, therefore, to be mixed together with a rather large dollop of judgement. It is hardly surprising if the optional ingredients added by the economic cook bring the dish to a flavour and consistency to accord with his taste.

In this section I have been concerned to suggest only that one of the causes of the less-than-optimal performance of the British econ-omy may have been wishful thinking and bias on the part of econ-omists of a mainly Cambridge extraction and Keynesian persuasion who, it is alleged, comprised the British economic Establishment in the years under discussion. It was not relevant in this context to say anything about the political disposition of non- or anti-Keynesians. But Keynesians have no monopoly of political inspiration: the po-

65

litical roots of monetarism are worth examination and to this we turn in Chapter 8.

Growthmanship

Growthmanship might be considered as one manifestation of arrogance and wishful thinking. It enjoyed a great vogue in the 1950s and 1960s when the whole profession appeared to have been taken over by growth economists, stimulated, in the first place, by the post-war problems of the 'under-developed'countries. As Professor Hutchison[1] puts it:

In terms of what is often called 'theory' by economists, or in terms more precisely, of non-empirical or quasi-empirical, analytical model building, the study of growth has, of course, been a major field of activity in Britain in this period. As regards the production of growth models, Britain must rank very high, quite possibly at the top, in any world league table of output per head or per man-hour. Perhaps the (quite invalid) presumption has gained ground that so much strenuous intellectual production must somehow have so enlarged the understanding of the causes of economic growth as to increase significantly the power to raise or regulate it by the application of a coherent, reasonably well tested and agreed theory, yielding reasonably definite conditional predictions regarding the effects of growth on alternative policies.

But

. . . a claim that the fast growing countries are indebted, for any significant measure of their success, to what is understood by 'dynamic' or growth theory, would seem impossible to entertain.

In the United Kingdom the growth vogue was at its peak from July 1962, when Mr. Maudling became Chancellor of the Exchequer, until the crisis measures of July 1966 killed stone dead the National Plan published 10 months earlier. Early in 1963 the newly-set-up National Economic Development Council approved a 4 per cent growth target (which was, to say the least, imaginative, but which the more enthusiastic growthmen regarded as unambitious), and the new Chancellor introduced an expansionary Budget.

He was urged by the growthmen to be bold and to 'drive straight through' any balance of payments difficulties. The overseas 'balance for official financing'deteriorated from a surplus of £192 million in 1962 to deficits of £58 million in 1963 and £695 million in 1964.[10]

The new Labour Government elected in October 1964 complained bitterly and with justification of the balance of payments mess they had discovered when they 'opened the books', but nevertheless set up, under the ebullient George Brown, the Department of Economic Affairs, dedicated to growth. The Treasury, it was felt, did not have its heart in growth, being overly-concerned with the balance of payments. The Treasury did, however, come in handy in November 1964 when, with the Bank, it negotiated a loan of $3 billion to save the pound. In September of the following year the National Plan was proclaimed, based on economic growth of 25 per cent between 1964 and 1970. It did not survive the announcement, in July 1966, of a six months standstill on wages and prices, to be followed by six months of severe restraint.

That was effectively the end of growth as a primary economic objective; but while it lasted the cult had added its measure to the pressures in the economy. It was seen by some as a logical extension of Keynesianism. The problem of unemployment was solved, for good and all. The next step was to stoke up demand beyond the existing capacity of the economy to produce and this demand would generate new supply *if everyone expected the high level of demand to persist*. By a process of collective autosuggestion, we could talk ourselves into higher rates of growth. It was, as someone put it, the economics of Christian Science.[13]

Ignorance, arrogance, bias, wishful thinking, and growthmanship; these, I suggest, were the ingredients of economic unwisdom. The judgement of Lord Robbins, speaking in the House of Lords in July 1966[11] was that:

The pickle in which we find ourselves is the product of confused thought rather than inferiority of will. It is the intellectuals who have fostered the belief that we can have growth without discipline, stable prices with unrestrained demand, over-full employment without inflation and balance of payments difficulties; it is these who are ultimately blameworthy if anyone is.

To paraphrase Macaulay on Lord Byron we could say that from the economics of Lord Keynes his successors drew a system compounded of profligacy and imprudence, in which the two great commandments were for the individual to abjure saving and the state to embrace spending.

Notes

1. *Economics and Economic Policy in Britain, 1946–66*, Allen and Unwin 1968.
2. Quoted by T. W. Hutchison in *Keynes Versus the 'Keynesians'* ...?

(The Institute of Economic Affairs 1977). This chapter owes much to that essay and to Professor Hutchison's work quoted at Note 1.

3. An average of 2 per cent means a lower percentage in some areas. In March 1966, for example, when the percentage rate of unemployment in Great Britain was 1.3 this figure was inflated by percentages of 2.8 in Scotland and Wales, and 2.5 in the Northern Region. The percentage in the West Midlands was 0.7, in the Midlands as a whole 0.8, and in London and the South East 0.9. Source: *Ministry of Labour Gazette*, April 1966.

4. House of Commons, 22 May 1979.

5. Churchill's budget speech, 1929.

6. 'Any policy measures deliberately designed to increase the level of unemployment are morally wrong . . . I prefer the Swedish target, which they cannot of course achieve fully, of having the unemployment at 0 per cent.' Sir Roy Harrod *Towards a New Economic Policy*, (1967 pp. 16 and 17). quoted by T. W. Hutchison in *Economics and Economic Policy*.

7. Final sentence of *Essays in Persuasion*, (Macmillan 1931).

8. Elsewhere in the same book he writes: 'In fact, what is disappointing for those who would like to see economics cultivated as a kind of discipline or 'serious subject' (not to say 'science') is that one can find considerably more examples of economists using economic arguments in support of their known political views than one can of those prepared to admit that the economic arguments ran counter to their political attitudes. Usually, though not quite always, if one knew a university economist's political attitudes, one could predict with quite a high probability what his or her assessment of the economic arguments would be.'

9. *On Economics & Society*, The University of Chicago Press 1975, p. 188.

10. The deficit improved to £353 m. in 1965 but then continued downwards: £591 m. in 1966, £671 m. in 1967 and £1410 m. in 1968.

11. Quoted by Hutchison in *Economics & Economic Policy*.

12. Although: 'I do not see how . . . (members of the public who survey the controversy) . . . can avoid the conclusion that economics is not a science concerned with phenomena, but a survival of medieval logic, and that economists are persons who earn their livings by taking in one another's definitions for mangling.'
From Lord Beveridge's farewell address as Director of the London School of Economics, 24 June 1937. Quoted by Richard Lipsey in *An Introduction to Positive Economics* (Weidenfeld and Nicholson 1963).

13. There is an interesting parallel here with the monetarists, who attach considerable importance to expectations as a factor making their policies speedily effective.

Chapter six

New theory in old bottles

New ideas win a public and a professional hearing, not on their scientific merits, but on whether or not they promise a solution to important problems that the established orthodoxy has proved itself incapable of, solving.

Harry G. Johnson[1]

In 1921 the percentage of unemployed in the United Kingdom was 12.9 and in 1938 it was 13.5. In between it rose to 22 per cent in 1932, and only fell below 10 in one year (1927). The number unemployed never fell below 1 million. In 1921 the retail price index was 47 and in 1938 it was 33 (1963 = 100). Chronic unemployment was a problem; inflation was not.

In 1950, out of a work-force substantially larger than in 1938, less than 300 thousand were unemployed, and the number remained below 500 thousand until 1967 and did not reach a million until 1976. The *percentage* unemployed remained below 2.5 until 1970, a figure to which it returned in 1973. Between 1950 and 1981 prices rose nearly nine-fold. Unemployment was not a problem; inflation was.

A nine-fold increase in prices in just over 30 years is serious enough. More significant for our story is that it took 18 years – from 1950 to 1968 for prices to double, but only seven years – from 1963 to 1975 – for them to more than double again. The last doubling took only five years (1976 to 1981). Inflation was proceeding at an increasing rate.[2]

Thus the new doctrines of monetarism[3], which promised a cure for inflation and which had been gaining acceptance in the United States of America since the 1950s, began to fall on increasingly receptive ears and minds in the United Kingdom; just as, one might suggest, without pushing the parallel too far, the new doctrine of the GT had found a more-than-ready acceptance in 1936 after 18 years or so of chronic unemployment.

We should not find it surprising that in economics, which is after all one of the social sciences, theories change as society and society's problems change.[5] It would be a barren discipline that produced solutions to non-existent problems or, worse perhaps, produced today's solutions for yesterday's problems. The accusation levelled now at unreconstructed Keynesians is that they are peddling yesterday's solutions for today's problems.[4]

The new paradigm of Keynes came all of a piece, neatly in one book, the very model of a tablet handed down. And his priests were quick to construct dogma out of theology and build the Keynesian cross, so that no one, except perhaps Keynes, had any doubt what Keynesianism stood for. True, there was endless (it still goes on) argument about what he meant, what he *really* meant and, indeed, about whether he had said anything new at all. Nevertheless, the new model was there, in the text books, for all to see.

It is not, alas for the expositor, the same story with monetarism. But monetarism is, as they say, 'associated with the name of Professor Friedman of Chicago', and as upon that, at least, everyone is agreed, let us start with him.

Since we value the horizontal man more than we honour the vertical one, encomiums for Friedman, who is alive, are fewer than for Keynes; but we do know that he is the holder of the 1976 Nobel Prize in Economics, and a prolific writer – not only in economics – with some 250 publications, including 27 books, to his name. He has received the accolade of a television series, which places him level with Galbraith and one up on Keynes. There are, as John Burton has noted[6] fascinating similarities between Friedman and Keynes:

... their prodigious output, their wide range of concerns combined with a central interest in monetary theory; their talent for controversy and anti-establishmentarianism; their international status; their exceptional mental acuity, and agility in debate; their noted personal charm.

Impressive as this catalogue is, I submit, with respect to Mr. Burton, that it omits two of the most striking things that the two have in common: a passionate concern for the individual and his freedom and range of choice; and a notable, indeed enviable, capacity for self-publicity.

Milton Friedman is associated not only with monetarism and the Chicago School but with the Quantity Theory of Money – a view encouraged, no doubt, by the titles of two of his earlier (1956) publications: *The Quantity Theory of Money – A Restatement* and (as editor) *Studies in the Quantity Theory of Money*[7]

As Professor H. G. Johnson has pointed out in his highly entertaining account of the characteristics of a successful revolution or counter-revolution in economics,[1] it is very helpful, if not essential, to be able to claim respectable antecedents among the early fathers. This adds authority and a certain gravitas to the proceedings and sooths apprehensions that the whole thing might be *too* revolutionary. Keynes appealed to Malthus, and Friedman to Irving Fisher (the great populariser of the Quantity Theory) and to 'the oral tradition of the Chicago School.' Both of Friedman's claims have been disputed: his monetary theory has little to do with Fisher's; and his claims to the Chicago oral tradition have been challenged by Patinkin.[8] That Friedman's theories have little in common with the traditional quantity theory may come as a surprise to many of his disciples, not least to those who try to put (what they believe to be) his theories into practice. Perhaps that is another thing that Keynes and Friedman have in common: they seem to be unfortunate in their disciples.

Since there is no *locus classicus* of monetarism upon which to draw we may best proceed by drawing up a list of propositions associated with the doctrine. The drawing up of such a list does not carry the implication that all monetarists agree with any item, or that any monetarist agrees with all items. The doctrine of monetarism is not a seamless robe, and we have to proceed in a somewhat patchwork way. It will help if we group the propositions under a few broad heads.

Methodological

1. It is better to have a theory that predicts than one that explains.
2. Small economic models are better than large.

Theoretical

3. The Fisherian Quantity Theory is valid: changes in the quantity of money change prices proportionately (and in the same direction).
4. The (transactions or income) velocity of money is stable.
5. The demand for money is a stable function of real wealth.
6. Money must be analysed as an asset, one among *many* alternative assets.
7. The mechanism through which changes in the quantity of money are transmitted to prices and output begins with assets and with people's efforts to change their holdings of assets, including money.

71

8. It is important to distinguish between real and monetary variables.
9. There are 'natural' rates of employment and of interest.
10. It is permanent, not current, income that matters for predictive purposes.
11. Changes in the quantity of money (QM) are the main cause of changes in nominal income; and, specifically, are more important than changes in autonomous investment.
12. The relationship between the change in QM and the change in nominal income is subject to a variable lag. The first change is in output with little effect on prices. If the change in QM is downwards, output falls after 6–9 months and a gap opens up between actual and potential output and this exercises downward pressure on prices, after a further lag of 6–9 months. So the total lag between a change in QM and a change in prices is 12–18 months. (But this lag now seems to have been extended to two years).
13. The causation always runs from changes in QM to changes in nominal income, not the other way round.
14. Even allowing for lags the sequence outlined above is far from perfect; and it does not tell us how the final short-run change in nominal income will be divided between a change in output and a change in prices.
15. But in the long run the effect is only on prices. Output depends upon real factors.
16. A change in QM affects interest rates perversely: a rise in QM will first lower interest rates and then, as output grows, they rise.

Policy

17. 'Fine tuning' is not possible: what we should aim for is a constant (low) rate of growth of the QM.
18. It is more important to control the QM than interest rates and the availability of credit.
19. Floating exchange rates are better than fixed.
20. Employment cannot be raised permanently by a fiscal deficit.

Inflation

21. Inflation is always a monetary phenomenon.
22. Government spending is inflationary only if financed by creating money.

Expectations

23. Expectations play a crucial role in the *speed* with which monetary policies take effect.

This menu, partial though it may be, gives a general flavour of monetarist thinking. Before we try to organise it into some sort of logical whole, two observations may be in order. First, proposition 3 can be safely ignored: it has no place in modern monetarist theory. Secondly, it is clear, if this selection of propositions is a representative one, and I believe it to be, that monetarism has more to offer than an explanation of inflation: many of the propositions are about the relationship between money and income, not money and prices.

The core of the monetarist system is propositions 6 and 7: money is seen as one asset among a whole range of assets. People and firms in the private sector of the economy have a 'desired portfolio of assets.' That is to say, they dispose of their wealth (wealth is not the same as income) in a balanced way so as to achieve the maximum satisfaction from it. The range of possible assets in which wealth might be invested is very wide indeed and would include property (real estate), shares in companies, government bonds, national savings, owner-occupied housing, antiques, stamps, education for oneself and children. The list can be extended according to taste. The point is that there is a wide range of choice. And one of the choices is, of course, money. Each of the chosen outlets for wealth will yield a return to the holder in one form or another: bonds and equities will yield a cash dividend, owner-occupied housing will yield security, status and a hedge against inflation, education will yield personal satisfaction, status and, possibly, higher income over a lifetime.

The returns from investment do not all accrue at once: they flow in over time. In making our choice we make a guess about the future. In making a choice we form a judgement not only about the future of one possible asset but about the future of them all. Our expectations form a vital part of the selection.

Now at first sight *money* (if we define it as cash in hand or in a current account at the bank) yields no return at all. Indeed, in inflationary conditions its return is negative because it buys less and less as time goes by. But in fact it yields one very important return, that of *liquidity*. It is true that some non-monetary assets, for example building society deposits, are fairly readily convertible into cash, but with others – antiques, for example – it is much more difficult, and the cash value in most cases uncertain.

Since our knowledge of the future is always and necessarily uncertain it is a great advantage to have one asset which is not, as it were, committed to the future. That asset is money. And the greater the uncertainty the more money shall we wish to hold. We shall need some money to meet current spending, and the amount we keep for this purpose will depend upon our habits and our income.

To generalise we can say that the demand for money will depend upon income, real wealth, the range of (other) assets, and expectations. Note that in Keynes the demand for money rested on a choice only between holding money and holding bonds.

Now we may suppose that at any given time, and given all the existing conditions, all members of the private sector will be as near as they can get to satisfaction with their portfolio of asset holdings. This 'equilibrium' will be a moving equilibrium, as are all equilibria in a dynamic economy.

Let us now suppose that there is an increase in the quantity of money. This is not a very satisfactory supposition, because the results will be different depending on how the increase is brought about and who gets it. But let that ride and just assume an increase in the quantity of money.

Since the private sector was previously in portfolio equilibrium it is now in portfolio disequilibrium and people will act to restore equilibrium – not all at once, perhaps, but as the extra money 'seeps through' and holders become aware of it.

To understand what happens next it is essential to grasp the idea, indeed the fact, that all the money in an economy (we are talking here of a closed economy) has to be held by someone. An individual can reduce his holding only if another individual is willing to increase his.

As Professor Friedman explains it:[9]

For all individuals combined, however, the appearance that they can control their own cash balances is an optical illusion. One individual can reduce or increase his cash balance only because another individual or several others are induced to increase or reduce theirs; that is, to do the opposite of what he does. If individuals as a whole were to try to reduce the number of dollars they held, they could not all do so, they would simply be playing a game of musical chairs. In trying to do so, however, they would raise the flow of expenditure and of money income since each would be trying to spend more than he receives; in the process adding to someone else's receipts, and, reciprocally, finding his own higher than anticipated because of the attempt by still others to spend more than they receive. In the process prices would tend to rise, which would reduce the real value of cash balances . . .

And he goes on to point to the opposite case: if people try to hold more cash in the face of an unchanged money supply this will result only in lower spending, lower income and lower prices. There is surely little here that Keynes would have disputed.

To return to the consequences of disequilibrium: the first effect is likely to be that interest rates will fall as holders of unwanted cash try to convert it into bonds. (With an unchanged stock of bonds, bond prices must rise to meet the new demand, and when bond prices rise interest rates fall). But part of the excess money will be used to buy other financial assets, non-financial assets, physical capital goods or consumption goods. If the economy is underemployed, i.e. not working at full capacity, there will be an increase in economic activity until a level of income is reached at which the community as a whole is a willing holder of the higher money stock. If the economy is fully employed so that no increase in output is possible prices will rise until a price level is reached at which all the stock of money will be willingly held.

Conversely, with a fall in the stock of money there will be a contraction in economic activity and downward pressure on prices until a level is reached at which money holdings are at their desired level.

If the economy is not closed but open, i.e. has foreign trade, then further options are open to people trying to rid themselves of money: they may buy foreign assets or foreign goods and services. This will lead to a balance of payments deficit if the exchange rate is fixed; or a fall in the exchange rate if it is floating. (There will also be secondary effects on the foreign sector arising from the changed level of domestic activity and the changed level of the rate of interest).

Monetarists argue that because of its liquidity money is a special sort of asset and changes in its quantity will be felt quickly throughout the economy. The ways in which the monetary effect is transmitted are many, and no precise mechanism can be, or need be, specified. (Proposition 1.) Changes in the money supply will affect nominal income but we cannot say at all precisely how long this will take nor how the effect will be distributed between changes in output and changes in prices. (Propositions 11, 12, 13, 14). But in the long run the effect will be only on prices (Proposition 15).

Since the effects of changes in the money supply are so powerful, it is unnecessary to use any other instrument for the control of the economy. Not only is it unnecessary, it is also either useless or harmful. It is useless, for example, to try permanently to raise the level of employment by running a fiscal deficit (Proposition 20), because the 'natural' level of employment (Proposition 9) is determined by 'real' forces. There is also a 'natural' rate of interest which it would be as well not to interfere with. The exchange rate must be determined by market forces (Proposition 19). If Governments cannot use fiscal policy, interest rate policy or the exchange rate as policy instruments 'fine tuning' of the economy becomes impossible. (Proposition 17). Not only does this not matter, it is desirable, because all deliberate policy action of this nature distorts the market mechanism and the 'natural' working of the economy. All that is required is to control the rate of growth of the money supply. Everything else then falls into place. Since one of the major variables that falls into place is the price level, it follows that prices and incomes policies are unnecessary; and, again, not only unnecessary but harmful because they cut across market forces.

In this chapter I have tried to do no more than display the central ideas of monetarism, and the implications of those ideas for policy. The argument will be pursued and expanded in later chapters, especially those on inflation and its control. It is already becoming clear that the monetarist view of the world and of the way the economy works is vastly different from the view Governments have taken in the post-war years. But is it so very different from the view that Keynes took?

Yes

Notes

1. 'The Keynesian Revolution and the Monetarist Counterrevolution' in *On Economics and Society* (The University of Chicago Press 1975, p.104.)
2. Even at what, these days, might seem an unattainable 4 per cent prices will double every 18 years, i.e. at the end of a normal life-span they will be 16 times higher than at birth. At a little over 10 per cent (10.4%) they double every seven years, i.e. ten doublings in a lifetime. (See Appendix to Chapter 11).
3. The term is nowadays often confused with Thatcherism and used pejoratively. I used it neutrally, for want of a better. Its invention is attributed to Karl Brunner in 1968.
4. Or even yesterday's solutions for yesterday's problems. H. G. Johnson writes 'The view that unemployment is the overriding social problem also lingers on among British Keynesians such as Joan Robinson, Roy Harrod and Thomas Balogh. . . . .'
    'The Keynesian Revolution and the Monetarist Counter-revolution', 1970 reprinted in *On Economics and Society*, University of Chicago Press.
5. Professor T. W. Hutchison has identified three sources of the decline of a once-successful theory or 'paradigm', the second of which is 'historical and institutional change':

'. . . in economics and the social sciences, a very important source, often cumulative, of weakness and inadequacy (unlike, usually, in the natural sciences) consists of changes in historical conditions and institutions. Such changes both give rise to new weaknesses and inadequacies and magnify old ones, by creating empirical anomalies or irrelevances in once more acceptable "orthodox" doctrines.'

Keynes versus the 'Keynesians' . . . ?

(The Institute of Economic Affairs 1977.)
It was, of course, just such 'empirical anomalies or irrelevancies' in 'the classics' that Keynes had attacked.

6. 'Milton Friedman' A discussion paper prepared for *Twelve Contemporary Economists*. (Macmillan).
7. University of Chicago Press.
8. Don Patinkin *The Chicago Tradition, The Quantity Theory, and Friedman*. Journal of Money Credit and Banking 1, Feb. 1969.
9. 'Statement on monetary theory and policy' in *Employment, Growth and Price Levels* US Government Printing Office, 1959.

Chapter seven

Looking-glass economics

Strange! that such high dispute should be
Twixt Tweedledum and Tweedledee

John Byrom

Liquidity preference or the demand for money?

From the dazzling display of Keynesian gadgetry the device selected by economists as his most lasting and original contribution to economic theory is the Liquidity Preference Function,[1] the function or schedule, which, in conjunction with the quantity of money, determines the rate of interest.

The cost of holding cash balances, or hoards, argued Keynes, was the interest foregone. The higher the rate of interest the greater the cost; and the lower the rate the smaller the cost. The propensity to hoard, or to hold cash, what Keynes called the Liquidity Preference function, could therefore be drawn as a demand curve of the usual shape relating the amount of money demanded to the rate of interest. See Figs. 4.8 and 4.9 and the diagrammatic Appendix to Chapter 9. Instead of 'Liquidity preference curve' we can write 'Demand for money'

Keynes recognised that an increase in the quantity of money could be spent in a great variety of ways: in the purchase of securities of all kinds, in the purchase of real capital goods, the purchase of non-monetary assets and in consumption. But what Keynes needed his demand-for-money function for was to determine the rate of interest, and to achieve this he had to have, as the alternative to holding money, an asset carrying a rate of interest denominated in money terms. He chose the rate of interest on Government Bonds.

In illustrating the power of the changes in the quantity of money to affect economic activity Friedman relies heavily on the fact that all money must be held by someone. Keynes makes exactly the same point[2].

For the decision to hoard is not taken absolutely or without regard to the advantages offered for parting with liquidity – it results from a balancing of advantages, and we have, therefore to know what lies in the other scale. Moreover, it is impossible for the actual amount of hoarding to change as a result of decisions on the part of the public, so long as we mean by 'hoarding' the actual holding of cash. For the amount of hoarding must be equal to the quantity of money . . . ; and the quantity of money is not determined by the public.

The effect of changes in the quantity of money on the rate of interest is one element in the monetarist scheme of things. Proposition 16 states: 'A change in the quantity of money (QM) affects interest rates perversely; a rise in QM will first lower interest rates and then, as output grows, they rise' (and conversely for a fall in QM). This fits neatly into Keynes's framework. For as may be seen from the diagrammatic Appendix to Chapter 9 the systems of Keynes and Friedman yield, in this respect, identical results (although the mechanisms are different.)

Much confusion and misunderstanding might have been avoided if Keynes had labelled 'Liquidity perference' 'Demand for money'; or if Friedman had called his work 'Studies in the liquidity preference theory of money' instead of 'Studies in the quantity theory of money'. But then, perhaps no one outside the profession would have taken any notice. And that would not have done: for what Friedman wanted to influence was not only theory but policy.

Money, output and prices

The similarities between the monetarist story and the Keynesian do not end with the rate of interest. We have seen that the monetarist view of the effects of a change in the quantity of money is that such a change leads to changes in output, and prices, in the same direction after a 'variable lag', but with an undetermined division as between the effect on output and the effect on prices separately (Propositions 12 and 14). It is illuminating to compare Keynes's account of the process, in Chapter 21 of the *General Theory*, 'The Theory of Prices'[3]

There will be a determinate amount of increase in the quantity of effective demand which, after taking everything into account, will correspond to, and be in equilibrium with, the increase in the quantity of money.

Thus, increasing output will be associated with rising prices, apart from any change in the wage unit.

Thus as output increases, a series of 'bottle-necks' will be successively reached, where the supply of particular commodities ceases to be elastic and their prices have to rise to whatever level is necessary to divert demand into other directions.

It is probable that the general level of prices will not rise very much as output increases, so long as there are available efficient unemployed resources of every type. But as soon as output has increased sufficiently to begin to reach the 'bottlenecks' there is likely to be a sharp rise in the prices of certain commodities.

Keynes can scarcely be accused of neglecting the supply side. After commenting that the elasticity of supply[4] will be greater after 'a sufficient interval for the quantity of equipment itself to change' he observes:

Thus a moderate change in effective demand, coming on a situation where there is widespread unempoyment may spend itself very little in raising prices and mainly in increasing employment; whilst a larger change, which, being unforseen, causes some temporary 'bottlenecks' to be reached, will spend itself in raising prices, as distinct from employment, to a greater extent at first than subsequently.

Note that Keynes talks of a *moderate* change in effective demand where there is *widespread* unemployment yet concedes that even this will have some effect in raising prices.

That the wage unit may tend to rise before full employment has been reached, requires little comment or explanation. Since each group of workers will gain, (other things being equal) by a rise in its own wages, there is naturally for all groups a pressure in this direction, which entrepreneurs will be more ready to meet when they are doing better business. For this reason a proportion of any increase in effective demand is likely to be absorbed in satisfying the upward tendency of the wage unit.

Note, a part of *any* increase in effective demand is likely to go in increased wages.

Thus (Keynes is very fond of 'thus') in addition to the final critical point of full employment at which money-wages have to rise, in response to increasing effective demand in terms of money, fully in proportion to the rise in prices of wage goods, we have a succession of earlier semi-critical points at which an increasing effective demand tends to raise money-wages though not fully in proportion to the rise in the price of wage-goods; and similarly in the case of a decreasing effective demand.

From the foregoing a number of conclusions may be drawn; first that Keynes was aware of 'the problem of the unions' at positions at or approaching full employment, an awareness that he subsequently made more explicit[5]; secondly that he was very conscious that to raise demand was not enough; there was also the problem of supply; and thirdly not only is an increase in the quantity of money a necessary condition for inflation (both 'creeping' and 'true') to proceed, but a reduction in the money supply (in effective demand) will cause prices to fall – see his last 10 words above. While Keynes was clear on all these points his disciples, unfortunately, were not.

Is there much in the Keynesian account of the relationship between changes in money, output and prices with which a moderate monetarist would disagree? It is true that Keynes gives priority to the rate of interest in the transmission mechanism but priority does not exclude other, direct, effects including those on consumption. The monetarists include the rate of interest but do not give it priority. It is a matter of degree. (There is a sense in which monetarists are concerned *only* with the rate of interest – but defined as the 'own rate' of interest or return on every alternative asset or form of expenditure.)

Nor need Keynes's *apparatus* stand in the way of accord. It is, as he says, a way of 'introducing order and method into our enquiry'. And elsewhere, after noting 'the extreme complexity of the actual course of events' he concludes:

If we examine any actual problem along the lines of the above situation; we shall find it more manageable; and our practical intuition (which can take account of a more detailed complex of facts than can be treated on general principles) will be offered a less intractable material upon which to work.[6]

It is astonishing that Keynes who was above all a monetary economist, whose major theoretical work in economics before the *General Theory* had been a two-volume *Treatise on Money*, whose major insight in the *General Theory* is acknowledged to have been his analysis of the demand for money, an insight upon which rests latter-day monetarist theory, should have placed upon him the label of a man who believed that money did not matter, and the stigma of being the theoretical father of mid-twentieth century inflation, and worse.

It is quite idle to speculate on what Keynes would have thought of modern monetarist theory or of monetarist policies as manifest in the United Kingdom from mid-1979: 45 years on from *General Theory* the world is not the world Keynes knew. Yet it is permissible to suggest that, on the evidence, there are several points at which he would have found the monetarist approach not uncongenial. Philosophically, he would have had some kindred feeling for Milton Friedman's passionate concern for the freedom of individual choice, while perhaps setting the market boundaries less wide than Friedman. Analytically, he might have seen monetarist 'demand for money' theory as an elaboration of his own liquidity preference concept, and found much to approve. Politically he might, on the evidence of his cautious approach in 1937, have shared the monetarists' doubts about the practicability of fine tuning the economy; and, on the same evidence, have shared the monetarists' rejection of much that was done in his name. In viewing the battle between Keynesians and Friedmanians which rages on the plains below it is a piquant thought that one might, through the smoke, discern the praetors not leading their armies but standing back to back fighting off their followers.

Notes

1. Hicks, for example, says 'A theory of money . . . must indeed accept Keynes's major insight – that money is an asset, which can be weighed up against other assets in a balance-sheet, substituted for them or substituted by them'. (*The Crisis in Keynesian Economics, p36*).
2. GT, 174.
3. It may come as a surprise to some that Keynes even had a theory of prices.
4. Supply is said to be elastic when a small change in price calls forth a large increase in supply; and inelastic when an increase in price, even if large, calls forth little extra supply.
5. Lord Kahn in his 'On Rereading Keynes', *Proceedings of the British Academy* Vol. LX 1974, give a number of examples of Keynes's view on the problem of reconciling full employment, union power and stable prices, as follows:

   'How much otherwise unavoidable unemployment do you propose to bring about in order to keep the Trade Unions in order? Do you think it will be politically possible when they understand what you are up to?' and 'other more reasonable, less punitive means must be found.'

   'The task of keeping efficiency wages reasonably stable (I am sure they will creep up steadily in spite of our best efforts) is a political rather than economic problem.'

   'One is also, simply because one knows no solution, inclined to turn a blind eye to the wages problem in a full employment economy.'

6. GT, p. 249.

Chapter eight
Political economics

... monetarism is not politically neutral, but may be regarded as an economic accompaniment to the liberal–conservatism associated with such thinkers as Hayek and Oakshott

... it seems to me to be quite inescapable that monetarists do tend to favour policies in other contexts which are connected with right-wing political attitudes.

Tim Congdon, Monetarism [1]

Before economics became economics it was called political economy, and it is quite clear that at the policy level economics necessarily has a significant political content; the mere choice of economic objectives will embody some value judgement on the relative desirability of different ends. And if there is, as there customarily is, a choice of means to achieve those ends, these too will involve value judgements. The obvious example, which has run throughout this book, is the choice, if choice it be – between stable prices and full employment as an overriding objective; and whether, if stable prices is the chosen objective, that is best achieved by monetary policy or incomes policy.

We have seen that Keynes's legacy was dissipated and his name traduced by people, some of them economists, calling themselves Keynesians. The distinguishing features of Keynesianism in this sense were a growth of the size and influence of the public sector, and the elevation of an unrealistic concept of full employment to the status of an overriding objective. The first feature led to a compensating contraction of the private sector and a higher level of taxation; the second nourished the power of the trades unions; and both nourished inflation. Prices and incomes policies introduced to contain inflation necessarily meant not only a distortion of markets and consequent misallocation of resources, but an encroachment on individual freedom of action.

That picture is, of course, a caricature: even bastard-Keynesianism was not all bad. But it was that vision of the way society had gone and was going which informed and inspired the conservative reaction.

What right-wing opinion required, and required rather desperately, was a natural law, a new hidden hand, an economic theory which would reinstate to their proper place the traditional conservaative values and, above all, remove so far as possible, any justification for the encroachment of the state on to the domain of private enterprise. If only new, and ostensibly impartial, economic laws could be enthroned, or re-enthroned, much might be done, and undone, in their name. What was required was an economic nostrum which could be sold to the people as a cure for all their ills, real or imagined, and yet which could be put into bottles bearing labels of academic approval.

The quantity theory of money came readily to hand. It had a number of virtues. It was rooted in antiquity, and so had natural appeal to conservatives. Impressive correlations could be demonstrated between the money supply and inflation – and few understood that a correlation said precisely nothing about cause and effect. It removed, at a stroke, the need for either thought or negotiation with the unions: for economic thought, always difficult, was substituted a simple rule of thumb; and no negotiation was either possible or necessary about the inexorable laws of economics. But above all, the quantity theory was capable of a double life; the old quantity theory, so easy to recognise, could be paraded for the common people who could believe that the old Emperor was reincarnated, and could wave their flags; while the Court could say, with truth, that this was an entirely new Emperor, much superior to the old pretender. Few would notice that neither the old nor the new had any clothes. And anyway some new imposter could scarcely be worse than the present tyrant.

If we wanted to be mischievous we could concoct an account of the theoretical genesis of monetarism that might run as follows: Economists of a right-wing persuasion were thoroughly distressed at the Keynesian analysis because it lent very powerful support to all the things they feared and disliked, Government spending, intervention, negotiation with unions, and all manner of things that got in the way of the pursuit of happiness and private profit.

Casting about for a stick to beat the Keynesians, they found one: inflation. Keynesian economics led to inflation. And what caused inflation? Well, obviously, too much money sloshing about. A quick search through the GT revealed that Keynes paid only lip service to the Quantity Theory, as a special case of his theory. That was it:

Keynes said that money did not matter. That was the stick to beat the Keynesians. There was another Keynesian weakness: the Consumption Function, an essential plank in his theory, had been shown not to perform very well as a fulcrum on which to rest the levers of investment and aggregate demand management.

So, suppose, putting these two ideas together, one could show that there was a stable demand for money. *That*, instead of the Consumption Function, could become the fulcrum and the Quantity of Money the lever. This killed several Keynesian birds with one stone. With no consumption function, there was no multiplier, no link between investment and aggregate demand, no rationale for public investment.

Empirical research showed that the demand for money *was* stable – well, reasonably stable. But a statistical result is not an economic theory. The demand for money had to be dressed in some respectable theoretical clothes, and the search was on for reasons why people did not go on accumulating money but got rid of it if they had too much. And, surprise, it was found that if people suddenly acquired more money than they needed – perhaps dropped to them by helicopter, a favourite monetarist method – they spent it, on all sorts of things: consumption goods, consumer durables, houses, stocks and shares, antiques, education. The list could be extended indefinitely.

But of course it is not much of an insight or any great advance in economic theory to say that, given money they do not need, people will spend it. So the theory had to be dressed up a bit more. Now Keynes had had one very good idea: money was an asset. To simplify his exposition he considered only two assets: money and bonds. Why not pinch that idea and extend it? When people spent money what they were *really* doing was equating their real returns on assets at the margin. That sounded much more impressive. So there it was: money was an asset, and if you gave people too much of it they rearranged their assets until their real rate of return on bananas was the same as on everything else, including money. Now there was something for the economics profession to get its teeth into, as a change from all those dreary Keynesian 45° diagrams.

But enough fun with the theorists; what benefits could the new theory bring?

Well, it could deliver private property from the hands of the politicians. As Mr Congdon[2] puts it:

The Monetarist advocacy of stable money is integral to the defence of private property;

Money is one of the principal kinds of private property and variations in its quantity have most effect on the private sector. The 'Friedman rule' is intended first and foremost as the answer to inflation, but it also performs the function of protecting the private sector from the politicians.

Since it is the private sector which elects the politicians in the first place (the public sector as such having no franchise) it is a little difficult to see why it should need protection. But Congdon explains:

. . . monetarists distrust the political authorities. . .Chicago school economists have tended to take a realistic and cynical view of politicians' motives. . .The monetarists are inclined to consider that politicians, far from watching over the interests of the community as a whole, put their own interest first: politics may be analysed, not as the maximisation of social utility, but as the maximisation of politicians' utility.

There seems to be an implicit assumption here that monetarist politicians are different from the other sort: for who but politicians will put monetarism into practice?

For the Right, one of the most attractive benefits of monetarism is that it does away with any need to treat with the unions. The only reason for so doing is to moderate wages and, through wages, inflation. But if, as monetarists believe, inflation is not caused by the unions or by wage increases, but can be cured and controlled only by controlling the money supply, then it is pointless to negotiate with the unions over wages and, *a fortiori*, over prices. Unions have, and should have, no place in the councils of the nation. Moreover, monetarist theory absolves the Government from *any* responsibility for unemployment. Any unemployment is entirely the result of the unions' refusal to match wage demands to the money supply. The more intransigent the unions are, the more unemployment there will be, and the weaker the unions become. A Government cannot even have an employment policy because there is a 'natural rate' of unemployment which it is impossible, in the long run, to tamper with. Economic management is thus simplified: there can be no conflict between an employment objective and any other objective because no employment objective exists or can exist.[3]

Mr Congdon[4] spells it out 'The implications are grim. An active employment policy is not merely futile or self-defeating, but downright harmful. The only realistic course is to abandon the full employment objective. . .'

Not only is it futile to have an employment policy it is also futile to try to manage the economy in any rational way. Monetarists argue, with some justification, that 'Keynesianism' endowed us with too much ambition, a false confidence in our economic knowledge and in our capacity to steer the economy.

Mr Congdon again:

> Debate and uncertainty are banished from this view of economic policy: Keynesianism is the embodiment of rationalism in political economy.
>
> Monetarism is in conflict with the rationalist tendency. . . it denies that enough is known for policies to be framed with the exactitude needed. . .This may be branded as obscurantist or applauded as prudent intellectual modesty, but either way it departs abruptly from a rationalist managerial approach to economics. . .

I am sure Mr Congdon does not intend us to infer from this that monetarism is the embodiment of irrationalism in political economy. But it does, in its populist form, offer an escape from the complexity and reality of economic life. It offers a defence of private property and freedom from the intrusion of politicians into economic affairs: it removes any need to treat with the unions, and any need to have an employment policy or, indeed, any economic policy at all beyond the control of the money supply. It is not surprising that, as Mr Congdon says: '. . .some monetarists would feel happier in the political climate of the 19th century than in today's'.

It is always likely to be misleading to hang political labels on to people and movements, for both are many-sided. It is, in some sense, not incorrect to say that monetarism is 'right-wing economics'; but it does very much depend upon what sort of image 'right-wing' conjures up. It will not be unfair to look at the matter through the eyes, and the words, of Milton Friedman.[5]

Professor Friedman is a zealot twinkling for freedom; and in a world seemingly increasingly ruled by zealots of an opposite kind all miserably dedicated to prohibiting almost everything, that is much to be thankful for. Professor Friedman's argument is a simple one, and it runs as follows: there is a crucial link between free enterprise and a free society. The more government there is, the less freedom there is. To preserve and enlarge freedom, therefore, government must be diminished and confined to those activities that government alone can perform. Among the things that government cannot do are create wealth, determine output, employment and prices. In economics the only thing a government can and *must* do – for no one else can – is regulate the supply of money.

In this book we must look more at the money supply than at the many faces of freedom. But in doing so we should not lose sight of Friedman's larger vision: it is not an ignoble one.

Notes

1. '*Monetarism, An Essay in Definition*', Centre for Policy Studies, 1978.
2. Op. cit., p. 82.
3. In a memorandum submitted to the House of Commons Treasury and Civil Service Committee (TCSC) 20 June 1980, the Chancellor of the Exchequer defined the Government's objectives, in part, as follows:

   '2. The main objectives of the Government's economic strategy are. . . . to reduce inflation and to create conditions in which sustainable economic growth can be achieved.'

   '5. It has become abundantly clear in this period that Governments themselves cannot ensure high employment. . .'

   '7. The Government has deliberately not set its targets in terms of the ultimate objectives of price stability and high output and employment because, as argued above, these are not within its direct control.'

   Third Report from the TCSC Session 1980–81, 24 Feb 1981. H of C 163–II
4. Op. cit.
5. See, for example, *Free to Choose* by Milton and Rose Friedman (Secker and Warburg 1980).

Part three

Chapter nine
The money supply and its control

If you can't define money
Then all that remains
Is a quantity theory
To boggle your brains.

Keynesian traditional[1]

As we saw in the section on Interest and Money (pp. 41, 42) the concept of money is an elusive one, with no clearly defined boundaries. One man's definition of money is as good – well, almost as good – as another's. Money is what money is defined to be.

Liquidity

In one view money is purchasing power, something of a known value which is more or less readily available for the purchase of goods and services and other assets. This rules out paintings and motor vehicles, which take time to dispose of and whose value is uncertain. But it covers a wide range of assets which can fairly quickly be turned into a known amount of cash assets which are, in short, 'liquid'.

Some of these assets are listed in Table 9.1 which shows the components of Private Sector Liquidity (PSL). The first section shows the items that conventionally count as 'money'. Note that this includes 'time' deposits as well as 'sight' or current account deposits. Then we have 'Other Money Market Instruments' – Treasury and bank bills, deposits with local authorities and finance houses. Below that are various savings deposits, the largest of which are deposits and shares with building societies. These alone are equal to over 60 per cent of the conventional money supply; and they exceed, by a substantial margin, money in the form of current accounts. Overall,

Table 9.1 Private Sector Liquidity 2 (PSL 2)

	£ million Amounts outstanding at end of		
	1979	*1980*	*1981*
1 'Money'			
Notes and coin in circulation	9,701	10,425	11,027
Sterling bank deposits			
Sight (or current)	20,345	20,805	23,274
Time (or savings)	25,744	34,391	40,856
Certificates of deposit	540	1,372	1,512
Total 'Money'	56,330	66,993	76,669
2 *Other Money Market Instruments (OMMI)*			
Treasury Bills	263	230	318
Bank Bills	1,858	800	411
Deposits with local authorities	3,431	3,662	3,053
Deposits with finance houses	521	530	521
Less finance houses holdings of 1 and 2.	75	67	74
Total OMMI	5,999	5,155	4,229
3 *Savings deposits and securities*			
Shares and deposits with building societies	36,972	42,378	46,909
Deposits with trustee savings banks	5,373	5,793	6,095
Deposits with National Savings Bank	3,363	3,611	4,541
National Savings securities	2,111	1,923	1,801
Less savings institutions holdings of 1, 2 and 3	2,601	4,163	4,286
Total savings deposits & securities	45,218	49,542	55,060
4 *Certificates of tax deposit* (*net*)	860	1,184	1,000
Total of above	108,407	122,874	136,958
Total PSL2 seasonally adjusted	107,730	122,236	136,090

Sub-totals may not add because of rounding
Source: *Financial Statistics* No. 240, April 1982, Table 7.6.

conventional money accounts for not much more than half the total of private sector liquidity. And that is not all, for the definition of private sector liquidity used here does not include unused overdraft facilities, which can be substantial in the British banking system; nor does it cover deposits with loan clubs, and insurance policies which can, at need, be converted into cash. It is clear that even if we could control those items designated as money we should be very far from controlling the purchasing power of the private sector. Money itself, moreover, is capable of doing more or less 'work' depending upon how quickly it circulates (its velocity).

The *locus classicus* of the liquidity approach is the *Report of the Committee on the Working of the Monetary System*[2], from which we may quote from paragraphs 389 and 390:

> Though we do not regard the supply of money as an unimportant quantity, we view it as only part of the wider structure of liquidity in the economy . . . A decision to spend depends not simply on whether the would-be spender has cash or 'money in the bank' . . . There is the alternative of raising funds either by selling an asset or by borrowing . . .
>
> The decision to spend thus depends upon liquidity in the broad sense, not upon immediate access to the money . . . The spending is not limited by the amount of money in existence; but it is related to the amount of money people think they can get hold of . . .

As we have noted, even if something generally agreed to be the supply of money could be identified, there still remains the little matter of its velocity of circulation. The Radcliffe Committee considered this, and reported:

> We have not made more use of this concept because we cannot find any reason for supposing, or any experience in monetary history indicating, that there is any limit to the velocity of circulation. (391)

These days the Radcliffe Committee is represented as a conclave of Keynesian cardinals and its Report their encyclical against money. Ironically, at the time, the report was seen by many as marking a revival of monetary policy, and indeed it did give much importance to such policy, although in a wider context than at present:

> The aims of economic policy to which monetary action is related are complex: they can be directly in conflict with each other in the short term and only by adjustment can be held in balance in the long. There is no single objective by which all monetary policy can be conditioned. With this complexity of aim goes only partial effectiveness in use. Monetary measures are aimed at the level of demand, but by their nature they are incapable by themselves of having an effect sufficiently prompt and far-reaching for their purpose, unless applied with a vigour that itself creates a major emergency. (980)
>
> Secondly, the factor which monetary policy should seek to influence or control is something that reaches beyond what is known as the 'supply of

money'. It is nothing less than the state of liquidity of the whole economy. (981)

Thus, by monetary policy the Radcliffe Committee meant not control of the money supply simply, but control of liquidity; and this was to be achieved by interest rate policy. '. . . movements in the rate of interest have a central part to play in bringing about changes in liquidity' (385). 'The authorities thus have to regard the structure of interest rates rather than the supply of money as the centrepiece of the monetary mechanism' (397g). The difference between then and now is that although interest rates are used now, and more vigorously, the object is to control not liquidity but the money supply, for which purpose they have proved ineffective.

The Committee specifically considered whether there was any monetary measure that ought to be considered in a state of 'headlong inflation' or 'a dangerously inflationary condition'. They concluded:

It is frequently suggested . . . that the solution is to find some up-to-date close parallel with the restriction of the note issue: some way of restricting by statute the supply of money . . . we are unable to find in any such proposal a convincing answer to our question. In a highly developed financial system the theoretical difficulties of identifying 'the supply of money' cannot lightly be swept aside. Even when they are disregarded, all the haziness of the connection between the supply of money and the level of total demand remains: the haziness that lies in the impossibility of limiting the velocity of circulation . . . Regretfully, we cannot identify any quantity, the statutory restriction of which would solve the problem . . . (523)

Money identified

Since Radcliffe reported, opinions have changed and, beginning in 1976, successive governments, even those that did not embrace the monetarist philosophy, have believed that there *is* a quantity which can be identified as a relevant measure of money and which can and should be controlled, albeit not by statute. Of several possible measures, the one selected by successive governments is Sterling M3, written £M3[3]. It comprises UK notes and coins in circulation with the public plus all sterling deposits (including certificates of deposit) held by UK residents in both the public and private sector. In common parlance, the money supply is notes, coins and bank deposits.

There are a number of things we might note about this definition. First that it includes *all* (residents') sterling deposits, that is to say 'time' deposits, which earn interest, as well as current deposits, which do not. This is a point of some relevance when we come to consider the effectiveness of interest rates in controlling the stock

The money supply and its control

of money. Secondly it covers only *sterling* deposits held by UK residents; which means that residents' deposits that are switched into or out of foreign currency automatically disappear from or enter in to the money supply. Finally, it is perhaps worth noting at this point – for we shall return to it later – that bank deposits are the assets of the holder, or owner, but the liabilities of the banks. With the money supply defined, the next step is to control it. Perhaps the best way to approach the problems of control, and they are considerable, will be to look at those things that influence changes in the money stock.

Changes in the money stock

Changes take place continuously, for a complex variety of reasons that interact with one another; but at the end of a period, say a year, it is possible to bring together what are termed 'the counterparts' to the changes in the money stock, and from the changes in the counterparts to see what were the main influences on the stock of money. This is done for the years 1979 to 1981 in Table 9.2.

Apart from the issue of notes and coin by the Government (which

Table 9.2 Counterparts to changes in money stock, £M3.

	£ million		
	1979	1980	1981
1 Public Sector Borrowing Requirement (PSBR)	12,564	12,289	10,658
2 Less Govt. borrowing from non-bank private sector	10,882	9,461	11,147
3 = Govt. borrowing from elsewhere	1,682	2,828	−489
4 Plus sterling lending to UK private sector	8,585	10,025	11,311
5 = Domestic counterpart to changes in money stock	10,267	12,853	10,822
6 Plus external and foreign currency counterparts	−3,050	−560	222
7 Plus non-deposit liabilities	−602	−1,379	−1,614
8 = Changes in money stock, sterling M3	6,615	10,914	9,430

Source: *Financial Statistics* No. 240, April 1982, Table 7.3

is, in effect, a form of borrowing from the public) money is created when the banking system lends money; and the banking system lends to two economic categories of borrower: the public sector and the private sector. It is customary to begin with the public sector. This sector, of which the central government is only a part, but the major part, has, self-evidently, to finance any excess of expenditure over revenue by borrowing. (If, as has been known, revenue exceeds expenditure, debt is repaid or extinguished.) The amount that the Government needs to borrow to finance the deficit of the public sector (as defined for this purpose) is known, not surprisingly, as the Public Sector Borrowing Requirement, or PSBR. It is a magnitude that in recent years has assumed some importance in the economic pantheon. So we put it at the top of the table.

The PSBR is a potentially powerful force for the creation of money, for the Government, any government, cannot be denied: the banking system will in the last resort supply whatever money it needs. But it is only a potential force. For if the Government can avoid borrowing from the banking system by borrowing instead from the public – from you, from me, from pension funds – no money is created. This is simply because the private (non-bank) lender, in the process of lending, runs down his bank deposit – which is part of the money stock – by the amount that he lends to the Government. To minimize the money-creating effects of its borrowing, therefore, every government tries, in the jargon, 'to maximise debt sales to the non-banks'; hence the very considerable effort that governments put in to providing a wide range of gilt-edged and savings outlets for the public. How successful they have been in recent years can be seen from line 2 of the table: in 1979 87 per cent, in 1980 77 per cent and in 1981 105 per cent of the PSBR was covered by borrowing from the non-banks. Only the remainder (line 3) adds to the money supply.

The second element in the creation of money is the lending by the banking system to the private sector, and this is shown in line 4.

These two items – the residual amount that the public sector needs to borrow from the banking system, and what the banking sector lends to the private sector – make up the domestic counterpart of changes in the money stock (line 5). (This item, or something close to it, used to be called domestic credit expansion, or DCE.)

In an open economy (one with transactions with the rest of the world – and especially one with no exchange controls operating) money flows back and forth across the exchanges and affects the money supply. The net effect of these transactions is shown in line

6. (This item, and the next, are shown as *additions* to the domestic counterparts but where the actual flows are negative they carry a minus sign, i.e. we have 'plus a minus quantity'. An alternative presentation would be to show '*Less* external and foreign currency counterparts, etc.', and remove the minus sign.)

Line 7 adjusts for changes in the liabilities of the banking system that do not count as money. And the bottom line shows the changes in the money stock.

Two things stand out from this account. It is clear that in every year the PSBR played a relatively minor role in changes in the money stock, contributing in 1979 and 1980 less than a quarter to the total and less than that to the domestic counterpart. Lending to the private sector, on the other hand, very nearly equalled the growth in the money supply in 1980, and in 1979 and 1981 exceeded it by a substantial margin. Yet in its strategy for controlling the money supply the Government places great emphasis on the PSBR.

Controlling the money supply

The PSBR

There can be no dispute about the absolutely central place that the PSBR occupies in the Government's strategy for monetary control, beginning with *The Conservative Manifesto 1979* (p. 8): 'To master inflation proper monetary discipline is essential, with publicly stated targets for the rate of growth of the money supply. At the same time, a gradual reduction in the size of the Government's borrowing requirement is vital.'

In January 1980, the then Financial Secretary to the Treasury made some observations on the PSBR which were considered so significant, or at least so descriptive of the Government's stance, that they became enshrined in the 'Questionnaire on Monetary Policy' sent out by the House of Commons Treasury and Civil Service Committee to potential witnesses in April 1980:[4]

Let me start with two simple facts. The first is a statistic. The PSBR is at present about 4½ per cent of total gross domestic product (GDP) – compared with an average of only 2½ per cent in the 1960s. The second is an economic relationship. That is, the PSBR and the growth of the money supply and interest rates are very closely related. Too high a PSBR requires either that the Government borrow heavily from the banks – which adds directly to the money supply; or, failing this, that it borrows from individuals and institutions, but at ever-increasing rates of interest, which place an unacceptable squeeze on the private sector.

In March 1980 the Government's consultative document 'Monetary Control'[5] said (paragragh 5):

The main instrument (or control) must continue to be fiscal policy and interest rates. The Government is satisfied that these provide the means to achieve its medium term objectives. In particular it intends to bring down over time in (sic) the Public Sector Borrowing Requirement (PSBR) as a proportion of national output.

The Government's Medium Term Financial Strategy (MTFS) published, with the Budget, six days later[6] linked the PSBR closely to the money supply, as follows:

It is not the intention to achieve this reduction in monetary growth by excessive reliance on interest rates. The Government is therefore planning for a substantial reduction over the medium-term in the Public Sector Borrowing Requirement (PSBR) as a percentage of Gross Domestic Product (GDP). The relationship between the PSBR and the growth of money supply is important but is not a simple one . . . But although the relationship between the PSBR and £M3 is erratic from year to year, there is no doubt that public sector borrowing has made a major contribution to the excessive growth of the money supply in recent years. The consequence of the high level of public sector borrowing has been high nominal interest rates and greater financing problems for the private sector.

The MTFS included a Table (Table 9) projecting the path of the PSBR forward to 1983–84, a path '. . . consistent with achieving the planned reduction in the growth of money supply over the medium-term with lower interest rates'. (paragraph 14). The MTFS published a year later[7] gave a new projection for the PSBR, but did not carry it forward beyond 1983–84, the terminal year of the first strategy.

The statement by the Financial Secretary to the Treasury says, quite correctly, that the relationship is between the PSBR, the money supply and *interest rates*; and the MTFS also brings interest rates into the picture. But at one point the MTFS states categorically that '. . . there is no doubt that public sector borrowing has made a major contribution to the excessive growth of the money supply in recent years. The consequence of the high level of public sector borrowing has been high nominal interest rates . . .'. The authors of the MTFS cannot have it both ways: *either* a high PSBR contributes to excessive monetary growth *or* to high interest rates. It will not do both. (Unless it is being argued that high interest rates lead to an *increase* in the money supply, rather than restrain it. There are those who argue that this is, in fact, what happens.) And as we shall see below there is impressive evidence that public sector borrowing has not made a major contribution to the growth of the money supply in recent years.

If I have laboured the point about the devotion of the Government to the PSBR, there is a reason for it. The fact is that the PSBR occupies a most curious position in the demonology of monetary control, for both Professor Friedman and Professor Lord Kaldor, at opposite ends of the monetarist debate, believe that it has little or nothing to do with the matter. Let us take Professor Friedman first.

In his response to the questionnaire referred to above[4] he writes[16]: 'The key role assigned to targets[18] for the PSBR . . . seems to me unwise for several reasons: (1) These numbers are highly misleading because of the failure to adjust for the effect of inflation; (2) There is no necessary relation between the size of PSBR and monetary growth.' He goes on to argue that 'emphasis on the PSBR diverts attention from the really important aspects of government fiscal policy.' In Professor Friedman's view it is 'total government spending, not taxes and not borrowing' that 'measures the true current cost to the citizenry of governmental activities'. Thus the professor's objections to the PSBR are strategic and political rather than purely technical. He reserves his fiercest criticism for the tactics of monetary control, a matter we shall come to presently.

Professor Lord Kaldor's attack on the PSBR in his written evidence to the Treasury and Civil Service Committee, is more uncompromising, a veritable Alamein of an offensive, focused on the Financial Secretary's speech of January (see above) and deploying forces of verbal argument, statistical tables, a regression equation and not a little rhetoric. It is all enormous fun and well worth reading. The first part of his case is that it is simply untrue that the PSBR has been the major cause of the growth in the money supply in recent years, a case he makes convincingly and at length. For our purpose here we can rely on one sentence from paragraph 95: 'These regression equations . . . show conclusively that the role of the unfunded PSBR was quite insignificant; it explains only 5 per cent of the change in £M3 in the last fourteen years.' The unfunded PSBR is that part financed by bank credit. The 'last fourteen years' are 1966–1979. Table 9.2 suggests that it was similarly insignificant in 1980 and 1981.

Ministers, as we have seen, do sometimes appear to assert that a high PSBR is both the major cause of an increase in the money supply *and* of high interest rates. In their more precise formulations they correctly present these as alternative consequences. Their reply to Kaldor, therefore, might be 'Even if the PSBR did not have much direct effect on the money supply, that was only because governments sold huge amounts of debt to the public. That could have been achieved only by pushing up the rate of interest to high and ever higher levels'.

Over recent years this is true, as Table 9.3 shows.

Table 9.3 Financing the borrowing requirement

Year	PSBR (£ million) 1	Financed by non-bank private sector (£ million) 2	Col. 2 as % of Col. 1 3	Net sales of British Government securities to non-bank private sector (£ million) 4	Col. 4 as % of col. 1. 5
1976/77	8,510	7,987	93.7	5,797	68.1
1977/78	5,595	7,798	139.4	4,914	87.8
1978/79	9,233	9,796	106.1	6,179	66.9
1979/80	9,902	8,968	90.5	8,328	84.1
1980/81	13,195	9,283	70.4	8,900	67.4
Total 1976–81	46,435	43,832	94.4	34,118	73.5

Source: *Financial Statistics*, No. 237, Tables 2.6 and 7.3; *Bank of England Quarterly Bulletin*, Vol. 21, No. 4, Table 8.

Of a PSBR totalling £46.4 billion over the five years to 1980–81, £43.8 billion or over 94 per cent was funded by the non-bank private sector; and of that £34 billion, equal to 73.5 per cent of the PSBR, was raised by sales of British Government Securities (and the remainder through National Savings and the issue of notes and coin). *Total* net sales of British Government Securities in the period were £41 billion, of which £26 billion (not shown in the table) were of a maturity of 15 years or more or undated. Yields on British Government Securities of 10 years or more maturity rose from 12 per cent in 1977 to 14.9 per cent in 1981.

Kaldor, if I may paraphrase him a little, argues that high interest rates are unnecessary, for two reasons. It is not high interest rates *per se* that induce holders of cash to buy marketable securities but *high interest rates that are regarded as temporary*. Funding is 'very much a matter of creating – and maintaining – the expectation of *falling* interest rates.' High – and ever higher – interest rates serve a purpose only because they may induce people to believe that the process cannot possibly go on.

The Treasury and the Bank of England would probably agree with this in principle. Indeed, it has for many years been the basis of debt management policy, known as 'The Grand Old Duke of York' strategy: the authorities marched the rate of interest to the top of the hill, selling gilts on the way, then marched it down again. And the document *Monetary Control* acknowledges the importance of expectations and that the Bank does try to influence them.[8]

Debt management is never an easy business, with the authorities and the market trying to outguess each other. Kaldor argues, as others do, that the publication of monetary targets makes the whole thing much *more* difficult because, as the document *Monetary Control* points out[9]: 'If the money supply starts to grow faster than the target range, investors will expect interest rates to rise and so hold back from buying: this further accelerates the growth of the money supply.' This may be no more than fund managers acting rationally, but it is known pejoratively as a 'buyers' strike' and 'holding the government to ransom'.

It is clear that, whatever the theoretical pros and cons of the matter, operationally the Government's view must prevail, and that in practice the size of the PSBR does have significant effects on monetary conditions. It follows that if the authorities are to have proper control over the money supply and interest rates they must have control of the PSBR.

Unfortunately, in 1980–81 they did not have that control: a PSBR that was set at £8½ billion in March 1980 and raised to £11½ billion as late as November turned out in March 1981 to be over £13 billion. As the Bank of England commented at the end of 1980[10], with the whites of its knuckles only just showing, 'While it is normal for the size of the PSBR not to be closely predicted, the fact that the scale of public borrowing in the first part of the year was considerably underestimated tended to increase the difficulty of operating monetary policy'.

As well as being used to control the monetary effects of the PSBR, interest rates are also the instrument used to influence the other main engine of monetary growth, bank lending to the private sector; the higher the rate of interest, it is argued, the lower will be the demand for bank credit. That may be true enough in normal times – whatever they are – but at times of boom or recession the demand for bank credit may become largely inelastic with respect to (i.e. insensitive to) the rate of interest, so that there emerges a perverse combination of high interest rates and excessive growth of the money supply. The Bank of England commented as follows on the 1980/81 experience:

The recession has not only enlarged the PSBR but, along with the high exchange rate and high wage settlements, has exacerbated the financial difficulties of companies, particularly those in manufacturing . . .
Companies have continued to be almost exclusively dependent for external finance on the banks . . .

The recession, and . . . high rates of wage inflation, have in degree . . . made monetary restraint more difficult . . . companies' financing needs have remained very large. The associated borrowing appears to have been particularly insensitive to high interest rates.[10]

The growth of broad money was indeed probably increased by the particular effects of recession – which inflated the scale of public borrowing and at the same time led to high borrowing by industry from the banks.[11]

The matter does not quite end there. For high interest rates are not only a consequence of recession (because the recession inflates the PSBR), but a cause, and would tend to prolong or deepen any recession.

We have now covered in broad outline the main sources of monetary growth and traditional methods of monetary control; and have noted along the way some criticisms not only of the methods but of the underlying philosophy. It was natural that a government heavily committed to the monetarist doctrine should examine the methods of control; and to that examination we now turn.

The search for new methods of control

The first results of the Government's examination were published in 'Monetary Control' in March 1980.[5] They contained proposals for improving short-term control and included the conclusion that the Supplementary Special Deposits scheme (the 'corset') should be phased out; and this was done in the following June. (The 'corset' was a device to restrict the banks' ability to acquire interest-bearing deposits. 'Corset' was an apt description, for its effect was to make the money supply look slimmer than it was.)

After a period of consultation the Chancellor of the Exchequer announced in the House of Commons on 24 November 1980 the broad outlines of new arrangements, and the Bank of England issued a background note.[12] This was followed by a further Bank paper on 12 March 1981, 'Monetary Control: next steps'.[13] On 5 August 1981 the Bank published 'Monetary Control: provisions'[14] setting out new arrangements, some of them already gradually introduced, that were to come formally into effect on 20 August 1981. Thus the whole process, from the publication of the Consultative paper to the institution of new arrangements took less than 18 months which, given the complexity of the subject and the amount of consultation that was required, was fairly rapid for a bureaucracy.

In broad terms the choice facing the authorities in seeking to improve control lay between a modification of existing methods, which relied heavily on interest rate movements, and a move to some form of 'monetary base control'. Monetary base control (MBC) works by regulating the base assets of the banking system on which the inverse pyramid of bank lending rests. It requires a fairly certain relationship between the base and the bank deposits founded on that base. In the end the authorities chose the former route, but pointed out that the modifications introduced '. . . would be consistent with a gradual evolution towards a monetary base system . . .'[15]

In addition to the earlier abolition of the 'corset' the main features of the new arrangements which became formally effective on 20 August 1981 were as follows:[19]

(i) The practice of continuously 'posting' a Minimum Lending Rate (MLR) was discontinued.

(ii) In future the Bank would aim to keep interest rates at the very short end of the market within an undisclosed band. It would do this by open market operations rather than by direct lending through 'the discount window.' ('Open market operations' are, as the name implies, operations whereby the Bank, by buying and selling securities in the open market, influences not only market conditions, i.e. interest rates, but the banking system's assets.)

(iii) The requirement on the banks to maintain a minimum reserve asset ratio was abolished.

These new arrangements represented 'a significant change' in the operations of the Bank of England in the money markets. The intention was that the market (as distinct from the Bank, via the former MLR) should have a much greater influence on short-term interest rates. As a corollary, interest rates were likely to fluctuate more widely; and the Bank would discount (buy) larger quantities of commercial and bank bills instead of, as formerly, mainly government paper. One result, at least in the early months of the new system, was that the Treasury no longer knew whether its monetary moves would be effective in the market. As one official expressed it, it was

'Like lighting the blue paper but not knowing whether the firework would go off.'

What are we to make of all this? Do the new arrangements mark, as claimed, 'a significant change'? Critics of the traditional methods of control would argue that they have been ineffective because the Bank of England has been reluctant to relinquish its traditional role in setting the level of interest rates. Given this reluctance, but given also monetary targets to hit, the Bank (or 'the authorities', which brings in the Treasury) have set interest rates that are believed to be *consistent* with the money supply targets. In short, they have sought to influence the *demand* for money by setting the *price* (the rate of interest) at which they would supply the desired *quantity* of money.

A move to full monetary base control would have reversed this relationship so that the authorities decided the *quantity* of money they would make available, leaving the market to determine the *price*. What the Bank and the Treasury have done is to adopt a half-way position, a position that, they claim, is consistent with a further move to some form of monetary base control. By open market operations in an expanded bill market they will influence the *supply* of bank liquidity (and hence the ability of the banks to lend and the quantity of money). This will leave it to the money markets to set the *price* of money, the rate of interest – provided it is within the 'undisclosed range'. How wide or narrow this range is, is of course, a crucial question. Thus the authorities have made a cautious step along the road to controlling the supply of, rather than the demand for, money. It is a step that monetarists should welcome, but it was not welcomed by Professor Friedman.

It is worth looking in some detail at what Professor Friedman has to say because this will expose the logic of the extreme (I do not use the word pejoratively) monetarist position and show how far away from that position the British authorities are.

In his evidence to the Treasury and Civil Service Committee, referred to above, Friedman comes to 'monetary tactics' and to the Treasury and Bank paper 'Monetary Control', on which he comments as follows:

I could hardly believe my eyes when I read, in the first paragraph of the summary chapter, 'The principal means of controlling the growth of the money supply must be fiscal policy – both public expenditure and tax policy – and interest rates.' Interpreted literally, this sentence is simply wrong. Only a Rip Van Winkle, who had not read any of the flood of literature during the past decade and more on the money supply process, could possibly have written that sentence.

What makes the professor so cross is the idea that the money supply can be controlled by interest rates. Interest rates can control only credit; and money, in his view, is not, for the most part, credit, nor credit money.

To manipulate the PSBR and interest rates, he argues, is to influence incomes (the PSBR effect) and demand for money-substitutes (the interest rate effect). Far better to control the supply of money directly and this, he believes, can be done through the use of a suitable (i.e. a narrow) monetary base. This, he concedes, might lead to volatile interest rates over short periods; but over periods of 'more than a few weeks' they would be stable.

Professor Friedman believes the practice of financing the PSBR through nominal gilt-edged long-term securities to be 'highly undesirable' and, like Professor Lord Kaldor, is strongly critical of high interest rates on long-term stock. The high nominal rate set by the government on such stock seems to indicate that it expects inflation to continue at a high level but '. . . if the Government succeeds in reducing inflation, it is saddling itself or its successors with unconscionably high future interest payments.'

As we noted above, between 1976/77 and 1980/81 the Government sold £26 billion of securities of 15 years maturity and longer at interest rates of between 12 and 15 per cent. Even if the rate of inflation is brought down no lower than 5 per cent (at which rate prices still double every 15 years) there will remain a very heavy *real* debt burden[17] for the future. We are already locked in to a future of *either* a continuing high rate of inflation *or* of a high real debt burden. The Government is, however, at last beginning to issue index-linked securities.

Controlling Assets or Liabilities?

In the language of supply and demand there is conceptually a choice between influencing supply through the monetary base or demand through the rate of interest; or, in Friedman's terms, controlling either money or credit. There is another way of looking at it: there is a choice between controlling the assets or the liabilities of the banking system.

The biggest single element in the money supply is bank deposits, which are a *liability* of the banking system; and bank lending to the public and private sector is an *asset* of the banking system. Assets and liabilities always balance.

Before people began to worry about the money supply and to

assign to banks' liabilities – the money supply, largely – a special significance, attention and control was focussed on the banks' assets, their lending. This lending was controlled by a mixture of directives from the Bank of England (acting, at least nominally, as the agent of the Government via the Treasury), and ear-stroking. Between 1965 and 1971, when this system was in use, bank lending and the money supply were kept within a growth rate of 10 per cent per annum. After 1971, with the introduction of Competition and Credit Control, this system was discarded, and the money supply went through the roof, reaching an annual rate of growth of 28.8 per cent in September 1973. This was the period of the Great Barber Boom, when property values, in strict accordance with monetarist theory, shot up with the money supply. To correct the weaknesses of the new system the Supplementary Special Deposits Scheme (the famous 'corset') was introduced in December 1973. The purpose of the 'corset', as we have noted, was to restrict the banks' ability to acquire interest-bearing liabilities. And in 1976, under Chancellor of the Exchequer Healey, monetary targets were introduced for the first time. Thus in the period after 1971 there was a movement away from the control of credit and interest rates towards a greater reliance on the market to determine interest rates (in 1972 the old Bank-imposed Bank Rate was replaced by the market-orientated MLR) and towards a concern for the monetary aggregates. With the advent in 1979 of a Government committed specifically to controlling the money supply attention, in theory, shifted wholly to the liabilities side of the balance sheet; but in practice, as we have seen, the authorities still relied heavily on influencing the assets (lending) side and are moving only very cautiously to effective control of liabilities. In the meantime, the one thing that has not been controlled is the money supply, the growth of which has consistently been well above target.

The paradox is that when, in 1965–71, nobody bothered about the liabilities side and the particular numbers for the money supply thrown up, the money supply was effectively controlled by controlling assets; and when attention switched from assets to liabilities, it was not controlled. It is, on the face of it, an odd story and one that your average visiting Martian, unfamiliar with the mysteries of the British banking system, might find puzzling. 'Why' he might ask, 'do you want to abandon the control of assets in favour of control of liabilities when the two are equal and experience shows that the control of assets is, so far, the only effective way of controlling liabilities?'

Summary

Money is what money is defined to be, and there are many definitions. The Radcliffe Committee decided that since money could not be defined, and because its velocity of circulation might vary, there was nothing called 'money' that was worth controlling. What mattered was not money but liquidity.

Money is largely bank deposits. Bank deposits are created by bank lending to the public and private sectors. To control bank lending is, therefore, to control the money supply at one remove. This amounts to the same thing as controlling banks' liabilities by controlling their assets. Between 1965 and 1971 when lending was directly controlled monetary growth was moderate (although no one paid any attention to the monetary numbers).

Under a completely new system, Competition and Credit Control (CCC) the money supply grew rapidly. More attention began to be paid to the money supply, and beginning in 1976 monetary targets were published. Interest rates were the primary instrument of control.

Present policy focuses on the PSBR as a major cause of monetary growth, although evidence suggests that it is not; but it has raised interest rates.

High interest rates are not a satisfactory method of control because they may not be necessary, they may actually increase the money supply, they will add to the real debt burden to the extent that inflation falls; and in times of recession they may prove ineffective because private borrowers become insensitive to them.

Monetarists argue that in any case what interest rates control is not money but credit and it is wrong to try to control money by controlling credit. The money supply should be controlled directly through a system of monetary base control. New arrangements for monetary control in the United Kingdom are consistent with a move in this direction.

In the language of supply and demand, to control credit through interest rates is to control the price and to supply the quantity (of money) demanded at that price. Monetarists prefer the control of money through a monetary base which sets the quantity (of money) supplied and allows the market to decide the price (the rate of interest).

Appendix

It may be helpful to display the different approaches to interest rates and the control of the money supply in diagrammatic form. This will also, incidentally, throw some light on the differing ways in which the economy is perceived to work by the different schools.

The different approaches turn partly on whether the money supply is seen as something determined independently 'outside the system' or at least firmly under the control of the authorities (in the jargon, is 'exogenous': a money supply dependent on the supply of bullion would be exogenous); or whether it is wholly or largely a product of the system itself ('endogenous') as it would be, for example, if the banking system more or less automatically supplied the quantity of money that people required to finance a given level of money gross domestic product (GDP).

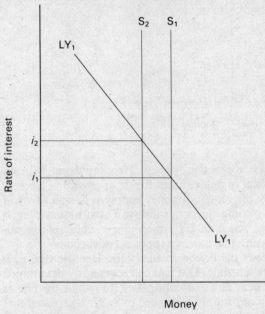

Fig. 9.1 Keynes

Figure 9.1 depicts the system of the GT. There is an exogenously determined money supply S_1 which, together with the Liquidity Preference schedule LY_1 related to a level of income Y_1, determines the rate of interest, i_1. If for some reason (unspecified, but outside the system) the money supply falls to S_2 the interest rate rises to i_2. This will induce a fall in income, Y, (via the investment demand schedule and the multiplier), a new Liquidity Preference schedule will emerge to the left of LY_1 (not drawn), and the rate of interest will move back towards i_1.

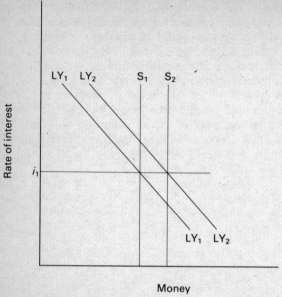

Fig. 9.2 'Keynesian'

Figure 9.2 shows 'Keynesian' policy. Here we *begin* with an interest rate i_1, set so as to induce a steady rate of growth of income, Y. At an income Y_1 the required money supply is S_1 and this will be forthcoming. As income moves upwards to Y_2 (with its associated Liquidity Preference schedule LY_2) the money supply accommodates to S_2. And so on. The money supply is endogenous.

Figure 9.3 illustrates the Friedmanian system. Here we start with a demand for money schedule, DM and an exogenously determined money supply S_1. Then, as a matter of policy (to reduce the rate of inflation, say) the money supply is reduced to S_2. (It is assumed that this can be done). The interest rate rises to i_2 and the authorities accept this. DM does not shift. The fall in the money supply lowers the price level, after a lag of 18–24 months, and the *real* money supply moves back towards S_1 and the rate of interest back towards i_1.

It is interesting to note the *differences* between Keynes and the Keynesians; and the *similarities* between Keynes and Friedman. Whereas in Keynes the money supply is exogenous, in 'Keynesian' it is endogenous. In both Keynes and Friedman it is exogenous and in each case the rate of interest at first rises as output falls and then falls as output rises. But the *mechanism* for the change in output is quite different.

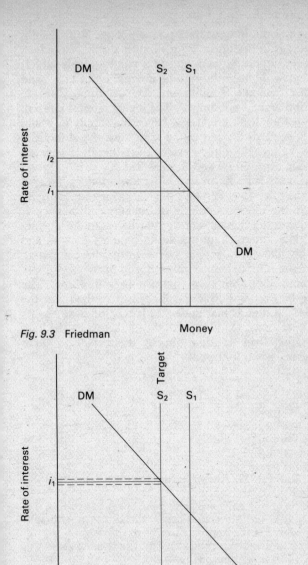

Fig. 9.3 Friedman

Fig. 9.4 British Monetarist

Figure 9.4 shows the intermediate position of the British authorities. We begin, as in Friedman, with a money demand schedule, DM, and a money supply S_1; and we add a money supply target, S_2. So, consistent with that, the rate of interest is set at a band around i_1 (higher than the 'equilibrium' rate determined by the intersection of DM and S_1, not drawn). The higher interest rate will reduce the *demand* for bank credit and hence the supply of it and this will push S_1 towards S_2; and at the same time the authorities will try to push the money supply towards the target by downward pressure on public expenditure and the PSBR.

Output, of course, falls. Recovery, and a lower rate of interest, come about as the price level falls and the *real* money supply rises.

In this system the money supply is still mainly endogenous. It might be looked at as 'Keynesian' in reverse: whereas in the 'Keynesian' version a (low) interest rate was set to promote growth, and the money supply allowed to accommodate, in the present system a (high) interest rate is set to reduce inflation, and the money supply allowed to accommodate, but in a contractionary direction. The main difference between the 'traditional' British method and the post-August 1981 position is that under the latter, the Bank, by its money market operations, tends to force the market to set the high interest rates, rather than set them directly itself. Thus, a slight element of exogeneity is introduced.

Notes

1. Some authorities prefer
    If you can't define money
    What have you got
    But a quantity theory
    Of God knows what?
2. Cmnd. 827, August 1959. Known as 'the Radcliffe Committee' and 'the Radcliffe Report'.
3. For a discussion of why only one target should be used and why that one should be £M3 see 'Monetary Control' Cmnd. 7858, paragraphs 8 and 9 (reproduced in the Appendix to Chapter 10)
4. Third Report from the Treasury and Civil Service Committee Session 80–81 Vol. II, House of Commons 163–II.
5. Cmnd. 7858, March 1980.
6. Financial Statement and Budget Report, March 1980.
7. Financial Statement and Budget Report, March 1981.
8. Cmnd. 7858, Annex A para 4.
9. Paragraph 1.4.
10. *Bank of England Quarterly Bulletin* Vol. 20 No. 4, Dec 1980.
11. *Bank of England Quarterly Bulletin* Vol. 21 No. 1, Mar 1981.

12. 'Methods of Monetary Control' reprinted in the *Bank of England Bulletin* Vol. 20 No. 4, December 1980.

13. Reprinted in the *Bank of England Bulletin* Vol. 21 No. 1, March 1981.

14. Reprinted in the *Bank of England Bulletin* Vol. 21 No. 3 September 1981. For a useful summary see *Economic Progress Report* No. 137 September 1981, (HM Treasury).

15. Chancellor of the Exchequer's Statement of 24 November 1980.

16. Treasury and Civil Service Committe Session 1979–80. Memoranda on Monetary Policy, House of Commons Paper 720, August 1980.

17. The question of the 'burden' of public debt is a tricky one. In 1981 of a total public sector debt held outside the public sector itself of £136.5 billion, over £120 billion (88%) was held by the domestic private sector. (Financial Statistics No. 238 Feb. 1982 Table S 11). Thus most of the debt is owed *by* residents *to* residents; the only 'national' burden is the part owed to foreigners. Nevertheless if the real value of interest payments to residents is high, so is the real cost of any taxation required to finance those interest payments. But the actual transactions (taxes raised and interest paid) will be in a currency that has in the meantime been devalued by inflation in the intervening years.

18. They were not, in fact, 'targets' but projections. Only the money supply figures were targets.

19. One consequence of the new methods of control was a major extension of the coverage of the banking statistics. The 'old banking sector' became the 'new monetary sector' on 18 November 1981 and this increased £M3 by £7.2 billion (9.5%) at a stroke. For a full explanation see *Bank of England Quarterly Bulletin* Vol. 21 No. 4 p. 531.

Chapter ten
The British experiment

I'm grateful to Britain for trying monetarism.

Professor J.K. Galbraith[1]

The Government's longer-term purpose, for the achievement of which monetary policy is but one instrument, is to arrest and reverse the decline of British industry. Given the long-or-medium-term nature of the objective it would be inappropriate to try to pass any verdict on a policy that has been in operation, at the time of writing, for less than three years. Nevertheless, an important economic experiment is in progress, and something must be said about it: 'What do you think of it so far?', as Eric Morecambe might ask.

The monetary experience

The centre-piece of the experiment, of the policy, is, of course, the control of the money supply, specifically £M3; accordingly the Government set targets for the growth of £M3. On the face of it this was nothing new, for targets had been set since 1976.[2] But there was something new, because this time the target was there to be hit, not just another ornament hung on the economic Christmas tree, a belt for the Keynesian braces. (It is not easy to get three metaphors into one sentence. The terminology of targetry becomes difficult to handle, quite apart from the dangers of getting targets entangled with ornaments, belts, fifth wheels, cornerstones and the like. Can a target be 'fulfilled' 'achieved' or 'exceeded'? Why should a fixed target seemingly be more difficult to hit than a moving one? Why should it be easier to hit if you move it further away? The monetary target range is no place for purists.)

At first, all went well. A target for growth in £M3 of 7–11 per cent (at an annual rate) between June 1979 and April 1980 was achieved with an out-turn of 10.3 per cent growth. After that, nothing went right. For the 16 months to October 1980 the actual rate of growth was almost twice the centre of the target range (17.8 per cent against 9 per cent). In November 1980, by which time £M3 was growing at an annual rate of 24 per cent, the *Financial Times* (5 Nov 1980) observed that '... such an erratic statistic makes a woefully shaky foundation for the Government's central economic strategy...'

Not only were the foundations shaky, the Treasury seemed unaware that the ground was trembling. In July 1980, in which month alone £M3 grew by £3 billion, or 5 per cent, the Deputy Secretary at the Treasury in charge of monetary policy twice asserted to a sceptical House of Commons Committee that the money supply was under control and that there was no intention to let it get out of control. Taxed with his statement in December, when it was apparent that the money supply was quite out of control, he conceded that '... it was not a very good forecast, but it was quite well based on the evidence'.[3] As by July much informed outside opinion was that the money supply was in danger of running away, this was rather like the pilot explaining to the crash enquiry that although the ground had seemed uncommonly close the altimeter *was* showing 500 feet.

In March 1980 the same annual growth rate, of 7–11 per cent (but on a higher base) was set for the 14 months to April 1981, and this target was reaffirmed in November 1980, a reaffirmation that showed a commendable degree of optimism for by then, as we have noted, the annual rate of growth since February had already reached 24 per cent. No doubt, however, it was 'quite well based on the evidence'. In the event this target, too, was overshot and by an even wider margin than the earlier one, the out-turn, at $18\frac{1}{2}$ per cent, being over twice the centre of the target range.

How did the Treasury, which controlled both the targets and the money supply, explain, or explain away, the unfortunate discrepancies that kept appearing between the two? The Treasury and Civil Service Committee, who enquired into the matter, reported as follows:[4]

In their evidence to us on 1 December, Treasury officials provided four explanations for the rapid growth of £M3. The first was the effects of removal of the corset which had been much larger than expected. The second was the unexpectedly rapid growth of the PSBR. The third was the effects of external finance following favourable movement in the current account of the balance of payments. The fourth was the continued high level of bank lending. This list covers virtually all the possible sources of monetary growth and is tantamount to saying that the money supply has

> risen because the money supply has risen. It does not hide the fact that the Government has not achieved the one target to which it was absolutely committed.
>
> It is clear to us that there has been a suspension of the money supply numbers . . . numbers the Government has said were central to its economic strategy.

Since monetarist theory predicates a relationship between the rate of growth of the money supply and the rate of inflation 18–24 months ahead this was all rather alarming. It was not surprising, perhaps, that Mr John Biffen, then Chief Secretary to the Treasury, should reserve his position on the matter: 'Those like myself' he said, in the House of Commons on 11 December 1980, 'who have been committed to the policy of the Government have always been extremely chary of trying to make a mechanical relationship between the money supply and the rate of inflation'.

The Treasury may have been justified in citing the unexpected growth of the PSBR as a factor contributing to the monetary explosion. But the growth was only unexpected in relation to the forecasts of the PSBR, forecasts which the Treasury itself had made; and the Treasury was, nominally, in charge of the PSBR.

But perhaps one of the most important causes of the increase in the money supply was that while the Treasury at one end of town was losing control of public expenditure and public borrowing, the Bank of England at the other was busy pumping money into the banking system. In its *Quarterly Bulletin* for September 1980 (pp. 283–284) the Bank catalogues a long list of measures that it took during the summer to relieve 'unusual stringency in the money markets and persistent pressure on banks' liquidity . . . because of continuing heavy tax payments and *large official sales of gilt-edged stocks*' (my italics).

Money market analysts argue that but for this assistance by the Bank of England banks would have been unable to increase their lending on the scale they did (sterling lending to the private sector totalled £10 billion in 1980, see Table 9.2). Moreover, it was certainly an odd situation in which the Bank of England was with one hand selling stock to the non-banks as fast as it could to finance the PSBR and with the other lending money to the banks to relieve the stringency thereby caused. It was not, on the face of it, the action of a Bank wholly committed to the control of the money supply. And what, one might ask, was the Treasury doing while all this was going on down in Threadneedle Street? Had they, perhaps, drifted off to sleep again? Or had the Governor, surveying the signals flying from the monetary flagship in Parliament Street, put the telescope up to his wrong eye?

On this episode the *Financial Times* in its Monetary Policy Review of 27 October 1980 commented:

For the whole of this year the Bank of England has been pumping money into the banking system to prevent interest rates rocketing sky-high. In mid-September a total of £2½ billion of such 'temporary' assistance was outstanding. Indeed, one of Mrs Thatcher's favourite jibes in the current monetary discussion is to remark that the Bank of England is now the lender-of-first-resort, not just the traditional lender-of-last-resort.

A month later (26 November 1980) they observed that:

... until banks are cut off from their supply of almost unconditional liquidity, broad monetary growth will remain excessive.

Over a year later, on 6 January 1982, after the introduction of the new monetary arrangements, the *Financial Times* returned to the theme:

What is certain is that it cannot make sense to try at the same time to control the broad money supply – the domestic sterling liabilities of the banking system – and to refuse to subject the banking system itself to any real constraint, and that in essence is the story of the last decade of monetary control in the UK.

The second year

Picking themselves up as best they could from the monetary debacle of the preceding year, the authorities re-formed around the Medium-Term Financial Strategy (it was, after all, a *medium*-term strategy) and in the Budget of March 1981 announced a new monetary target for the 14 months to April 1982. In accordance with the strategy the monetary target was moved down from an annual growth rate of 7–11 per cent to one of 6–10 per cent, but again, of course, on a higher base.

By November 1981 the rate of growth of £M3, at 17¾ per cent per annum, was over twice the mid-point of the range. The authorities, however, could fairly claim that there had been special circumstances. The prolonged civil service strike, which delayed tax collection, distorted most of the monetary aggregates. Despite this distortion the Bank of England[5] was confident that there had been a sustained increase in bank lending to the private sector. Mortgage lending by the banks had grown particularly fast. The rise in the money supply, although distorted by the civil servants' strike, was real.

The exchange rate

The second complicating factor was the fall in sterling. The sterling/dollar rate, which had stood at $2.4 to the £ in January 1981 (daily average) had fallen steadily throughout the year to just over $2 in early June. On 4 June 1981 a world-wide wave of selling forced the rate down by over 7 cents in one day to $1.94. The fall continued throughout the summer and by September the daily average was down to $1.82.

This fall in sterling placed the authorities in a very considerable dilemma. At first the fall was welcomed because although the authorities wanted the rate down from $2.40, monetarist market principles decreed that they could not intervene to bring it down.[6] When, however, sterling continued in free fall below $2 a new problem arose. The halving in the rate of inflation (from 21.9% to 10.9%) that had taken place between May 1980 and July 1981 (despite the growth in the money supply) was largely attributable to the high exchange rate, which kept down import prices in sterling. Moreover the Government's forecast of the rate of inflation, as measured by the retail price index, was that it would be down to 8 per cent in the second quarter of 1982. And this forecast was based on the policy assumption that 'The exchange rate, which will be determined by market forces, is assumed for the purposes of this forecast to remain unchanged'.[7] Now between the time that forecast was made and September the dollar rate had fallen by some 20 per cent and the effective rate (the rate against all currencies) by some 13 per cent. Since, roughly speaking, every 4 per cent fall in the exchange rate means a 1 per cent rise in the price level (after a lag) the implication was that the rate of inflation would be between three and five percentage points higher than forecast: the rate would cease its downward movement and begin to rise again. Since the Government's colours (and electoral prospects) were nailed firmly to the anti-inflationary mast this was clearly a prospect that it could not tolerate.

Accordingly, when the effective exchange rate fell by 5 per cent between the end of August and mid-September the Bank of England engineered a rise in bank base rate (MLR having been abolished) by 2 per cent to 14 per cent. A further rise, of 2 per cent to 16 per cent, occurred on 1 October. An interest rate hoick (whether by Bank Rate, MLR or, now, base rate) is the classical defence against a falling exchange rate or a balance of payments crisis. In this case the more specific purpose was to correct the large differential between American and British rates. The Government was also obliged to abandon its declared policy of non-intervention and to intervene in the foreign exchange markets to support sterling.

It is impossible to say with any certainty what effect these two measures – raising the rate of interest and intervening in the exchange markets – taken together, would have on the money supply. On the face of it they should be depressive; but if, for example, those who had moved out of sterling into foreign currency when sterling was falling now moved back, that would inflate the money supply. The significance of the measures was that they pointed to the limits that conditions in the real world placed upon theory, and to the conflict of objectives. In theory an independent monetary and interest rate policy requires a freely floating exchange rate and, given that, will 'work'. In practice shorter-term considerations may make it expedient to override theory.

In the $2\frac{1}{2}$ years between June 1979 and November 1981 (the last month of the old statistical series, before the banking sector was enlarged) the money stock grew by £23 billion, or 44 per cent. This experience, in relation to targets, is illustrated in Fig. 10.1. To gaze on this picture is, perhaps, to intrude on the private grief of those who have struggled to control the money supply, forever leaping up to plant the base of their targets at the place where the money supply was last seen, only to watch it bound away again out of reach.

Attitude to wages

The elimination of inflation is a primary aim of policy; and in the monetarist canon there is only one cause of inflation – an excessive growth in the money supply – and, therefore, only one cure – the elimination of that excessive growth. Since the rate of inflation is determined solely by the money supply it follows that incomes policies are not only undesirable (for reasons set out in Chapter 12) but unnecessary. It follows, too, that trades unions do not and cannot cause inflation. By the same token, as John Biffen, then Chief Secretary to the Treasury, said on 24 September 1979, 'Trade unions cannot prevent the Government curing inflation'.[8]

How, then, did the new government propose to deal with wages and 'the problem of the unions'? In a series of speeches between May and November 1979 Sir Geoffrey Howe, the new Conservative Chancellor of the Exchequer, spelt out how costs and prices would be determined under a strict monetarist regime.

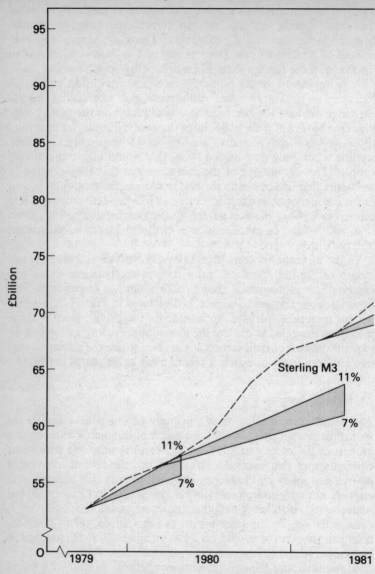

(Source: *Financial Statement and Budget Reports
Bank of England Quarterly Bulletin*)

Fig. 10.1   Sterling M3 and targets (sterling M3£billion, seasonally adjusted.
Target ranges, annual growth rates per cent.)

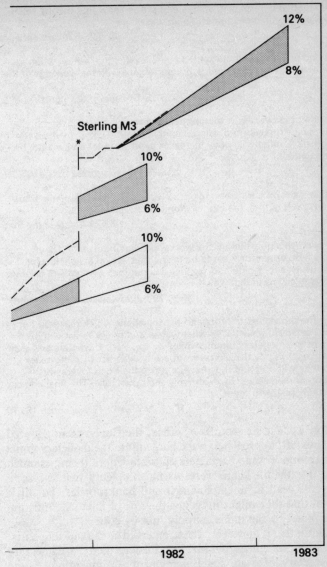

Sterling M3

12%

8%

10%

6%

10%

6%

1982   1983

* New monetary sector introduced November 1981

'Those engaged in determining wages and prices know that money will not be available to finance impossible increases.'

22.5.79 Hansard col 900

'Costs and prices need to be settled at the level of the firm or, when appropriate, the sector, with minimum interference with the workings of the market.'

23.7.79 Treasury press notice 114/79

'Any attempt to overthrow that monetary dicipline must result in higher prices, more bankruptcies and rising unemployment. That is my message to trade unionists . . . inflationary pay increases simply cannot and will not be accommodated.'

8.8.79 Treasury press notice 125/79

'If people insist on bargaining for extra wages and salaries that are not earned from extra output, the money won't be there to meet it.'

13.8.79 Article in the Sun

'It's very much a question for the workers in that industry to decide whether it's wise or not for them to be taking that (strike) action. It' s for people themselves to decide how far they can put their own jobs at risk by striking for pay claims in that way.'

9.10.79 Interview on BBC, Panorama

'It is for the thousands of firms and organisations which make up our economy to establish realistically what wages and prices to set within the framework of the monetary targets which we have set. If workers and their representatives take pay decisions which are unwise because they seek too much, they will find that they have crippled their employers and gravely harmed themselves by destroying their own jobs. The final choice must inevitably rest with them.'

16.11.79 Treasury press notice 173/79

Thus, in its first six months of office, the Government adopted a very 'hands-off' approach to wage bargaining: the monetary limits were known and if wage-bargainers chose to ignore them, so much the worse for them. There were warnings aplenty that excessive awards would lead to unemployment and bankruptcies, but little recognition that they might influence the rate of inflation. Inflation was determined by the money supply, not by costs.

Six months later, however, there emerged a shift of emphasis, heralded by a statement by Mr Jim Lester, then Parliamentary Under Secretary of State for Employment. Commenting on the Retail Price Index published on 16 May 1980 he said: 'While a number of factors is responsible for the current high level of inflation, excessive pay settlements which are not offset by higher efficiency and increased output *are still the main cause*.' (My italics.) The statement as it stood was a nonsense, because if settlements *were* offset by higher efficiency and increased output they would not be excessive. But his meaning was clear, and The Treasury did not like it. The formulation, they thought, did not reflect the broad thrust of government policy.

Four days later, however, the sentiment was repeated, in more careful language, in a speech by Sir Geoffrey Howe to the Confederation of British Industry, in which he said: ' . . . we need pay settlements below the rate of increase in the Retail Price Index. That's essential if we are to keep inflation on a downward trend without continuing increases in unemployment.'[9] The next day Sir Geoffrey Howe spoke in similar vein to a Conservative Women's Conference: 'Excessive pay settlements are making the current position a good deal worse than it need have been . . . the need for greater restraint is inescapable if monetary policy is to work as directly and quickly as it could . . .'

This shift of Ministerial emphasis did not pass unmarked by the press and other commentators: in an article of 31 May 1980 the *Economist* wrote that the Prime Minister and Chancellor of the Exchequer were now sounding 'like Messrs Callaghan and Healey (1978–79 period)' and 'Mrs Thatcher has been exhorting workers not to demand wages awards they have not earned, as if tight monetary control would not automatically take care of that'. Graham Searjeant in the *Sunday Times* of 18 May (following Mr Lester's statement but before Sir Geoffrey's speeches) hoped that Ministers would now abandon their illusion that inflation – something to be taken care of by restricting the money supply – was different from actual price rises.

Stockbrokers Simon and Coates were also quick to pick up the new emphasis. In their weekly policy statement of 20 May 1980 they wrote: 'The myth that all that was needed was proper control of the money supply for inflation to fade steadily away has dominated government policy up to now. The fact that, while a firm monetary stance is essential, an anti-inflationary strategy needs support elsewhere has become blindingly obvious to all but the purest theorists of monetarism.'

Six months later (8 November 1980) the *Financial Times* in a leading article said: 'Over the past few months, the emphasis of Government policy has moved slowly but steadily away from the financial markets and towards the real economy. By almost imperceptible steps, Ministers seem to have transferred their attention from the monthly money supply figures to the prospects for the coming wage round.' If, however, the commentators expected a drift into some sort of incomes policy, they misread the signs. The doctrine was still that in the end excessive wage demands caused unemployment. It was, characteristically, the then Financial Secretary, Nigel Lawson, easily the Government's most lucid monetarist expositor, who set the matter straight in a speech on 24 October 1980. After identifying two causes of unemployment as 'world recession' and 'decades of resistance to economic changes' he went on

The third cause of today's unemployment is excessive pay increases pricing people out of jobs. Or, put another way, the attempt to secure higher living standards than we have in fact earned. That path leads either to higher inflation – if the Government allows it to by printing more money to accommodate the higher wages – or higher living standards for some with unemployment for the rest. Or both.

No government in a free society, with free trade unions, can guarantee full employment. Indeed, it is perhaps instructive to consult that most revered of sources on this subject, the Seminal Employment Policy White Paper of 1944. This explicitly identified three essential conditions of a high level of employment. The second of these is particularly worth quoting: 'The level of prices and wages must be kept reasonably stable.' In other words, those who determine the level of wages are also determining, in large measure, the level of employment.

Thus, there was no change of policy, but there was some change of emphasis, away from the suggestion that costs (including wages) would be held down simply because the money would not be there or made available, and towards an implicit admission that excessive wage increases could occur but to the extent that they did they would cause unemployment. (For a full discussion of employment, real wages and the money supply see Chapter 13.)

When the Government began to apply 'cash limits' to the public sector (the largest part of whose expenditure is on wages and salaries) this was seen by some as an 'incomes policy for the public sector'. This was an incorrect interpretation: cash limits (which were in operation before the Conservative Government came to power) are merely a logical extension to the public sector of the monetary squeeze on the private sector. One of the major criticisms of the results of the Government's policies in its first two years was that because of its 'commitment to Clegg' (an election undertaking to honour certain promises made to the public sector unions) and its general failure to come to grips with public expenditure, the Government's tough monetary policies bit *only* on the private sector, laying waste substantial areas of private industry while leaving the public sector largely untouched.[11]

The reader may see a contradiction here: if the rate of growth of the money supply was not only not reduced but bounded away at an alarming rate, how could it be said that there was a severe monetary squeeze on the private sector? The answer is that almost everyone (Samuel Brittan was a notable exception) is agreed that although £M3 ran away, other monetary indicators and the very high exchange rate that existed until the summer of 1981 reflected a considerable tightness of 'monetary conditions'. More specifically, industry was squeezed by an exchange rate that made exports difficult and imports cheap, the high cost of borrowing and a depressed home market. Some industries may additionally have been squeezed by wage settlements, but overall these settlements were surprisingly moderate, given the going rate of inflation, as employees increasingly came to see that there *was* a real choice between 'money and jobs'. There is a further point to be made here, which is that, fierce as the squeeze was, it might have been worse but for the action of the Bank of England. The Bank has been criticized for its 'half-hearted monetarism' and its over-eagerness to relieve pressure on the banking system. A more charitable interpretation is that it came to regard the needs of the real economy as of more importance than the control of a number – £M3 – that it had perhaps come to regard as a misleading and unreliable indicator. The Treasury concede that in 1980 at least £M3 was not a good indicator of monetary conditions and that in future it would have to look at wide range of financial indicators including, possibly, the exchange rate.[10]

There, for the moment, we must leave the matter. It is far too early to bring in any verdict, even a Scottish one, on the British Experiment. Monetarists, however, could fairly say that there can be no verdict because there has been no experiment; for it is of the essence of monetarism that the money supply should be controlled. And that the authorities have shown themselves, so far, incapable of doing.

Nor might there ever be an experiment. Some unofficial oracles who have reflected on the matter see a future of a monetary regime that retains the MTFS and which is strict in intention, but which does not focus policy on, or measure success or failure by, any one money supply figure. Such a regime might be sensible, pragmatic and might well achieve some or all of the objectives of monetarism. But, we should be in no doubt, it would not be monetarism. Monetarist theory says that there is a thing called money which can be identified and controlled and for which there is a (stable) demand. If we empty the bath of all the muddy water of practical monetarism, the theoretical baby goes down the plug hole with it.

When Professor Galbraith remarked that he was grateful to the

British for trying monetarism he may not have been unmindful of the nation's impressive history of economic mismanagement, its genius for snatching penury from the jaws of plenty. A nation equipped with both British unions *and* the British Treasury, that had made Keynesianism a dirty word, could surely be relied upon to bury Professor Friedman.

If in the end the British monetarist experiment were deemed to have failed because of the monetary fiasco that might be an incorrect verdict, but not an unfair one. For the monetarists, by placing so much emphasis on the money supply, have dug a pit for themselves.

The most important part of monetarist philosophy is that concerned with the efficiency of markets and the need to let those markets function. Yet the monetarist salesmen have chosen to fill their shop window with the gewgaws of monetary technicalities, distracting attention from the more durable goods inside.

Appendix

The Medium-Term Financial Strategy [12]

The Chancellor of the Exchequer, Sir Geoffrey Howe, launched the Medium-Term Financial Strategy (MTFS) in his 1980 Budget Statement with these words: 'The strategy sets out a path for public finance over the next few years. At its heart is a target for a steadily declining growth of the money supply'. The strategy laid down a growth path for the money supply (£M3) of 7 to 11 per cent in 1980–81 and 6 to 10 per cent in 1981–82. Yet over the two years the money supply grew by some 38 per cent. The heart of the strategy had been overactive.

The purpose of the strategy

Introducing the strategy, the Chancellor said that it was ' . . . by no means to be confused with a national plan, for it is concerned with only those things – very few of them – that the Government actually have within their power to control'. The Chancellor's confidence that the Government could actually control the elements of the strategy turned out to have been misplaced. But the intention was laudable: it was to set out a medium-term path for public borrowing that would be consistent with the money supply targets. Since our economic problems were long or medium-term it was sensible to have a strategy that looked more than one year ahead. Note that only the money supply figures were *targets* to which the government was firmly committed. All else were *projections* – 'illustrative' was the word that came increasingly to be favoured to describe them.

The thinking underlying the decision to publish the strategy was that to commit the Government in this way would influence *expectations* and thus speed the process of adaptation. It would convince people (economic decision makers) that the Government was serious in its medium-term purpose. The plan having been published, there could be no back-sliding without embarrassment. Politically it could be interpreted as a preemptive strike by the hard-line monetarists in the Treasury, supported by the Prime Minister, to commit the Government to monetarist policies for a period of years. The monetarist flag was nailed firmly to the mast. It was not envisaged that in the rough weather ahead someone would have to make an embarrassing trip up the mast to prize the nails out again.

The construction of the strategy

In simple terms the strategy is built up in the following way. First, targets are set for a steadily declining growth of the money supply (the 'heart of the strategy'). Then General Government expenditure and revenue are projected to yield a General Government Borrowing Requirement (GGBR). Independently a second GGBR is projected which is consistent with money supply growth and (declining) interest rates *and* with the requirement that the Public Sector Borrowing Requirement (PSBR) should fall progressively as a percentage of Gross Domestic Product (GDP). The difference between the two GGBRs (if any) forms what the Treasury, with its ear for a catchy phrase, describes as the 'implied fiscal adjustment'. What this means is that if the first GGBR is smaller than the second then, in that year, either taxation can be lower or public expenditure higher (or some combination of these).

To illustrate, let us look at the 1982–83 figures as projected in 1980 (Table 10.1). The PSBR falls to $2\frac{1}{4}$ per cent of GDP (item 6) and this yields a PSBR of £$3\frac{1}{2}$ billion at 1978–79 prices (item 5) and a GGBR of £4 billion (item 4). But expenditure, £71 billion (item 1) exceeds receipts, £$69\frac{1}{2}$ billion by only £$1\frac{1}{2}$ billion. To raise this deficit of £$1\frac{1}{2}$ billion to the allowable one of £4 billion either expenditure must exceed £71 billion or receipts must fall below £$69\frac{1}{2}$ billion (or a bit of both), to the value of £$2\frac{1}{2}$ billion; this is the 'fiscal adjustment'. In the next (1981) MTFS this fiscal adjustment was revised downwards to £1 billion (at 1979–80 prices), and in the out-turn it worked out at £$1\frac{1}{2}$ billion 'cash' and was, by

Table 10.1 Medium-term financial strategy (£ billion)

	Year of projection	Price basis
1. General Government expenditure	1980	1978–79
	1981	1979–80
	1981	cash
	1982	cash
2. General Government receipts	1980	1978–79
	1981	1979–80
	1981	cash
	1982	cash
3. Implied fiscal adjustment*	1980	1978–79
	1981	1979–80
	1981	cash
	1982	cash
4. General Government borrowing requirement (GGBR)	1980	1978–79
	1981	1979–80
	1981	cash
	1982	cash
5. Public sector borrowing requirement (PSBR)	1980	1978–79
	1981	1979–80
	1981	cash
	1982	cash
6. PSBR as % of GDP at market prices	1980	
	1981	
	1982	
7. Money GDP at market prices	1982	cash

* + means lower taxes or higher public expenditure than assumed in lines 1 and 2.
† Fiscal adjustment eliminated by 1982 Budget measures.
.. Not available.

definition, eliminated by the 1982 budget measures. Item 3 might be called 'the Budget line' because it indicates the budget balance: the March 1982 projections indicate scope for £½ billion of tax cuts in 1983 and £2 billion in 1984. But the margins of error are very large and the projections only 'illustrative'.

The development of the strategy

As we have seen, there are two parts to the strategy: the monetary

1980–81	1981–82	1982–83	1983–84	1984–85
74½	73	71	70½	
91½	91½	90	87½	
..	119½	127	132½	
107.9	119½	131½	138	148
−67½	−67½	−69½	−71	
−79½	−82½	−84	−85	
..	107½	119	128½	
−94.0	−109	−121½	−130	−143
—	—	+2½	+3½	
—	—	+1	+2	
..	—	+1½	+3	
—	—	−†	+½	+2
7	5½	4	3	
12	9	7	4½	
..	12	9½	7	
13.9	10½	10	8½	7
6	5	3½	2½	
11½	8	6½	4	
..	10½	9	6	
13.2	10½	9½	8½	6½
3¾	3	2¼	1½	
6	4¼	3¼	2	
5.7	4¼	3½	2¾	2
231.0	255	280	307	336

Source: *Financial Statement and Budget Reports*, 1980, 1981 and 1982

part and the fiscal part. The fiscal side got away to a bad start, with the PSBR in 1980 at 5.7 per cent of GDP instead of the planned 3¾ per cent. Because of this and the general difficulty of controlling revenue and expenditure (nominally within the 'power of control') the downward path of the PSBR was significantly modified in subsequent projections: in 1984–85 it would be (as a percentage of GDP) above the level originally planned for 1983–84. Nevertheless the general thrust of the fiscal policy was maintained; the PSBR did begin to fall progressively as a percentage of GDP.

Table 10.2 Medium-term financial strategy Targets for growth of £M3.*
(Range of percentage change during the year)

Year target set	1980–81	1981–82	1982–83	1983–84	1984–85
1980	7–11	6–10	5–9	4–8	
1981[†]		6–10	5–9	4–8	—
1982[†]			8–12	7–11	6–10

* The targets set in 1982 apply also to PSL2 and MI.
† The 1981 base was 20 per cent above the 1980 base; and the 1982 base approximately 15 per cent above the 1981 base (after adjustment for the change in the monetary sector).

It was quite other with the monetary side, the heart of the strategy (Table 10.2). The Government recognised from the beginning, quite rightly, that to make projections three or four years ahead was a hazardous business and that the projections would fall 'within a wide range of possible outcomes'. It listed a number of 'outcomes' that 'could significantly change the growth rate of the economy over the next few years, and hence the finances of the public sector'. It conceded that: 'To maintain a progressive reduction in monetary growth in these circumstances it may be necessary to change policy in ways not reflected in the above projections. The Government would face a number of options for policy changes to achieve this aim, including changes in interest rates, taxes and public expenditure.'

Thus the Government sensibly acknowledged that some flexibility of policies would be necessary to meet events as they developed. The money supply, however, was specifically excluded from this flexibility. For the first MTFS concluded: 'But there would be no question of departing from the money supply policy, which is essential to the success of any anti-inflationary strategy'. The commitment to control the money supply was absolute. The monetary flag was attached to the mast with six-inch nails.

But between February 1980, the base month of the first target, and March 1981, when the next MTFS was published, the money supply rose by over 20 per cent. Growth of the money supply at this rate had, in monetarist theory, serious implications for the rate of inflation 18 to 24 months ahead. Except that it didn't, because:

Some of the factors that have been identified as contributing to the rapid growth of £M3 in 1980–81 mean that it should not have the implications for future inflation which generally follow an increase in money supply.

And anyway

Taken on its own . . . £M3 has not been a good indicator of monetary conditions in the past year.

However

. . . over the medium-term its velocity of circulation has been broadly stable, and for such a period the growth of £M3 can be more readily related to the growth of nominal income and overall fiscal stance. It can, therefore, provide a guide to the levels of public expenditure, revenues and borrowing likely to be consistent, over the medium-term, with the objective of bringing down monetary growth and interest rates. £M3 is accordingly being retained as the main target variable in the medium-term financial strategy . . . .

Sterling M3 was reprieved. Nor was the experience of 1980–81 going to panic the authorities into modifying their monetary targets; these were to be as set down the previous year, which meant that the 1981–82 target would be *lowered* from a 7–11 per cent range to one of 6–10 per cent, albeit from a base 20 per cent higher. And not only that; it was the Government's intention ' . . . to consider clawing back some of the past year's rapid growth of £M3 by permitting an undershoot as and when the opportunity arises'. These were fighting words; but they seem to have covered some inner doubts, for the concluding sentence of the 1981 MTFS contented itself with an intention merely ' . . . to hold firmly to the main thrust of the financial strategy . . . ' An admirable sentiment, but lacking something of the conviction of the 'no question of departing' of the previous year.

By March 1982, and the time for a second update of the MTFS, £M3 had risen by a further $14\frac{1}{2}$ per cent (from its base 20 per cent above the original 1980 base) with, presumably, the usual implications of monetarist theory for the rate of inflation towards the end of 1984. There was a fair amount of explaining to be done, so in the 1982 MTFS the Treasury began to rake over the wreckage, looking for the black box to see what had gone wrong this time. It could not be put down to pilot error, for the pilot was still alive.

There had been, it was noted, the civil service dispute, which had 'made interpretation of all the aggregates difficult'. There had been 'institutional changes'; the 'removal of artificial constraints on money and credit markets (was) having far-reaching effects on bank behaviour'. And the banks had gone into mortgage lending.

But if the banks were behaving strangely, so too were the public. According to monetarist theory people have a stable demand for money: if they have too much they will try to get rid of the excess (although, collectively, they cannot). But they were not spending £M3; they were saving it, as the MTFS explained:

The demand for liquid balances as a medium for saving, rather than spending, seems to have increased significantly in the last three years, implying a shift in velocity. The growth of the wider monetary aggregates has been part of a marked rise in the private sector's total holdings of financial assets relative to income. It may . . . be the result of the private sector's attempt to restore the real value of financial assets eroded by past inflation.

The public were not playing the monetarist rules. (Although even if they had been the only way they could collectively have got rid of any £M3 would have been to shift it into some wider measure of money).

With all this fluidity in money and credit markets, the Treasury now began to have second thoughts about £M3: 'The case for looking at a range of measures is especially strong when the financial system is undergoing rapid change.' And so £M3 was demoted; the new monetary targets (higher than before and, of course, starting from a base raised yet again) were to apply not only to £M3 but to Private Sector Liquidity 2 (PSL 2) and to M1. This decision to look at at least three measures of the money supply, each of which was, on past evidence and the Treasury's own admission, certain to move differently from the others, contrasted strangely with the firm view in *Monetary Control* that targets were best set in terms of a single aggregate:

The Government believes that its monetary policy can best be formulated if it sets targets for the growth of one of the aggregates, against which progress can be assessed. This gives the clearest guidance to those concerned in both financial markets and domestic industry, on which to assess the direction of Government policy and to formulate expectations. It is for this reason that in recent years the United Kingdom, along with most other industrial countries, has published monetary targets.

As no one aggregate is by itself a sufficient measure of monetary conditions it could be argued that there should be targets for several or all. But this would make it much more difficult for the market and the public to appraise the determination of the authorities to meet their monetary objectives. In the short run, the various aggregates respond differently and with different speeds to changes in interest rates so that seemingly inconsistent measures might be needed to meet the various targets. The Government therefore believes that targets are best set in terms of a single aggregate.

So, in the monetary targets stakes the Government was now going to have three horses running for it, significantly increasing its chances of finding a winner (although on the trainer's past record no one was going to put his shirt on any of them). And, of course, the Government would continue to use interest rates as a guide to the tightness or otherwise of monetary conditions.

Nor was that to be all: a fifth horse was wheeled out, in the shape of the exchange rate:

The exchange rate also normally gives useful information on monetary conditions . . . (and) . . . its effects on the economy and, therefore, its behaviour, cannot be ignored.

The behaviour of the exchange rate can help in the interpretation of monetary conditions, particularly when the different aggregates are known to be distorted. The exchange rate is a route through which changes in the money supply affect inflation. It can also be an important influence on financial conditions. External or domestic developments that change the relationship between the domestic money supply and the exchange rate may therefore disturb the link between money and prices, at least for a time. Such changes cannot readily be taken into account in setting monetary targets. But they are a reason why the Government considers it appropriate to look at the exchange rate in monitoring domestic monetary conditions and in taking decisions about policy.

Interpretation of monetary conditions will continue to take account of all the available evidence, including the behaviour of the exchange rate.

There was also a glimpse of a sixth and even darker horse that might be slipped into the race at some stage, in the shape of 'money GDP'. The Chancellor mentioned it in his speech, as something with which the new target 'should be consistent'; and references to it were sprinkled throughout the MTFS. But its precise role in the matter was unclear. Perhaps if even the wider monetary aggregates failed to perform satisfactorily they too would be abandoned and replaced by money GDP as a target. You can't get much wider than that.

The 1982 MTFS closed on a note even more modest than that of the 1981 version. The intention 'would be to hold firmly to the central purpose of the strategy by steady, but not excessive, downward pressure on the monetary variables'.

The degeneration of the MTFS

After the first year of the MTFS its authors were badly shaken by their total failure to control £M3, but they still believed that it could be controlled and that it was the right measure and should be the only measure. There was even brave talk of clawing back some of the excessive growth. After a second year of failure they were in retreat on all fronts. First, the target range was raised from 6–10 per cent (5–9 per cent in the original version) to 8–12 per cent. Secondly, the policy of focusing on one indicator was abandoned. Thirdly, the exchange rate was introduced as an additional indicator. Fourthly, the object of control was no longer the money supply but 'monetary conditions' or the 'underlying rate of monetary growth'. Monetary policy was to be 'realistic' and 'responsible' (having previously been unrealistic and irresponsible?). The monetary targets were going to have to be 'consistent with' a number of things, including money GDP and the exchange rate; whereas one had fondly supposed that it was these other things that were going to have to be consistent with the monetary targets. That, one had supposed, was the whole idea. It was all a far cry from MTFS Mark I where there 'would be no question of departing from the money supply . . . '.

Mr Denis Healey, the former Chancellor of the Exchequer, could place his hand upon his heart, or any other part of his anatomy, and declare that in making policy judgements he had had regard to all the monetary aggregates, interest rates and the exchange rate. Nor is it to be doubted that any future Chancellor, of whatever persuasion, could truthfully say the same. What, then, distinguished Sir Geoffrey's strategy from rival brands? On the evidence, only one thing: his determined and successful assault upon the PSBR. That, and not the money supply, was the heart of the MTFS. After March 1982 the monetary element of the MTFS had been so modified that the Cheshire cat of monetarist doctrine had disappeared, leaving only a pragmatic smile.

Notes

1. *Observer* 31 August 1980 p.15.
2. Targets for growth of £M3, 1976–1982.

| | | Annual rates of growth | |
| | | £M3 target | £M3 out-turn |
Date Target set	Period of target		
December 1976	12 months to April 1977	9–13%[1]	7.7%
March 1977	12 months to April 1978	9–13%	16.0%
April 1978	12 months to April 1979	8–12%	10.9%
November 1978	12 months to Oct. 1979	8–12%	13.3%
June 1979	10 months to April 1980	7–11%	10.3%
November 1979	16 months to Oct. 1980	7–11%	17.8%
March 1980[2]	14 months to April 1981	7–11%	18.5%
March 1981	14 months to April 1982	6–10%	13.0%
March 1982	'During the year'	8–12%[3]	

Notes:
1. Range consistent with DCE limit
2. Same target reaffirmed in November 1980
3. Applies also to PSL2 and M1.
Sources: Third Report from the Treasury and Civil Service Committee 1980–81, H of C 163–1. *Bank of England Quarterly Bulletin. Financial Statement and Budget Reports.*

3. Third Report from the Treasury and Civil Service Committee Session 1980–81, House of Commons 163–II, questions 344 and 1103.
4. Second Report, 1980–81, H of C 79, paragraph 39 Dec. 1980.
5. *Quarterly Bulletin* Vol. 21 No. 4 Dec. 1981.
6. When, on an earlier occasion, a remark by the Prime Minister about prospective lower interest rates had been misinterpreted by the markets and brought sterling down quite sharply, she is reported to have said that if that was the effect she would say the same next week.
7. *Financial Statement and Budget Report* 1981–82, p. 26.
8. Treasury Press Notice No. 140/79. He added 'Nor, to be fair, do they want to do so'.
9. We may compare this formulation by TweedleHowe with a similar sentiment by TweedleHealey in the House of Commons on 14 June 1978: 'The control of inflation depends not only on moderation in pay settlements but also on firm control of the monetary aggregates.'
   In his speech to the CBI (TPN no. 95/80) Sir Geoffrey Howe went on to say '. . . (moderation in pay demands) is one of the subjects which we have now discussed several times at the National Economic Development Council. And which we are willing and anxious to discuss, in that forum or any other, with the TUC and with anyone else who is willing to listen'.

10. See *Financial Statement and Budget Report* 1981–82, p. 16; and 5th Report from the Treasury and Civil Service Committee 1980–81 H of C 232–II, pp.13 and 64.

11. 'The curb in money supply growth affected only marketed output or, in effect, the private sector, while leaving the public sector quite unscathed.'

    'Since industry in Britain is (still) predominantly in private hands, it was industry, and not the public services, which was obliged to shed most labour. By this mechanism the ... policies adopted ... simultaneously featherbedded the public sector and penalized industry. The monetary squeeze, combined with the public spending explosion, rendered the "new industrial strategy", designed to shift resources towards industry, quite impossible to achieve. Since the strategy became something of a music hall joke for other reasons this may seem a rather unnecessary debating point.'

    'The traumas of the private sector illustrate most effectively that monetary and real forces on (*sic*) the economy cannot be separated from each other into analytically watertight compartments.'

    The interesting thing about these passages is that the words elided between 'adopted' and 'simultaneously' are 'by the Labour Government', and the period is 1974–77. (*Monetarism, An Essay in Definition*, Tim Congdon, Centre for Policy Studies 1978, p.59)

12. All quotations, except one, are from the Chancellor of the Exchequer's Budget Statements of 1980 and 1982 or from the *Financial Statement and Budget Reports* 1980, 1981 and 1982. The exception is the quotation from *Monetary Control* Cmnd 7858 20 March 1980.

Chapter eleven
Inflation

The idea that inflation is a single phenomenon, yielding to a single cure is itself simply a fashionable over-simplification. It arises from the monetarist observation that inflation is a monetary phenomenon, which on its own is about as interesting as saying that fever is a thermodynamic phenomenon.[1]

Anthony Harris[1]

Inflation, in one form or another, has always been with us. Long before economics was established as a separate subject for study people were concerned about, and wrote about, prices – why they were high, and the causes of the rise thereof. It is probably the oldest identified economic problem; yet despite the millions of words written on the subject there is still no agreement on its causes and cure. The accelerating world inflation of the 1970s stimulated new interest, and more books and articles. Economics has its own inflationary problem, probably originating more on the supply side than the demand.

In the early post-war years the most head-hanging solecism a young economics student could commit was to describe inflation as 'Too much money chasing too few goods'. A good, punchy slogan and good enough, no doubt, for the common people, but sloppy. The correct formulation, we were instructed, was 'Too much *demand* chasing too few goods'.

Neither 'definition' is satisfactory because neither is neutral: each implies a cause of inflation. If we are to investigate causes in a properly objective fashion we need an impartial definition. Such a one is 'inflation is a process of continuously rising prices'. Not very exciting perhaps, but it does sum the matter up.

But even this anodyne formulation may not be entirely neutral. For exactly the same meaning can be expressed by saying that 'inflation is a process of a continuously falling value of money'. This clearly indicates that money is involved somewhere in the matter, and indeed it is: for money in all its uses is central to the functioning of modern economics, and the value of money is of much greater importance than the value of peanuts, baked beans or motor cars. In this narrow sense inflation is, as Milton Friedman says, 'always and everywhere a monetary phenomenon'.

The costs of inflation

Most people will readily accept that inflation is 'a bad thing'; but there are those who do not. And the longer inflation goes on, the higher it is, and the more we adapt to it, the weaker is our instinctive and positive reaction against it. So some assessment of its costs is worthwhile; and not least because the *elimination* of inflation also has its costs and we need to be able in some rough and ready way to balance the costs of having inflation against the costs of not having it. This may not be easy if the costs of eliminating inflation are short-term and the benefits long-term.

The costs of inflation may be conveniently divided into economic costs and social costs although, as usual, there is some interaction between the two.

Economic costs

The economic costs derive essentially from uncertainty – uncertainty about future absolute and relative prices. Since the future is unknowable anyway, we already have quite enough uncertainty to cope with without the additional uncertainty introduced by a changing value of money. One of the important decisions that people have to make is how much of their wealth they will consume now and how much they will consume later. Uncertainty about future prices makes this choice more difficult and, if their guesses are wrong, less than optimal. Investment choices are made even more difficult. Investment decisions depend upon the balancing of a present cost against a future income stream.

It can be argued that inflation does not matter if all contracts, for example for wages, pensions, loans, taxes, etc., are indexed to the rate of inflation so that they retain their real value at some base date. But there are problems and drawbacks. For one thing, what is the rate of inflation? Since everybody has a different pattern of expenditure, everybody has his own inflation rate. To apply one, or even several rates to all contracts would be bound to have inequitable results. Universal indexation *can* make inflation easier to live with; but by the same token it weakens the incentive to deal with it. Once adopted, it builds inflation into the spiral of costs-incomes-costs. It implies a steadily falling exchange rate as the domestic price level rises (unless, of course, the whole world is indexed). In short, universal indexation is very much a second-best solution, to be adopted only if the elimination of inflation seems either impossible or improbable.

With inflation, not only will the future income stream be difficult to estimate but the rate of interest to use to discount this stream to present value will be uncertain. Moreover the very existence of inflation will add to any project an additional risk premium which will mean that some projects become unviable which without inflation would have been viable. Thus, investment may be less than it would have been.

In a properly functioning market economy resources are allocated by *relative* prices. Inflation does not operate uniformly over all prices, so relative prices become distorted, with a resultant misallocation of resources. (We may note in passing that an inflation suppressed by price and wage controls also distorts relative prices).

Social costs

The social costs of inflation also relate, in part, to uncertainty: people like to know where they are, they like a degree of stability in the world they occupy, and inflation introduces instability and the need to adapt to change. Inflation causes an arbitrary redistribution of income and wealth which may not be that which society would choose, given the choice: there is a redistribution from lenders to borrowers, from those with monetary assets to those with real assets and property.

There will be redistribution from taxpayers to Government if tax allowances are not fully indexed. There may be a redistribution from wives to husbands if the husband does not pass on to his wife the appropriate proportion of his inflation-induced wage increase.

The uncertainty costs of inflation are related to its variability, not to its level: clearly if we had a stable or a varying-but-known rate of inflation there would be no uncertainty. But in practice we do not have this knowledge.

We may conclude that a relatively stable value of money is to be preferred. Of course, what reasonable men regard as 'relatively stable' may be influenced by their experience: the Germans regard anything over 5 per cent as pretty alarming while Israelis or Brazilians would think of that as positive stability.

Finally we should note again that whilst inflation has costs, its elimination also has costs. Whether these costs are, or are not, too high is essentially a matter for political, not economic, judgement. This is unlikely, however, to inhibit some economists from lending the authority of their profession in support of their political predilections.

Causes

If we ask 'what causes inflation?', that is to mis-specify the question. For inflation is essentially a *process* and what we want to know is what engine propels the process and how it can be stopped. We can readily specify events, occurrences, actions, which will start an inflation – and indeed we shall be obliged to do so in the process of analysis – but what starts an inflation is much less important than what keeps it going. It is the dynamics rather than the genesis of inflation with which we are concerned.

We know from the elementary theory of price that price is determined by the interaction of supply and demand, operating like the two blades of a pair of scissors. A rise in 'price' may be occasioned by an upward shift of demand or a diminution of supply associated with a rise in costs, or both. For this analysis to be valid demand and supply must be independent of one another, and for this reason we cannot use it to determine the price level of supply and demand in the economy as a whole, because total supply and demand are not independent of one another; the incomes generated in the production of supply also constitute demand. Nevertheless, it is helpful and legitimate to look at those inflationary forces which originate mainly on the demand side and those that have their origins in supply or, more particularly, in the costs of supply.

Demand inflation

Keynes's theory of inflation, which we looked at earlier, appears at first blush to place the main emphasis on the side of demand. But this is only because he is tracing out the effects of an increase in (effective) demand in a severely underemployed economy. In that case, he says, an increase in demand will spend itself at first almost entirely in an increase in output and very little in a rise in prices. He assumes, that is, that in a greatly underused economy supply is completely elastic – given an increase in demand, supply will increase without the inducement of higher prices.

This is entirely consistent with the identity of exchange of the quantity theory, $MV = PT$. It means that all of the increase in M (associated with the increase in demand) is absorbed by a change in

T (V being assumed constant) leaving P unchanged.

But the situation changes completely once we reach the point where the economy is fully employed. Indeed, as Keynes made quite clear, it begins to change long before that, because the under-use of productive resources of men and machines is not spread evenly throughout the economy. As production expands, bottlenecks will be met, or will emerge, whatever it is that bottlenecks do. Once the economy is fully employed the conditions of supply or production form, as it were, one huge (or is it narrow?) bottleneck – no further production is, by definition, possible. When this point is reached, any further increase in demand or in the money supply is wholly reflected in an increase in prices. Thus there is at one extreme a condition of fully elastic supply where, in response to an increase in demand only output changes; and at the other extreme a condition of totally inelastic supply where only prices change. In between is an area where both change.

That prices must rise once full employment output has been reached can be seen by considering our income identity, $C + I = Y$, i.e. total expenditure on consumption and investment equals total income. Suppose that expenditure is £100 m, generating income of £100 m at existing prices. If the expenditure is raised by 10 per cent to £110 m then for the identity to be satisfied incomes must also rise to £110 m. And since output is at its limit, equality between expenditure and income can be achieved only if prices rise by $\frac{110}{100}$, i.e. by 10 per cent.

Again, this is wholly consistent with the quantity theory identity $MV = PT$. Full employment means that T, the volume of transactions, is at its limit. Any change in M (with V assumed constant) must be wholly reflected in P, prices.

Thus, whether we think in terms of the Keynesian framework and changes in demand or of the old quantity theory framework and changes in the money supply we arrive at the same result which is, to repeat, that when there is an increase in demand/money, only output changes until we approach the limits of capacity and then only prices change. In between there is an area where both change.

The analysis, or explanation, of how the changes work through the economy would differ according to one's framework of thought – according to one's implicit 'model' of the economy, and according to how the extra demand, or money, first entered the economy. A Keynesian would argue that new demand entering the economy though higher investment, by either the private sector or the public sector, would spread through the economy via the multiplier process. New demand arising from, say, a reduction in taxation would raise the average propensity to consume (because consumption is out of disposable income)[2], and therefore total consumption[3].

There would also be some tendency for the rate of interest to fall as a result of higher cash balances and this would tend to stimulate further investment.

For an account of how an (old) quantity theorist might envisage the process we can turn to the language of David Hume:[4]

> Though the high price of commodities be a necessary consequence of the increase of gold and silver yet . . . some time is required before the money circulates through the whole state . . . it is only in this interval or intermediate situation, between the acquisition of money and a rise of prices that the increasing quantity of gold and silver is favourable to industry. When any quantity of money is imported into a nation, it is not at first dispersed into many hands, but is confined to the coffers of a few persons, who immediately seek to employ it to advantage . . . they are thereby enabled to employ more workmen than formerly, who never dream of demanding higher wages, but are glad of employment from such good paymasters. If workmen become scarce, the manufacturer gives higher wages, but at first requires an increase of labour; and this is willingly submitted to by the artisan, who can now eat and drink better, to compensate his additional toil and fatigue. He carries his money to market, where he finds everything at the same price as formerly, but returns with greater quantity and of better kinds, for the use of his family. The farmer and gardener, finding that all their commodities are taken off, apply themselves with alacrity to the raising of more; and at the same time can afford to take better and more cloths from their tradesmen, whose price is the same as formely, and their industry only whetted by so much new gain. It is easy to trace the money in its progress through the whole commonwealth; where we shall find, that it must first quicken the diligence of every individual, before it increases the price of labour.
>
> Accordingly we find, that, in every kingdom, into which money begins to flow in greater abundance than formerly, everything takes a new face: labour and industry gain life; the merchant becomes more enterprising, the manufacturer more diligent and skilful, and even the farmer follows his plough with greater alacrity and attention.'

The new quantity theory is not the old. But it is difficult to believe that a modern quantity theorist – or, for that matter, a modern Keynesian – would find much to disagree with here. An increase in the quantity of money affects first output with 'everything at the same price as formerly', and prices rise only after an (unspecified) lag. There is, obviously, an assumption that there are unemployed resources to begin with (workmen are 'glad of employment').

Hume hints at how a rise in prices is induced by increased demand. Producers find 'all their commodities are taken off'. In the modern economy many prices are not flexible in that they respond *immediately* to an increase in demand. The first effect is on stocks, working back through the chain of production and distribution; retailers' stocks fall, then wholesalers', then producers', then producers' merchants (and importers', in an open economy). When we get back to the markets in commodities, the raw materials of production, we are into markets which *are* highly sensitive to demand, and any increased pressure of demand (especially if it is worldwide or stems from a powerful buyer such as the United States of America) will be reflected in higher prices. These higher prices feed back through the chain of production and distribution. Although there is a certain stickiness in manufacturers' and retailers' prices, these traders will both have to pay higher prices for their inputs and will become aware that demand is sufficiently buoyant to accept higher prices. This consciousness of buoyant demand may also induce some suppliers to raise their prices even though they have, as yet, incurred no increase in costs.

It is thus possible to conceive of a rise in prices originating entirely from an increase in demand: and, by the same token, we can argue that but for the increase in demand beyond a certain level the rise is prices would not have occurred. It also follows that the more excessive is the demand, the greater will be the rise in prices.

Demand-induced cost inflation

But it is clear that we cannot stop there. Because of the rise in prices some people somewhere will be better off. And the remainder will be worse off, to a like extent. Those who are worse off will seek to restore their position by raising the price of what *they* sell; and in the case of the vast majority of people what they sell is their labour; so the asking or selling, price of labour will rise. And because the employers of labour perceive conditions of buoyant demand in which higher prices will not lead to a fall in demand they have a diminished incentive to resist demands for higher wages. Wages will rise. And not only wages: the recipients of profit incomes will also seek to restore their purchasing power.

The higher incomes of those receiving wages and profits now add to the pressure of demand. If the disturbance which gave the initial impetus to demand is now, as it were, withdrawn, the situation may stabilise at a new level of prices and incomes. But the adjustments are bound to be imperfect, there are lags in the adjustment process and, moreover, there is now an *expectation* that prices will rise; so a new stability is not assured.

The process just described may be termed a demand-induced

cost inflation. The impetus came from demand but once the process was established it held both demand and cost elements within it which interacted. The process is not reversible, a fall in demand would not restore the previous price level. It would, however, be aborted by not allowing or by neutralising the initial increase in demand – strangling it at birth, as it were.

An alternative version of a demand-induced inflation has the extra pressure of demand feeding directly on to factor prices, i.e. in the main, wages, rather than to factor prices via the prices of goods.

A prime cause of the British inflation of the post-war years was, as we have seen, an over-estimate by economists of the flexibility of resources, an under-estimate of the amount of free resources required for the smooth running of a dynamic economy and, as a result, the attempt to run the economy far too close to the limits of its capacity. The inflationary consequences of this were either ignored, miscalculated or accorded a very low priority.

Cost inflation

The initial impetus to inflation can come from the cost side. By costs we mean all those factors which make up the selling price of goods, which are: the cost of materials, the cost of labour, profit, the cost of using equipment, and any taxes on spending, e.g. a value added tax. In what follows, we shall ignore the cost of using equipment. Since we are assuming, so far, that we have a closed economy we can also ignore the cost of imported materials. As all materials, therefore, originate within the economy these costs too can be ignored, because purchases within the economy equal sales from elsewhere in the economy, and cancel out in the aggregate. We are left with labour costs, profit and spending taxes as the elements of cost.

The ability to raise costs independently of an increase in demand rests essentially on the possession of power. Labour must have the power to raise wages, profit-takers must have the power to raise prices; Governments must have, and clearly do have, the power to raise taxes. We know that labour unions have power; and we know that some profit-makers, i.e. industries, have power. In each case this power derives from some degree of monopoly.

Thus by the exercise of power unions can raise the price of labour, industries can raise profits (by raising prices without raising wages) and Governments can raise taxes. Clearly the most propitious conditions for raising costs occur when a union exercises its power in an industry which enjoys the position of a monopoly seller. (The

combination of the National Union of Mineworkers and the National
Coal Board springs to mind.)

We assume some system of 'mark-up' pricing so that any increase
in production costs is immediately passed on in higher prices. When
prices are raised all those who have to pay those prices (other than
those within the price-raising industry) are worse off. The real
demand of those enjoying higher prices has risen and the real
demand of those facing higher prices has fallen. There has been a
redisbribution of income in favour of monopoly groups.

Passing on

If those who are made worse off were prepared to accept this the
matter would end there. But it is unlikely that they would be – they
will attempt to restore their position. The crucial question, from the
point of view of the propagation of inflation, is whether they will be
able to do so.

In the analysis of cost inflation we are always asking: 'can the cost
be passed on?'. Whether it can or not will depend on whether policy
is 'tight' or 'accommodating' and how policy is perceived by those
involved in the bargaining process.[5]

All the operators in the system, all the bargainers and price-
setters, are aware of the environment in which they are working.
They will know both what Government policy is and what it is declared to be; they will know to what level or range of unemployment it is committed, if any; they will know whether fiscal policy[6]
is accommodating or tight; they will know whether monetary
policy is accommodating or tight, how easy or difficult it is or is
likely to be to borrow money, pass on prices. Not only will the operators in the system know the policy stance of the 'authorities' (the
Government and the Bank of England) they will know something
of how other operators are reacting.

Tight policy

The tighter policy is perceived to be, the more difficult will it be
seen to be to pass on increases in costs. Sellers of goods will recognise
from their assessment of market conditions that it will be difficult
or impossible to raise prices without loss of trade. A lot will depend
on the degree of competition in particular markets. Unions will
recognise the position of their firms and industries and will be aware
that if claims are pressed too hard firms will close down. Public servants may come to believe that the Government intends to keep to

its cash limits. The high interest rates associated with the tight monetary policy will inhibit new investment, discourage stockbuilding, and have particularly severe effects on the housing market and the construction industry, which will also be hit by the public expenditure constraints that are a necessary part of the tight fiscal policy. Statistics will show rising unemployment, falling production and a falling rate of increase of prices and wages. People will come to expect that the rate of inflation will continue to fall.

In this sort of climate a cost inflation cannot proceed very far or very fast. Indeed, in the extreme it cannot proceed at all. It is theoretically possible that the assumed rigidity of the money supply could be wholly offset by an increase in the velocity of circulation, but there is little motive for any mass movement in this direction: there is no obvious reason why the demand for money should fall, especially in the light of the expectation that the rate of decline in the value of money will slow down.

Accommodating policy

In the 'accommodating policy' case, all is reversed: demand is high, money is plentiful, interest rates are low, unemployment is low, prices and wages rise steadily, and there is a general perception that all cost increases can be readily passed on. Employers will readily accede to trade union demands because on the one hand they will see that the cost can be passed on, and on the other they do not want to be cut off by a strike from a booming market.

The monetarist view[7]

There are several different schools of monetarism, with important differences between them which we shall discuss later. But in broad terms the monetarist analysis of inflation is as follows.

Inflation is always a monetary phenomenon and can be cured or controlled only by monetary action. The important relationship is between the demand for and the supply of money. Economic agents have a stable demand for money. If the supply exceeds this demand, agents will act to get rid of the excess and this, by various routes, generates and perpetuates inflation. The appropriate counter-inflationary action, therefore, is to reduce the money supply. As agents try to accommodate to the reduced supply, forces are set up which tend to reduce the rate of inflation. Market forces will operate to eliminate any discrepancy between the supply or stock of money and the quantity that agents want to hold. One way would be for the private sector to reduce its demand for goods and services; or to attempt to reduce its holdings of securities, an attempt that would drive up interest rates.

Actions such as these will depress first output and later, after a lag, prices. There will be other effects: the exchange rate is likely to rise and this will lower import prices and, for a time, depress activity in the export industries and put pressure on costs in these industries.

The precise mechanism through which a reduction in the money supply brings down the rate of inflation will vary according to circumstances, and it is unnecessary to specify it too closely. The *speed* with which monetary policy takes effect depends very much on people's expectations: the more generally it is appreciated that monetary control will bring down inflation and that the authorities are resolute in their monetary policy, the quicker will inflation come down and the smaller will be the cost in lost output.

The monetarist analysis carries the implication that inflation is demand-induced, not cost induced. Hence there is no room in the monetarist prescription, in its purest form, for incomes policies.

Inflation in an open economy

The foregoing analysis of inflation has for the most part assumed a closed economy. The external influences on inflation are important, particularly in the monetarist analysis, and these are discussed more fully later.

Summary

Inflation has significant economic and social costs. For analytical purposes we may identify three types of inflation: demand inflation, demand-induced cost inflation, pure cost inflation. But inflation is essentially a reactive process and the extent to which an inflation, once begun, can proceed depends upon the actual and perceived tightness or laxness of policy.

Appendix

The statistics of inflation

1. The time it takes for the value of money to halve at different rates of inflation may be seen from Table 11.1.

Table 11.1   Rates of inflation and value of money

Annual rate of inflation (%)	1	2	3	4	5	6
Number of years to halve value of money	70	35	24	18	15	12
Annual rate of inflation (%)	7	8	9	10	12	15
Number of years to halve value of money	11	10	9	8	6	5

2. The purchasing power of the pound over time may be looked at in two ways. If we want to know the erosion of our purchasing power over time we ask what is, say, a '1970' pound worth today. Or we can turn the question round and ask how much we would need now to buy what a pound would have bought in 1970.

Both answers may be read off from Table 11.2; the first by reading across and the second by reading down. Moving along the 1970 *row* to the 1970 *column* we find our base of 100 (call it £100). Then moving along the row to the 1981 column at the end we see that it is worth 25.4 (£25.4). The *erosion* of purchasing power has been

$$100 - 25.4 = 74.6\%.$$

Moving down the 1970 *column* to the 1981 *row* at the bottom we find that to buy now what £100 would have bought in 1970 we should need £393.9.

The two figures are, of course, related, and may be derived from each other via the base:

$$\frac{100}{393.3} \times 100 = 25.4 \qquad \frac{100}{25.4} \times 100 = 393.9$$

3. There are a great many price indices. The one customarily used to measure 'the cost of living' is the Retail Price Index (RPI). This is the index commonly used in wage bargaining. It does not, however, contain any element for direct taxation (income tax) although income tax is clearly a factor in the standard of living. Accordingly Mr Healey, when he was Chancellor of the Exchequer, bargained with the unions along the following lines: if you will restrain wage demands I will cut taxes. Such a pact was to almost everybody's advantage: there was some loss to the Exchequer, but wage-earners would have extra take-home pay without industrial costs being raised.

The Conservative Government carried this idea a stage further: if, as seemed the case, workers bargained for an 'after tax' in-

Table 11.2 Purchasing power of the pound 1920–1981 (January figures). Source: Barclays Review

Erosion of purchasing power

Equivalent purchasing power

	1920	1925	1930	1935	1940	1945	1950	1955	1960	1965	1970	1971	1972	1973	1974	1975	1976	1977	1978	1979	1980	1981
1920	100	125	135.5	157.2	129.4	111.4	98.0	75.9	66.0	56.3	45.6	41.8	38.8	36.0	32.1	26.8	21.7	18.6	16.9	15.5	13.1	11.6
1925	80.0	100	108.4	125.8	103.5	89.1	78.4	60.7	52.8	45.0	36.5	33.5	31.0	28.8	25.7	21.4	17.4	14.9	13.6	12.4	10.5	9.3
1930	73.8	92.3	100	116.0	95.5	82.2	72.4	56.0	48.7	41.5	33.7	30.9	28.6	26.6	23.7	19.8	16.0	13.7	12.5	11.4	9.7	8.5
1935	63.6	79.5	86.2	100	82.3	70.8	62.4	48.3	42.0	35.8	29.0	26.6	24.7	22.9	20.4	17.0	13.8	11.8	10.8	9.9	8.3	7.4
1940	77.3	96.6	104.7	121.5	100	86.1	75.8	58.7	51.0	43.5	35.3	32.3	30.0	27.8	24.8	20.7	16.8	14.4	13.1	12.0	10.1	9.0
1945	89.8	112.3	121.7	141.2	116.2	100	88.0	68.2	59.2	50.5	41.0	37.6	34.8	32.3	28.8	24.0	19.5	16.7	15.2	13.9	11.8	10.4
1950	102.0	127.5	138.2	160.4	132.0	113.6	100	77.4	67.3	57.4	46.5	42.7	39.5	36.7	32.8	27.3	22.2	19.0	17.3	15.8	13.4	11.8
1955	131.7	164.6	178.5	207.1	170.4	146.7	129.1	100	86.9	74.1	60.1	55.1	51.0	47.4	42.3	35.3	28.6	24.5	22.3	20.4	17.3	15.3
1960	151.6	189.5	205.4	238.4	196.1	168.8	148.6	115.1	100	85.3	69.2	63.4	58.8	54.6	48.7	40.6	32.9	28.2	25.7	23.5	19.9	17.6
1965	177.7	222.1	240.8	279.4	229.9	197.9	174.2	134.9	117.2	100	81.1	74.3	68.9	63.9	57.1	47.6	38.6	33.1	30.1	27.5	23.3	20.6
1970	219.2	274	297.0	344.7	283.6	244.1	214.9	166.4	144.6	123.4	100	91.7	85.0	78.9	70.4	58.7	47.6	40.8	37.1	34.0	28.7	25.4
1971	239.1	298.9	324	375.9	309.3	266.3	234.4	181.5	157.7	134.6	109.1	100	92.7	86.0	76.8	64.0	52.0	44.5	40.5	37.1	31.3	27.7
1972	258.0	322.5	349.6	405.7	333.8	287.3	252.9	195.9	170.2	145.2	117.7	107.9	100	92.8	82.9	69.1	56.1	48.1	43.7	40.0	33.8	29.9
1973	277.9	347.4	376.6	436.9	359.5	309.5	272.5	211.0	183.3	156.4	126.8	116.2	107.7	100	89.3	74.4	60.4	51.8	47.1	43.1	36.4	32.2
1974	311.3	389.1	421.8	489.5	402.7	346.7	305.2	236.4	205.3	175.2	142.0	130.2	120.7	112.0	100	82.3	67.7	58.0	52.8	48.3	40.8	36.1
1975	373.5	466.9	506.1	587.3	483.2	415.9	366.2	283.6	246.4	210.2	170.4	156.2	144.8	134.4	120.0	100	81.2	69.6	63.3	57.9	48.9	43.3
1976	460.1	575.1	623.4	723.4	595.2	512.4	451.1	349.4	303.5	258.9	209.9	192.4	178.3	165.6	147.8	123.2	100	85.7	78.0	71.3	60.3	53.3
1977	536.8	671	727.4	844.0	694.4	597.8	526.3	407.6	354.1	302.1	244.9	224.5	208.1	193.2	172.4	143.7	116.7	100	91.0	83.2	70.3	62.2
1978	590.1	737.6	799.6	927.8	763.4	657.1	578.5	448.1	389.2	332.1	269.2	246.8	228.7	212.3	189.6	158.0	128.3	109.9	100	91.5	77.3	68.3
1979	645.1	806.4	874.1	1014.3	834.5	718.4	632.5	489.8	425.5	363	294.3	269.8	250.0	232.1	207.2	172.7	140.2	120.2	109.3	100	84.5	74.7
1980	763.3	954.1	1034.3	1200.2	987.5	850.0	748.3	579.6	503.5	429.5	348.2	319.2	295.9	274.7	245.2	204.4	165.9	142.2	129.4	118.3	100	88.4
1981	863.4	1079.3	1169.9	1357.5	1116.9	961.5	846.5	655.6	569.5	485.9	393.9	361.1	334.7	310.7	277.4	231.2	187.7	160.8	146.3	133.8	113.1	100

crease in pay then the appropriate index would be one that included income tax (although it was denied that *any* index should be used: wage increases should be related to productivity, not the cost of living). Accordingly in August 1979 they introduced a new index, the Tax and Price Index, which was based upon the RPI but included income tax. By August 1982 the Tax and Price Index had risen by 47.1 per cent since August 1979 while the RPI had risen by only 39.9 per cent. Sources: *Economic Trends Annual Supplement, 1982*, p. 118. *Economic Trends*, No. 347, Sept. 1982, p. 5.

Notes

1. *Financial Times*, 25 June 1981.
2. 'Disposable income' is what the name implies: income at the disposal of the recipient. It must therefore be measured *after* all deductions beyond his control.
3. Note that the *marginal* propensity to consume, and hence the multiplier, need not change.
4. Essay 'Of Money', quoted in O'Brien *The Classical Economists*, p.162. Note that his 'increase of gold and silver' must come from abroad, although our analysis is conducted in terms of a closed economy.
5. Keynesians would be likely to measure or judge tightness or laxness primarily by reference to the pressure of demand; and monetarists primarily by reference to monetary conditions.
6. By fiscal policy we mean policies on taxation and expenditure which determine the size and direction of the public sector balance – whether it is in surplus or deficit, by how much and in which direction it is planned to move.
7. For a useful short account of the monetarist view as interpreted by the Government see *Economic Progress Report* No.123, July 1980.

Chapter twelve

The control of inflation

The main point is that the objective of the authorities, pursued with such means as are at their command, should be the stability of prices.

Keynes[1]

... we must make it a prime object of deliberate State policy that the standard of value, in terms of which they (savings) are expressed should be kept stable ...

Keynes[1]

The prime task for any Government must remain the control of inflation.

Denis Healey[1]

We have seen that inflation may, conceptually, originate on either the demand side or the cost side but that, once established, it is essentially a reactive process, the main reactive force being the drive of those made worse off by inflation to protect their real incomes. The problem of controlling inflation, therefore, reduces to a matter of finding the best way to interrupt this reactive force.

There are two choices. The force may be contained by a 'tight' policy. Or action may be taken to modify behaviour (in the English translation, incomes policy). If 'tight' policy is chosen it matters little whether the name on its collar is the Tweedledee of demand constraint or the Tweedledum of monetary control. In practical application they amount to much the same thing.

The two choices are not mutually exclusive: *so far as the control of inflation* is concerned there is no reason why they should not be used in combination. But there are other considerations, not directly related to the control of inflation, that will influence the choice.

The tight policy option

This is the route preferred by monetarists with the tight policy operating on and through the money supply. The mechanism through which this works was outlined at the end of the last chapter, and on this mechanism alone pure monetarists would rely. Some monetarists, however, believe that the process can be speeded up and made less painful with the aid of incomes policies. We need to say a word, therefore, on why the purer monetarists reject incomes policies. Later we shall consider why trade unionists may also reject incomes policies.

Monetarists reject incomes policies because they believe above all in free markets. Incomes policies suspend market mechanisms and prevent relative prices from allocating resources as the market indicates. The result is a misallocation of resources and an arthritic economy. Even less, and for the same reasons, do they believe in *prices* and incomes policies. Since wages are part of the set of market prices, wage earners must be allowed to bargain freely in the market. Efficient firms meeting a market demand will be able to pay higher wages to attract labour. Others will not. Thus the market will direct resources in the direction that society, expressing its wishes through the price mechanism, requires. Any interference with this process will lead to a misallocation of society's resources.

The rationale of the 'tight policy' is that a cost-generated inflation cannot proceed very far unless the authorities permit it by allowing increases in demand or the money supply. Most economists (the extreme anti-monetarists excepted) accept this analysis with, possibly, some rider about social costs. Keynesians, it is true, tend to favour incomes policies but it would be incorrect to conclude from that that they deny the effectiveness of tight monetary policy. A well-known Keynesian textbook of the 1950s[2] concluded a chapter on 'The Level of Prices', with these words:

The fact is that monetary economics is too complicated to be dealt with by theories as simple as the Quantity Theory. The most important conclusion we can derive from it is that big rises in the level of real or of money incomes are not possible unless there are more or less equal rises in the quantity of money; an inflation can always be brought to an end if the supply of money is limited. This is an important fact, but it is only a small part of the theory of inflation.

Before we leave the 'tight policy' option and move on to incomes policies we must consider one possible escape from tight policy, a hypothetical set of circumstances in which tight policy could be circumvented.

Trade unions are a combination of labour, a form of labour monopoly. But we have implicitly assumed that each union acts independently. If, instead, we assume that labour unions act *in con-*

cert to demand higher wages, the situation changes. For if *all* labour demands higher money wages and if *all* employers perceived that this was so *and* believed that the demands were likely to be met, then the inflation could continue, despite a tight policy; because the higher money incomes also constitute higher money spending power. This spending power will sustain the demand for goods and services and hence the demand for labour: no unemployment need ensue. Unless the process happens simultaneously over the whole economy, firms will need some credit to bridge any gap between paying higher wages and receiving the income generated by all the higher wages paid by other firms. But such credit is likely to be required for only a short period and whatever the rate of interest the cost will be small (one month at, say, 15 per cent is less than $1\frac{1}{4}$ per cent p.a.) Costs of that order will not deter a firm if the alternative is to face a long strike or go out of business.

It is theoretically possible for a tight policy by the authorities to be thwarted in this way but *only* if all labour acts in concert *and* if all employers perceive that all other employers will concede higher wages. Once the tight policy is established and perceived to be so these conditions are unlikely to be met, especially if employers, too, act in concert to resist wage claims.

The 'escape' is possible because, under the restrictive assumptions made, enough credit would be available to ensure that higher money wages were passed on in higher prices. No one could 'price himself out of a job'.

This conclusion, however, needs to be modified in the case of an open economy, where it *can* be true that we can 'price ourselves out of jobs' because we sell our goods on world markets in competition with others. Nor would any loss of jobs be confined to the export industries: there would be 'ripple' effects on other domestic industries. Moreover, many domestic industries are in direct competition with foreign imports.

The relationship between domestic costs and prices and foreign costs and prices is not, however, straightforward, because in between the two comes the foreign exchange rate. The immediate effect of following the 'escape strategy' would be for the exchange rate to fall. Whether this would reduce, maintain or increase employment, it is impossible to say, a priori. (But certainly it would add to inflation).

Incomes policies: the nature of wage bargaining

The foregoing has led us to a number of important conclusions, or, if conclusions is too strong a word, to certain working hypotheses upon which the discussion may be moved forward.

We can conclude, or hypothesise, that an inflation can be brought to an end by a strict monetary regime – subject to the condition that all parties to the wage bargain do not act in concert to thwart it. We can agree that this process will be more prolonged and will create greater unemployment if trade unions do not acquiesce in it. It follows that with trade union co-operation an inflation can quickly and more-or-less painlessly be brought to an end by a strict monetary policy.

But Keynesians, or non-monetarists – anyone who favours the incomes policy approach – would argue that *if* you have the full co-operation of the unions you do not need a strict monetary regime. Other things (e.g., in an open economy, import prices in sterling) being equal, trade union co-operation is a sufficient condition to end an inflation.

It seems, then, that in the monetarist case trade union co-operation is highly desirable and in the incomes policy case it is necessary – and necessary, one should note, not for one or two years, but for always.

The crucial question for both policies, therefore, is this: is co-operation likely to be forthcoming on a long-term basis?; and this, in turn, resolves itself into the question of the nature of trade union bargaining. In pursuing this question, we should first note the institutional fact that we are talking about trade unions, with an 's', and not 'the trade unions' acting collectively. In bargaining matters they do not act collectively, except exceptionally and for short periods.

What a trade union bargains for is an increase in the real (i.e. price adjusted) after-tax earnings of its members. (Within 'an increase in earnings' we subsume other benefits, including a reduction in hours).

Trade Unionists realise that the increase in the money wage must at least keep pace with the rise in the price level if real earnings are to be maintained. It is not, however, always clear whether the rate of inflation they take into account is the past rate, or the expected rate. (To the extent that it is the expected rate it becomes an important part of an anti-inflationary policy to lower expectations.) Over and above the increase in money wages required to keep pace (over some period) with inflation they require a 'real' increase. And they are aware that the total of the money increase will be subject to income tax at the marginal rate, i.e. at the highest rate of tax to which they are liable or will become liable after the increase. Their final demand in money terms must be designed, therefore, to yield a net gain after allowing for inflation and taxes.

This, of course, is normal short-run maximisation behaviour, designed to maximise the 'profits' of members, behaviour such as would be followed by any other price-setting organisation.

Every union acting in isolation is compelled to act in this way. Trade unions are, on the whole, democratic organisations and there is pressure on leaders from the membership to act in the way prescribed. Now, if an individual union is to act in any other way it has to be persuaded either (in the monetarist case) that to act in an ostensibly maximising way will produce unemployment for its members, or, (in the incomes policy case) that to act in that way is to perpetuate an inflation that is bad for its members. It also has to be persuaded that all other unions will *act in the same way*.

There are a number of reasons why it need not be so persuaded.

1. It may not believe in monetarist theory, even if it understands it. (It will note that economists themselves are divided).
2. Even if it understands and believes in the efficiency of monetarist theory it may not believe in the Government's resolve to carry that policy through.
3. It may not believe that the defeat of inflation should be an overriding objective.
4. Union members may not be convinced, or may not want to be convinced, that excessive pay claims are the largest single factor contributing to inflation. At any one time it may well be true that other factors – oil prices, import prices generally, indirect taxes – are adding to inflation and union members do not see why they should be selected as both the main culprit and the instrument of salvation. Even if there is no very strong evidence that other factors are important it is always easy (for any of us) to blame others first – especially if these others are seen as hostile and despised groups such as bosses, politicians and foreigners.
5. Even if it is accepted that excessive wage increases are the proximate cause of inflation, and that the defeat of inflation is desirable, union members may nevertheless observe that a fall in their real incomes is a necessary part of the cure (because wages must fall before prices) and they may just decline to accept this. As W. A. Morton has put it:[3]

What was wanted by the critics of labour was a sacrificial wage policy for the purpose of keeping down prices. This fanciful policy would have reduced demand for food and clothing, but it would also have created a large wage lag...and lessened inflation wholly at the expense of organised labour...Why anyone would have expected organized labour to follow voluntarily a sacrificial wage policy, in view of the abandonment of price control, is a problem for social psychology, not economics. Indeed, the implementation of such a policy would have been possible only within the framework of the corporative state.

6. It may believe, correctly or not, that a wage increase can 'come out of profits', i.e. without any need to raise prices or cut jobs.

7. It may be bloody-minded and decline to co-operate with government policy. (Here, much depends on union leadership. But, as we have learned, not all union leaders support even Labour Governments).

8. Recognising that any benefit follows only if all unions exercise restraint it may not be convinced that other unions will be restrained.

9. It may (correctly) believe from past experience that, even with inflation, gains in money wages yield *real* gains.

10. It may know that its own or its industry's (monopoly) position is so powerful that high prices can be passed on and that there is no risk of unemployment.

11. Even if a risk of unemployment is acknowledged it may not be seen as either a high or an immediate risk, and will be discounted.

12. Even if there is the certainty of some unemployment within a given firm/industry a union may still accept, say, a 15 per cent wage rise against 10 per cent redundancy. (Everyone believes that the sack is something that happens to everyone else: and if it comes to a vote those most at risk – the old, the very new – are likely to be heavily outvoted).

13. With unemployment pay, supplementary benefit, income tax relief and, possibly, redundancy pay, even unemployment may not seem too much to be feared.

14. Incomes policies, with their norms and general conditions, severely delimit the scope for bargaining. Indeed, that is the purpose of incomes policy. Trade Union leaders correctly see this as an emasculation of their power and status, a cutting away of the very reason for their existence. This effect should not be underestimated: trade union leadership confers power, status and, these days, for some, high income. This effect does not operate, indeed is reversed, where the constraint is monetary policy rather than incomes policy. It is not difficult to see why the call for 'free collective bargaining' – responsible, of course – has a certain appeal.

This is a formidable list which makes it clear that for a variety of reasons, many of them wholly rational in terms of self-interest, many of them wholly respectable, and all of them understandable as human responses, trade union 'co-operation' is not a thing likely to be easily come by.

This conclusion is more comforting to a monetarist approach than to an incomes policy approach. Trade unions are inherently unable to co-operate and the only solution is to impose some outside constraint that applies pressure more-or-less-evenly on all. It is hell-fire economics: possessed by original sin, the sinners cannot repent and walk the paths of righteousness and incomes policy. They must therefore be made to fear God.

But if the conclusion is more favourable to the monetarists it does not follow that salvation through monetarism will be painless. There are some, alas, who would not wish it to be. But, union co-operation can minimise the pain. As ministers say, *ad nauseum*, the sooner unions recognise that strict monetary control is here to stay ('we will not print money to validate excessive wage claims') and that excessive wage claims can cause only unemployment, the quicker the cure will be.

In the event, such union recognition is likely to be reluctant, slow and partial. In a fight, with no incomes policy, the strongest will come off best. Strong unions in strong industries will make real gains without loss of employment. Others will suffer loss of real income and jobs. The result will be some fall in inflation, some rise in unemployment, some redistribution of income and a considerable loss of national product. Some firms and industries will not survive but if the market test is valid they should not survive anyway. Monetarism is about market economics, not just about defeating inflation. But one large part of the economy, the public sector, is not subject to market forces. It is therefore crucial to the success of monetarist policies that the Government should apply to the public sector – which comprises a set of monopolies – those disciplines which the market cannot. Otherwise the outcome will be that all the inflation will be in the public sector and all the unemployment in the private sector. But if that is the outcome it will ill-become those who reject incomes policies to abuse the public sector unions for using their bargaining position.

There has been, perhaps, almost as much politics as economics in this chapter and I make no apology for that. Inflation is, as Keynes recognised long ago, a political problem. Frank Blackaby[4] put it thus:

I can well imagine the comment on this paper, that large parts of it have nothing to do with economics. I think that is true. There are powerful non-economic elements in the determination of the rate of inflation, and certainly the problem of devising workable methods for dealing with it is also a problem mainly outside the field of technical economics.

Trade union psychology may not fit easily into an equation but that does not mean that it has nothing to do with economics in the broader sense.

Even if the monetarist solution is in some sense successful that does not mean that an incomes policy is not needed. If we accept that real incomes are determined by real production and that there is now very little scope for labour to make any significant gains at the expense of capital, it follows that labour is essentially bargaining against itself. The bargaining is not about increasing labour's share but about the distribution of that share.[5] There ought to be a more sensible way of deciding this than by a process that generates no real gains, only losses in the form of inflation or unemployment.[6]

Notes

1. Keynes, *Essays in Persuasion*, pp. 92, 216, 217. Macmillan 1931. Healey, House of Commons, 14 June 1978, Hansard Vol 951 No 132, col 1028.

2. *Outline of Monetary Economics* by A. C. L. Day, Oxford, Clarendon Press, 1957.

3. 'Trade Unionism, full employment and inflation', *American Economic Review*, Vol. 40 (1950). Excerpts reprinted in *Inflation* Ball and Doyle (eds), Penguin Books 1969.

4. 'Incomes and Inflation' in *After Keynes* (ed). *J. Robinson*.

5. As usual, Keynes had recognised this: 'In other words, the struggle about money wages primarily affects the *distribution* of the aggregate real wage between different labour-groups, and not its average amount per unit of employment, which depends, as we shall see, on a different set of forces. The effect of combination on the part of a group of workers is to protect their *relative* real wage. The *general* level of real wages depends on the other forces of the economic system'. GT, Chap. 2

6. In a speech to the Birmingham Chamber of Commerce on 26 June 1981 (the opening shot, presumably, in a campaign to influence the 1981–82 'pay round' which would commence on 1 August) the Chancellor of the Exchequer, Sir Geoffrey Howe, pleaded for considerably lower pay rises. The next day the *Financial Times* devoted its leader to the issue raised, under the heading 'Money versus real incomes'. It said:

'The present Government came to office with the view that pay was no concern of ministers, and should be left to market forces . . . we have now reached the stage in the life of Mrs Thatcher's administration when Ministers decide that pay is after all a political issue. The Chancellor, the Bank of England, a whole parade of junior ministers, and in the end, we may be sure, all the Queen's horses and all the Queen's men are praising the virtues of restraint'.

'If only people understood that money increases without increases in real output can buy nothing but inflation, and that output would grow faster under more stable circumstances, a deeply worrying problem would melt away. The logic of such arguments . . . is always faultless; but it rests on a basic misunderstanding. The problem is not that people do not understand. . . . The problem is rather that people feel compelled to behave in a way which they know to be foolish'.

'What the politicians overlook is the basic problem of politics in all times: the interest of individuals is not the same as the good of society as a whole. Everyone may agree with the Chancellor . . . but everyone striking an individual bargain wants to be at least in line with the average'.

Chapter thirteen

Employment, real wages and the money supply

It is to the question of union power and union behaviour, rather than undue restriction of the money supply, that we should look for the most important causes of high unemployment.

Prof. Harold Rose[1]

This chapter differs from others in that it develops a more formal economic model. The general reader may find it helpful to look first at the summary at the end to see how the argument is structured.

Keynes showed that, where there was unemployment, employment could be increased by increasing effective demand and the money supply. He acknowledged that as full employment was approached, prices would begin to rise until, when full employment (not defined) was exceeded, prices only would rise, and a 'true' inflationary situation exist.

In the United Kingdom for the past several years we have had both unemployment (in the 'involuntary', Keynesian, sense) *and* inflation; and unemployment has now (1982) reached a level comparable to that experienced in some of the pre-war years. The question we have to ask, and answer, is why it is that Keynes's remedy cannot be used to reduce this unemployment.

The classical theory of employment, according to Keynes[2], was based on two fundamental postulates:

I   The wage is equal to the marginal product of labour.
II The utility of the wage when a given volume of labour is employed is equal to the marginal disutility of that amount of employment.

Keynes rejected the second postulate but accepted the first, insisting on its importance as follows:[2]

In emphasising our point of departure from the classical system, we must not overlook an important point of agreement. For we shall maintain the first postulate as heretofore, subject only to the same qualifications as in the classical theory; and we must pause, for a moment, to consider what this involves.

It means that, with a given organisation, equipment and technique, real wages and the volume of output (and hence of employment) are uniquely correlated, so that, in general, an increase in employment can only occur to the accompaniment of a decline in the rate of real wages. Thus I am not disputing this vital fact which the classical economists have (rightly) asserted as indefeasible[3]

According to classical theory, said Keynes:

. . . the volume of employed resources is duly determined . . . by the two postulates. The first gives us the demand schedule for employment, the second gives us the supply schedule; and the amount of employment is fixed at the point where the utility of the marginal product balances the disutility of the marginal employment.

Keynes's objection to the second postulate was that it was plainly not in accordance with the observed facts, the facts at least of the 1930s. At that time, and no doubt today, the millions out of work would have been only too willing to work at or about the going real wage. Yet the classical theory implied that a small rise in prices, which (with money wages unchanged) would lower the real wage, would lead to a *withdrawal* of labour (because the real wage no longer compensated those in employment for the disutility of working). This was not plausible. The classical analysis could be true only if everyone, or nearly everyone, who wanted to work was working. It might then be the case that those who only just found it worth working at the going real wage would withdraw from work if the real wage fell. Any resulting unemployment would clearly be voluntary. But if unemployed people were willing to work at the going real wage but no work was available such unemployment would be involuntary. And involuntary unemployment clearly existed.

Keynes's argument comes to this. The first postulate correctly establishes *one* demand curve for labour and hence establishes a real wage for a certain amount of employment. But this demand curve is formulated by employers *on the basis of the demand they actually see, i.e. on effective demand*. It is not a demand curve based on full employment unless there happens to be full employment. The amount of labour they demand at the going real wage can, therefore, fall (far) short of the amount of labour which *would be willing to work* at that real wage; and if effective demand is deficient it *will* so fall short. The classical schedules for the demand for and supply of labour determine the real wage and the level of employment *only when there is full employment.*

The theory assumes what it is meant to determine. As Keynes had it: 'Obviously, however, if the classical theory is only applicable to the case of full employment, it is fallacious to apply it to the problems of involuntary unemployment – if there be such a thing (and who will deny it?).'[5] Keynes' analysis effectively disposes of the argument that when workers are involuntarily unemployed they can increase employment by lowering the real wage. There are two strands to his argument. The first, the one that we have just examined, is that the cause of the unemployment is not a real wage that is too high, but a level of effective demand that is too low. The second is that workers do not, in any case, have it in their power to lower their real wage; because workers can influence only their money wage; and if they lower their money wage, prices will fall, thus tending to restore the real wage.

If workers attempt to lower their real wage, the result will be a progressive decline in the price level. If the actual stock of money remains unchanged this will have the effect of increasing the *real* stock of money. The end result will be the same as if the actual stock of money had been increased at the former price level. But, of course, it is much easier, simpler and quicker to increase the stock of money than to go through the painful and time-consuming process of forcing down wages.

So, the Keynesian solution to involuntary employment is to increase effective demand up to the point where full employment is established at the going real wage, the going real wage being set by the productive capacity of the economy. Effective demand can be increased by pumping money into the economy in one way or another, so we may say that equilibrium can be restored at the full employment level when the stock of money is in balance, or compatible with, the real wage.

It is important to understand that the upper limit to the real wage is set by the 'real' factors in the economy, that is, by the state of technology, capital investment, natural endowment and all those factors that determine what an economy is capable of producing (and, in an open economy, by the terms of trade). It is obvious, for example, that the real wage in the United Kingdom will be higher than, say, the real wage in Tanzania. What happens if labour unions, by the exercise of monopoly power, seek to achieve a real wage higher than is technically possible?

If the monetary policy is accommodating, union power can

achieve a rise in money wages and, in the short run, in real wages. The aggregate real wage of all those employed (the average real wage multiplied by the numbers employed) is now greater than the real output of the economy. In a closed economy (i.e. no possibility of the excess's being met by imports) equilibrium can be restored only if prices rise, thus reducing the real wage. As prices rise the real value of the money supply falls until equilibrium is once more restored between the real wage, employment and the money supply. The original position, or something close to it, has been restored, but with a greater quantity of money and a higher price level.

The new equilibrium, however, can be maintained only so long as unions do not press for higher real wages. If unions continue to press for higher real wages the process continues *ad infinitum*, generating inflation but no permanent increase in real wages.

There is, however, no reason why, in a closed economy, any unemployment should ensue.

The economy is now in a state of continuing inflation. Monetarists believe that the rate of inflation can be brought down by reducing the rate of growth of the money supply. If, in pursuit of this belief, they react to the inflation by reducing the money supply below the point where it is in equilibrium with real wages and employment, unemployment will result. Now it is important to note that this unemployment does not arise because real wages are too high; because, by assumption, full employment previously existed at this level of real wages. The unemployment stems from the reduction in the money supply. And the money supply has been reduced because of the *attempts to achieve* an unrealistic real wage (i.e. a real wage that the economy is just unable to support). The distinction between a real wage that is too high and the attempt to achieve a real wage that is too high may at first sight appear a fine one, but it is crucial for policy.

Now, let us back-track in the analysis to the point where unions first attempted to enforce a higher real wage. The subsequent analysis began with the assumption 'If the monetary policy is accommodating . . . .' But, of course, it need not be. If the monetary policy were not accommodating then the inflationary process outlined would have been stopped in its tracks. This illustrates another important distinction: that between a tight (or 'non-accommodating') monetary policy to *prevent* an inflation, and a contractionary monetary policy to *end* an inflation. It is only the latter that results in unemployment.

A decision not to accommodate union pressure for a non-achievable real wage by an increase in the money supply is, obviously, a monetarist policy choice. There is, however, an alternative, an alternative that goes further back to the root of the problem. It is to persuade the unions not to press for a non-achievable real wage in the first place. This is the incomes policy approach. As we have seen from our analysis of wage bargaining, this is not likely to be easy.

To rely solely on incomes policy is a non-monetarist prescription. But some monetarists invoke the idea as a supplement to monetary policy. They argue, correctly, that if unions do not demand an unrealistic real wage then a tight monetary policy will not result in unemployment. But if unions do not demand an unrealistic real wage a tight monetary policy is unnecessary: there is no problem.

There are thus four policy combinations: the 'authorities' may adopt either an accommodating or a tight monetary stance; and the unions may demand either a realistic or an unrealistic real wage. The consequences of the adoption of these stances is summarised in Table 13.1.

Table 13.1.

Unions' real wage stance	Authorities' monetary stance	
	Tight	*Accommodating*
Unrealistic (i.e. for an excessive real wage)	Prevents inflation. But if inflation in progress: Lower employment, Lower inflation in the end leading to Higher employment	Higher employment, Higher inflation leading back to Lower employment
Realistic (i.e. for a real wage within the capacity of the economy)	No unemployment No inflation	

The most favourable result appears to be achieved by a combination of a tight monetary policy and a union policy that accepts a realistic real wage.

But the analysis above is the monetarist analysis. The fourth option has been left blank because it is the pure incomes policy approach. It is clear that an incomes policy that achieved acceptance of a realistic real wage would achieve exactly the same results as a 'realistic wage' combined with 'tight' monetary policy, i.e. no unemployment and no inflation. With such an incomes policy the need for an accommodating monetary policy does not arise: there is nothing to accommodate to.

Thus, an incomes policy is a sufficient condition to achieve the desired objectives. In the case of a tight monetary policy it is a necessary condition. All that a tight monetary policy is is a necessary condition to achieve one policy objective, namely lower inflation, given non-cooperation on the part of the unions.

The answer to the question with which we began is, then, that we cannot increase the money supply to reduce involuntary unemployment because to do so would be to accommodate unions' demands for an unrealistic real wage, and perpetuate inflation. This was one problem that did not exist when Keynes wrote, although he was fully alive to it as a potential problem.

That, however, is not quite the end of the matter. We have been thinking in terms of equilibrium positions in which real wages, employment and the money supply are in consonance with one another. But there is, unfortunately, the little matter of the transition from one equilibrium point to another.

The objective of tightening the money supply is to eliminate inflation or to reduce the rate of inflation. By definition that means that prices must fall; and prices do not just fall on their own (except in so far as, in an open economy, import prices fall). Prices are formed from costs and costs must fall before prices. And the largest single element in costs is the cost of labour. Therefore the fall in wage costs must precede the fall in prices, and this means a fall in real wages. Thus the *process* of ending inflation does require a fall in real wages. That is one reason why it is, understandably, so difficult to get union acquiescence in the matter.

In the absence of such acquiescence a tight monetary stance is the only alternative open. But if as part of a tight monetary and fiscal policy (the two should march together) it is found necessary to raise indirect taxes that exacerbates the problem, because indirect taxes raise prices and thus further reduce the real wage.

Summary

The conclusion of classical labour market analysis that unemployment was always voluntary because it could be eliminated by the acceptance of a lower real wage is invalid because it assumes full employment.

When, as in the 1930s and now, there is unemployment yet more people would accept work at the going real wage, then such unemployment is involuntary, the only sort that Keynes was concerned with.

With real wages stable, involuntary unemployment can be eliminated by increasing the money supply. When full employment is reached there is equilibrium between the real wage and the money supply.

If at this point there is effective union pressure for a higher real wage an imbalance will emerge between the real wage and the money supply. There are now two possibilities: either the real money supply is increased to match the higher real wage; or it is not. If it is, the process is repeated and inflation is established. If it is not there is unemployment.

This unemployment is involuntary in the sense that more people would be willing to work at the new real wage; but voluntary in the sense that it stems from pressure for an unrealisable real wage. In principle, this unemployment could be eliminated by an increase in the money supply. But if the elimination of inflation has priority over the elimination of unemployment, it must not be, because to increase the money supply in these circumstances would perpetuate inflation.

If unions demand an excessive real wage, inflation can be eliminated only by a tight monetary policy. If unions do not demand an excessive real wage, a tight monetary policy is unnecessary.

If the real wage is excessive and the real money supply fixed the process of restoring balance between them requires a fall in the real wage.[4]

Appendix

The analysis of this chapter may be helpfully presented in diagrammatic form.

Figure 13.1 is the classical case. DD is the demand curve for labour, SS the supply curve. The supply curve rises vertically to indicate *absolute* full employment at that point. 'Practical' full employment is taken to be a point slightly to the left of this. E_1 is full 'practical' employment.

If the real wage is reduced from W_1 to W_2 employment falls from E_1 to E_2. This is voluntary unemployment because at a real wage W_2 the demand for labour exceeds the supply, i.e. the unemployment could be eliminated if labour would accept a wage W_2.

Figure 13.2 is the Keynesian case. At a wage W_1 workers would supply labour up to employment E_1, full employment. But at wage

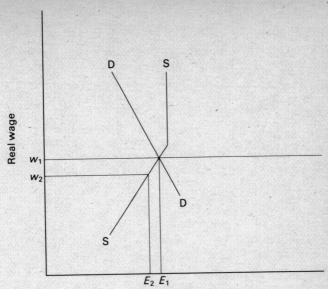

Fig. 13.1   Employment

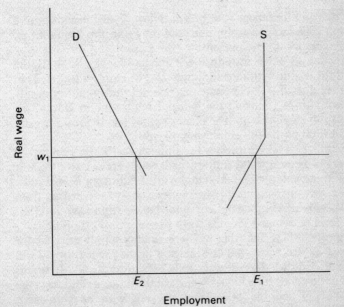

Fig. 13.2

Employment

165

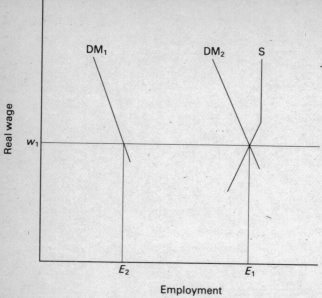

Employment, real wages and the money supply

Fig. 13.3

W_1 the demand for labour is only E_2. (Below W_1 the demand curve for labour falls away sharply, not fully drawn in the diagram.) E_1 E_2 is involuntary unemployment.

In Figure 13.3 we introduce the money supply. DM_1 is the demand for labour with money supply M_1. Unemployment is, as in diagram 13.2, E_1E_2. To eliminate this unemployment money supply is increased to M_2, moving the demand for labour to DM_2. This produces full employment. The money supply and the real wage are in equilibrium at the full employment level.

In Figure 13.4 labour presses for a higher real wage, signified in the diagram by an upward shift of the labour supply curve from S_1 to S_2. With a money supply M_2 employment falls from E_1 to E_2. To eliminate this unemployment the money supply is increased from M_2 to M_3 moving the demand curve for labour from DM_2 to DM_3. At this level of demand the real wage rises above W_2 (not drawn).

It appears at first sight that by increasing its supply price labour has raised its real wage. But the increase in the money supply will raise prices, so that the real wage falls back towards W_1. If labour persists in demands for a higher real wage the process continues; the money supply and the price level rise but with no permanent increase in the real wage.

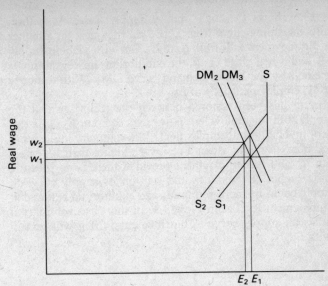

Fig. 13.4

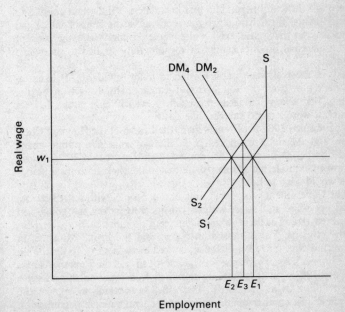

Fig. 13.5

Figure 13.5 shows the 'tight money supply' case. As before, labour shifts its supply curve from S_1 to S_2 in the quest for a higher real wage. Employment falls from E_1 to E_3. But with a labour supply curve of S_2 and a real wage of W_1 the equilibrium money supply is M_4 represented by the labour demand curve DM_4. With a money supply of M_4 employment falls to E_2.

Equilibrium has been restored between the real wage and the money supply, but unemployment now exists equal to E_1E_2. Is this voluntary or involuntary unemployment? It is voluntary in the sense that the economy cannot sustain a real wage higher than W_1 but it can sustain W_1 and full employment provided there is no pressure for anything higher. If labour would stay on its supply curve S_1 money supply could be increased to M_2 and equilibrium restored at the full employment level as in Fig. 13.3. In short it is voluntary if labour insists on supply curve S_2 but involuntary if it will remain content with S_1.

Notes

1. *Barclays Review*, May 1981
2. GT, Chap. 2.
3. There is a difficulty here. The first postulate is valid when applied to the individual firm. And since the economy is the sum of individual firms it is, in that sense, true of the whole economy. But the concept of the marginal product cannot be meaningfully applied to the whole economy.
4. A fall in the real wage implies a fall in living standards. It is extraordinary how even the toughest Governments shy away from saying plainly that living standards must fall or even remain static. It is as though it were a taboo subject, like death.

   On 1 February 1982 Mr Francis Pym, the Leader of the House of Commons and the minister in charge of the Government's public image made a speech in which he warned that there could be no early improvement in living standards and that in the short term these standards would have to fall.

   As the Government was at that time urging people, with some success, to accept wage and salary awards considerably below the going and projected rate of inflation this might seem no more than a statement of the obvious. Yet it caused an outcry and the Prime Minister, in answering questions in the House, backed away from it. In defending her minister's speech, as she was bound to, she, as the *Financial Times* (3 Feb. 1982) put it 'pointedly refrained from quoting the passages about falling living standards'. Her office 'was trying to present the speech as just another manifestation of Mr Pym's innate pessimism'.

It is, of course, unfortunate, and less than tactful, that ministers who make such speeches often seem to do so in full evening dress in front of the television cameras and behind a high table awash with food and drink.

5. GT, Chap.2, p.16.

Chapter fourteen
The foreign sector

If everybody minded their own business, the Duchess said in a hoarse growl, the world would go round a deal faster than it does.

Lewis Carroll, Alice's Adventures in Wonderland

Each nation, minding its own business, certainly makes the world's trade go round faster. To some of the consequences of living in that world, and not in a closed economy, we must now turn.

The balance of payments

The object of the United Kingdom's balance of payments accounts according to the Central Statistical Office, which compiles them, '... is to identify and record transactions between residents of the United Kingdom and residents overseas (non-residents) in a way that is suitable for analysing the economic relations between the UK economy and the rest of the world'[1]. Thus the accounts are seen as a tool of analysis. It is also implicit in this statement that there is more than one way of arranging them.

The word balance suggests the possibility of imbalance, and imbalance is certainly possible in some sectors of the accounts; but overall the accounts must balance. The question is not whether they balance but how. For economic policy the question is whether it is necessary or desirable to restore or improve a particular balance and, if so, what policy instrument should be used. As is usually the case in macroeconomics, one policy objective may conflict to a greater or lesser degree, with another. The problem then is to choose the optimal mix of policy. There is a respectable school of thought which holds that the balance of payments is not itself a problem – only the symptom of other, more fundamental, problems.

The full accounts are immensely detailed and complex, but for broad descriptive purposes they may be grouped into three blocks

I   The current account.
II The capital account.
III The balance for official financing.

The current account

The current account is our 'earnings' account; it shows whether we are paying our way in terms of goods and services bought and sold. It has two main elements: the balance of visible trade and the balance of invisible trade. Invisible trade includes receipts and payments for sea transport, civil aviation, travel, financial services, government services, interest, profits and dividends.

The current account links directly with the other income and expenditure accounts of the economy: exports (visible and invisible) are a source of income to UK residents; imports (visible and invisible), are a component of the expenditure of UK residents. Since income and expenditure must, in equilibrium, balance overall, it follows that if exports and imports are out of balance there must be an offsetting imbalance somewhere else in the economy.[2]

The capital account

The capital account records the flows, inwards and outwards, of long-term and short-term capital. It includes official long-term capital, overseas investment in the UK public and private sectors, UK private investment overseas, overseas currency borrowing or lending by UK banks, and trade credit. If, overall, outflows exceed inflows, then we are increasing our overseas assets (decreasing our liabilities); and conversely. Also included in the capital account is 'the balancing item'. This is really 'errors and omissions', a catch-all repository for unidentified transactions. It is sometimes very large.

The balance for official financing

The balance for official financing is the amount which the authorities have to provide to balance the accounts. In its very simplest manifestation it is the change in the reserves of gold and foreign currency: if the current and capital accounts together show a deficit the shortfall is made good from the reserves. With a current-plus-capital surplus the reserves rise. (A rise in the reserves is known as 'financing the surplus', although no finance, in the usual sense, is called for.)

The balance of payments as a constraint

The balance of payments limits a country's freedom of action in its domestic policies; and clearly this constraint bites hardest when a country is in persistent deficit and has continually to find official financing to meet that deficit. Deficits can be met by running down the reserves of gold and foreign currency, by borrowing from the IMF, and by borrowing from other sources. But reserves are finite, and the IMF and others will not lend without limit. Also, loans have to be repaid.

It will be as well to clear out of the way an ambiguity in 'official financing'. In its accounting form it is the item below the current and capital accounts which brings these accounts into balance. But the authorities can influence the capital account by encouraging capital inflows by, say, maintaining interest rates higher than required for purely domestic reasons. If the authorities, by one device or another, can induce additional capital inflows they are, in effect, financing a balance of payments deficit. But, on the conventions used, this does not count as official financing.

So, a persistent deficit on current account has to be dealt with.

Correcting a current account deficit

There are three basic options:

I   Physical controls.
II   Deflation of the domestic economy.
III Movement of the exchange rate.

Physical controls

These include import licencing, control over access to foreign exchange, import 'surcharges' and other taxes on imports and subsidies on exports. Nearly all such devices contravene international agreements, and their imposition, except in the most exceptional circumstances, would provoke ill-will and, possibly, retaliation. More fundamentally, they interfere with the normal operation of markets and, economists argue, lead to a sub-optimal pattern of trade and allocation of resources.

There is general, but not universal, agreement among economists and politicians that physical controls are the least efficient way of dealing with a balance of payments deficit on current account. One powerful argument is that if, as seems probable, the deficit arises, at bottom, from the inefficiency and relative uncompetitiveness of the domestic industry, then to insulate that industry from foreign competition is likely to make the root cause of the deficit worse rather than better. By dealing with a symptom import controls divert attention from the cause.

The economic argument that controls interfere with the market can be extended to the political argument that they interfere with personal liberty, since they must carry with them, for enforcement, legal powers (e.g. of search and enquiry) and penalties. The political argument against the enforcement of laws of this nature is often put most vociferously by people who, in other areas, call loudly for the rigorous enforcement of laws passed by Parliament.

Deflation

The deflationary solution to a deficit on current account rests on the link between expenditure and imports. There exists a propensity to import such that as income, and therefore expenditure, rises so do imports. A deflation which reduces incomes will therefore also reduce imports. If the economy is fully employed a deflation will also free resources, i.e. productive capacity, which may be used to increase exports. The argument applies *a fortiori* to both imports and exports if the economy is over-fully-employed. In an economy stretched to the limits of its capacity, purchasers of everything from consumer goods to capital equipment will be forced more and more to look to foreign suppliers for what the domestic economy cannot supply. The pressure of domestic demand, enabling anything to be sold on the home market, diminishes the incentive to manufacture for export. A deflation, then, will reduce imports and will create conditions for an increase in exports.

If, however, an economy is inefficient in that it produces goods of poor quality and poor design, and does not at least keep pace with technological advance, then it will find it difficult to export, and will be driven to import more of all those products that domestic industry cannot supply.

In these circumstances the level of income at which imports and exports would be brought into balance might be very low indeed, so low as to be politically impracticable. In such case deflation might be reinforced with physical controls of one sort or another, no doubt with the proclaimed intention that these should be temporary.[7]

Deflation has its main effect through *incomes*. But it may also affect *prices* in some degree if a reduction in demand reduces an existing inflationary pressure. A deflationary package of measures would also almost certainly include higher interest rates and these, while doing nothing for the current account, would tend to attract capital inflows. This would be helpful in the short run but if the capital inflows were merely footloose funds looking for the highest rate of return they would flow out again when interest rates went down again.

Movement of the exchange rate

The exchange rate is the instrument through which domestic prices are changed into foreign currency prices, and vice versa. An exchange rate may be fixed or flexible. A fixed rate, however, may be allowed to fluctuate within a known range; and a flexible rate may not, in practice, be flexible outside a certain (usually undeclared) range. In between fixed and flexible rates is the so-called 'crawling peg' variety, which is a 'fixed' rate that moves from one fixed point to another. This is at present not a candidate and we shall not discuss it further.

A *fixed rate* is a mechanism which links the domestic price level directly to the price level of the rest of the world. If the £ sterling always exchanges for French francs at the same rate then a price in sterling is also a price in francs, and it cannot become, say, cheaper in francs without first becoming cheaper in sterling. But the price level in different countries *does* tend to change, in response to a whole lot of influences, and adjustment to the change needs to be made. When the exchange rate is fixed the whole burden of adjustment is thrown on to those variables in the domestic economy that are *not* fixed – the level of prices, the level of wages and the level of employment.

If the adjustment is not made then balance of payments difficulties ensue. Since an exchange rate tends to become, especially in the UK, a national virility symbol, Governments are very reluctant to devalue.[3] Hence a fixed exchange rate has the effect of enforcing a certain discipline on the domestic economy and – if nearly all countries are on fixed rates, as was the case in the 25 years from the end of the war – on the world as a whole.

When adjustments are not made, it eventually becomes apparent to all that a currency is out of line, i.e. is over-valued or under-valued. Then 'speculators' (or people and firms taking purely self-protective action) step in and reinforce the wrong valuation – selling an over-valued currency and buying an under-valued currency. The weight of speculative pressure eventually becomes irresistible and the currency 'goes' – is devalued or revalued. It was this sort of pressure, on a huge scale in the late 1960s and early 1970s, that led to the breakdown of the so-called Bretton Woods fixed-rate system, established after the war. The members of the European Community now have their own fixed rate regime, in which the United Kingdom does not participate (although it is a member of the European Monetary Union).

A *fully flexible rate* is one entirely determined by market forces. It implies no intervention by the authorities and, therefore, no loss or gain to the reserves of gold and foreign currency. In principle the United Kingdom at present has such a rate but in practice movements in the rate are 'smoothed' by intervention by the Bank of England, on the ground that violent movements (caused, say, by a big movement of funds by one big holder) are undesirable and do not, anyway, reflect the 'true' or 'underlying' trend.

If a fixed rate provides a direct link between the world price level and the domestic price level, a flexible rate severs it: a country can have whatever price level it chooses, and the exchange rate will take care of it, will, as it were, absorb the difference between the domestic and foreign price level. As the price level rises the exchange rate will fall, and vice versa. For this reason some regard flexible rates as offering less of an obstacle to inflation than fixed rates; but monetarists, who very much favour flexible rates, will have none of it. They argue the inflation is caused, and controlled, by monetary factors and that a flexible rate can help in the control of the money supply.

Because a flexible exchange rate reflects the internal price level it tends to set up its own corrective process. Suppose the price level in the United Kingdom is rising faster than elsewhere. Foreign demand for British goods will fall and British demand for foreign goods will rise (because they are becoming relatively cheaper). As a result foreigners will demand less sterling and UK residents will demand more foreign currency (offer more sterling). The exchange rate falls and goes on falling until the fall offsets the higher British price level. The perceived falling exchange rate may induce holders of sterling to sell, or stop potential buyers from buying, thus depressing the rate further. The sterling price of imports rises as the exchange rate falls and *to the extent that money incomes do not rise as fast*, real incomes fall, and the result is deflationary.

If the inflation is allowed to continue at a faster rate than elsewhere the exchange rate will continue to fall. With a fixed exchange rate the pressure on the authorities to take remedial action is applied by the falling reserves of gold and foreign currency; with a flexible rate it is applied by a falling rate of exchange. The more an exchange rate falls, the poorer is a country likely to become because the terms of trade are likely to be moving against it.

The *terms of trade* are more important, as a factor in a country's real wealth, than the attention given to them would suggest. Moreover the domestic adjustment to a sharp fall in the terms of trade, such as that brought about by the big rise in oil prices, has important consequences for policy. Accordingly an appendix to this Chapter explains the matter in more detail.

We must return now to the analysis of a flexible exchange rate. As an escape from, or insurance against, a current account deficit, a flexible rate operates by providing a moving adjustment of external and internal price levels. As we can see from our analysis of the terms of trade, the effect on the balance of trade depends upon the responses of traders; but there has been a general presumption that a lower rate helps the balance of trade at the expense of the terms of trade. Increasingly, however, this is seen not only as an 'easy option' (easy because a falling rate enables exporters to pass on cost increases instead of trying to contain them) but also as an ineffective one in the long run.

Even if a flexible exchange rate (falling or rising) offered an escape from a current account imbalance, the option may not be there, because although the current account is greatly influenced by the exchange rate, and the exchange rate is influenced by the current account, the current account by no means determines the exchange rate. It is thus possible to have an exchange rate that is quite out of line with the real or perceived needs of the current account. This was the case in the United Kingdom in 1980, and the first five months of 1981 when an exchange rate kept high and rising by capital inflows is believed greatly to have impeded exports. Our possession of North Sea Oil makes sterling a 'petro-currency' and stronger than it would otherwise have been. This will make it harder for exporting industries to export and some may lose markets or cease to trade altogether. There is a fear that by the time the oil runs out, towards the end of the century, export industries may be so damaged that there would be great difficulty in sustaining a viable current account. Against this view is the argument that a strong exchange rate will force exporting (and import competing) industries to become more efficient, so that those that survive will emerge stronger. If an industry needs a very low exchange rate in order to survive it is probably uncompetitive anyway.

To summarise so far: the balance of payments has to be looked at as a whole: an imbalance, even a persistent deficit in the current account, does not necessarily have to be corrected. If corrective action is deemed necessary a number of policy instruments are to hand: physical controls; deflation or expansion of incomes, and therefore of imports; the devaluation or revaluation of a fixed exchange rate; a resort to a flexible exchange rate (implying no change in the reserves); policies, including interest rate policy, to encourage or discourage capital flows. A fully flexible exchange rate is determined by the supply of and demand for sterling over the whole range of monetary transactions with the rest of the world, not by current account transactions alone. The terms of trade affect real incomes and any change in real incomes must be accompanied by appropriate fiscal and monetary policies.

Correcting a capital account deficit

There is by no means the same urgency about correcting a capital account deficit. For one thing it is usually the counterpart of a current account surplus ('you can't invest a deficit'), usually accounted a good thing. For another there is no 'loss' because in exchange for the net outflow of capital there is a net acquisition of foreign assets. Indeed, a capital account surplus is more to be worried about because its counterparts are a current account deficit and the sale of assets to foreigners. But in principle the capital account can be influenced by physical controls, movement of the exchange rate, and movement of interest rates: but not, directly, by contractionary or expansionary policies.

The monetary approach to the balance of payments

This approach is still in the process of development. It is apparent that the balance of payments is in one sense a monetary account since, in the current account all movements of goods and services in one direction are matched by a movement of money in the other; and in the capital account all movements of securities, claims and other bits of paper are matched by a counter-flow of money. (The same, of course, is true of domestic transactions.)

The monetarist approach to the balance of payments follows the same general lines as their approach to domestic transactions. Economic units (people, firms, institutions) have a certain demand for real money balances. If more money exists, or is created, than people want to hold, they will dispose of it in the purchase of goods, services, real assets, financial assets, including foreign goods, services, real assets and financial assets. Thus a deficit on the balance of payments signifies that people are trying to reduce their money balances. No action, *apart from a strict control of the domestic money supply*, is required to halt this process because it will come to an end once people have reduced their money holdings to the desired level. It follows that one can take a relaxed view of a balance of payments deficit because not only is it self-correcting, it relieves the domestic economy of excess money more quickly than would otherwise be the case.

The exchange rate and the money supply

It is important to understand that a country cannot at the same time control its exchange rate and its money supply. This is because the exchange rate reflects the supply of and demand for the domestic currency in terms of foreign currency, and the authorities can influence the rate thrown up by the market only by buying or selling their own currency. If they sell their own currency (to bring the rate down) then this increases the amount of that currency in existence (because the money is borrowed, i.e. created by the Government). Conversely, if the Government buys its own currency (to support the exchange rate) then the currency so acquired is available to reduce the amount the Government has to borrow, and thus to reduce below what it would otherwise have been the amount of money created. It should be noted that a Government can only buy its own currency in the foreign exchange market with foreign exchange and, therefore, its ability so to do is limited by the depth, or otherwise, of its foreign exchange pocket, i.e. by its holdings of gold and foreign currency. Or by the amounts of foreign exchange that it can persuade others, notably the International Monetary Fund, to lend it. All the United Kingdom's many borrowings from the IMF have been to enable Governments to support sterling above the level dictated by the market at the time (see also Appendix 2 to this Chapter).

It cannot, however, be inferred from the above that if the government does *not* intervene that the foreign sector has no influence on the domestic money supply. It does, but the effects are complex, and they depend, essentially, on the sectors of the domestic economy from which sterling comes and to which it goes. For example, if foreigners buy Government debt then that finances the Government's borrowing need and reduces, by a like amount, what the Government has to borrow from domestic sources. To the extent that the Government would otherwise have had to borrow from the banks, the money supply is reduced below what it would otherwise have been. It is possible to envisage a hypothetical situation in which the Government sells its own currency (to depress the exchange rate) and yet the domestic money supply is unchanged. But this does not invalidate the general proposition with which we began, that a Government cannot at the same time control the exchange rate and the money supply. That, in essence, is why monetarists favour floating exchange rates, and why the United Kingdom Government, commited to money supply targets, has chosen not to participate in the exchange rate mechanism of the Europen Monetary Fund (EMS). (It was at first thought that participation would have meant frequent intervention to *support* a sagging sterling rate, but as it turned out, we should have had to have intervened heavily to keep the sterling rate down. This illustrates the impossibility of any Government's being able to know what is the appropriate rate for its currency.)

Appendix 1

The terms of trade

The effect of a movement in the exchange rate is usually to change the terms of trade, a higher rate improving the terms and a lower rate worsening them.

Suppose that the UK exports an item worth £100 to the United States, and imports from the US an item worth $400. To make matters easy, assume that the rate of exchange is £1 = $4.

The rate now depreciates to £1 = $2. The effect of this depends on what happens to prices. The change in the exchange rate opens up a range of choices to the exporters in both countries, which may be summarised as follows:

1. The exporter may keep his price unchanged in his own currency, implying, necessarily, a change in the foreign currency price.
2. The exporter may keep his price unchanged in the foreign currency, implying a change in the price in domestic currency.
3. The exporter may make some change in both prices.

Given two exporters (one in each country) each of which has a choice of three strategies, there are nine possible combinations of strategies, and it would be tedious in the extreme to work through them all. For illustrative purposes it will be sufficient to see what happens if both adopt strategy 1 and if both adopt strategy 2.

1. Prices are unchanged in the domestic currency, i.e. the UK item is priced at £100 and the US one at $400. The UK item costs $200 in the US and the US item costs £200 in the UK.

179

To earn the $400 required to purchase the US item the UK has to export twice as many UK items. The *terms* of trade have moved against the UK.

The effect on the *balance* of trade depends on what happens to quantities following the change in prices. The lower dollar price of the UK item should enable dollar sales to increase. The higher sterling price of the US item should reduce UK purchases.

How big this effect will be will depend upon how *elastic* are the respective demands, i.e. whether a fall in the dollar price of the UK good will much increase sales, and whether the rise in the sterling price of the American good will much reduce sales. The total effect on the balance of trade will depend upon the sum of these two effects, after a lapse of time.

2. Prices are unchanged in the foreign currency, i.e. the UK item sells for $400 and the US item for £100. Since the UK item still earns $400 it will still purchase the US item even at its original domestic price of $400. The $400 will be worth £200 to the UK exporter, and for £200 the UK importer can now buy $400. But he now needs only £100 to buy the American item. To put it another way the UK exporter now needs to export only half as many items to earn enough sterling to buy the American article. The terms of trade have moved in favour of the UK.

Since prices in the foreign currency are unchanged there are no changes in quantities sold. The sterling receipts of the UK exporter have doubled and the dollar receipts of the US exporter have halved, so, with quantities unchanged, profits have about doubled in the UK and halved in the US.

The sterling receipts of UK exporters have doubled and the sterling payments of UK importers are unchanged so the *balance* of trade, measured in sterling, improves.

Despite the complexity surrounding the analysis of the terms of trade effects of a change in the exchange rate, involving as it does elasticities of demand and supply and the preferred strategies of exporters (and importers) we can say that a falling rate is likely to make the terms of trade worse and a rising rate to improve them.

Changes in the terms of trade do not come about only through changes in the exchange rate. They follow from any change in the real price of the things we import and export, especially import. The most dramatic recent example of this is, of course, the huge increase in oil prices since 1972.

Adjustment to adverse changes in the terms of trade

If a country becomes poorer through a deterioration in the terms of trade, whether this deterioration comes about through the exchange rate or real prices, it means that real incomes have fallen, and an adjustment to the new situation must be made.

Essentially, policy must be aimed at making the fall in real incomes bite, either by a tight fiscal and monetary regime or an effective incomes policy. From our analysis of inflation we know that this will not be an easy thing to do. Failure will mean that money incomes go on rising in futile pursuit of an unattainable real income, and inflation will result, or continue. If, following the oil price rise, oil importing countries had recognised and accepted the loss of real income instead of trying to offset it, much subsequent inflation might have been avoided. The huge rise in oil prices was *deflationary* in essence and only become *inflationary*[4] because the response allowed it to be.

Appendix 2

Intervention, the exchange equalization account (EEA)[6], and the money supply

The demand for and the supply of currencies is governed by the same laws of supply and demand as apply to other goods: the lower the price the more will be demanded, the higher the price the more will be supplied. We may therefore draw the usual curves to represent the free market demand for and supply of currency (Fig. 14.1).

The price of a currency is measured by the price of another currency, that for which it is exchanged. In our simplified example we assume there are only two currencies, pounds and dollars, so we measure the price of pounds in dollars.

Since, by assumption, those demanding pounds offer only dollars, and those supplying pounds want only dollars, the demand curve for pounds is the supply curve for dollars and the supply curve for pounds is the demand curve for dollars.

At an exchange rate (price) of r_1, Q_1 pounds and dollars are demanded and supplied. That is the rate that clears the market of pounds and dollars. At an (over-valued) £ exchange rate of r_2 the supply of pounds (= demand for dollars) exceeds the demand for pounds (= supply of dollars).

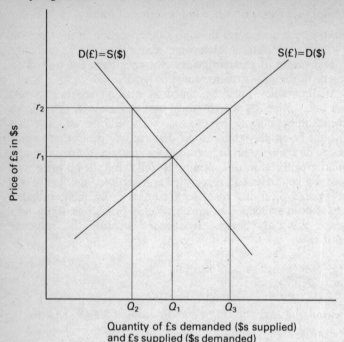

Fig. 14.1

If the authorities want to maintain that exchange rate an additional demand for £s (supply of dollars) must be forthcoming from somewhere. In the United Kingdom that can be only from the Reserves, operating through the Exchange Equalization Account. So the EEA supplies dollars equal to Q_2Q_3. Clearly the EEA cannot go on doing this indefinitely. When the Reserves (of gold and foreign currency) are exhausted, or at a dangerously low level, further support can be given only by borrowing more foreign currency (usually from the IMF).

Conversely if the authorities try to maintain a rate for sterling below the market rate (which would be represented in the diagram by a line below r_1) then there would be an excess demand for sterling that could only be met from outside the market, i.e. from the EEA. The EEA would buy dollars and sell sterling, as a result of which the Reserves would grow. Note that there is an asymmetry between the authorities' ability to support an over-valued and an under-valued currency. In the former case a limit is set by the availability of foreign currency. In the latter case there is, in principle, no limit to the amount of its own currency that a Government may create. But the more it creates the more, in general, (although it is not a one-to-one relationship) will it add to the money supply. (See below).

Implications for the money supply

When an over-valued exchange rate is being supported, the EEA is selling $s and acquiring sterling. This tends to reduce the money supply.

In the contrary case, when, that is, the authorities are trying to force the sterling rate down, the EEA is selling sterling to buy foreign currency. This increases the amount of sterling in existence and tends to increase the money supply.

Appendix 3

The Keynesian theory of the balance of payments

We saw that in the *General Theory* there is a relationship between income and expenditure on consumption such that changes in income lead to changes in expenditure on consumption. A similar relationship holds between changes in income and changes in expenditure on imports. Just as there is a propensity to consume so is there a propensity to import.

This may be exhibited on a diagram relating expenditure to income by a line showing that as income rises so does expenditure on imports, but not by as much.

Exports however, being paid for by the expenditure of foreigners, are not a function of domestic income, but are determined largely by the relative price, in foreign currency, of home produced and foreign goods and services; and by the level of world trade. Exports may be represented on our diagram by a line showing a fixed amount of expenditure on exports. Since exports are not related to income and do not change as income changes this line will be parallel to the income axis, in Fig. 14.2:

At income OY the balance of payments on current account is in balance but if OY is not the full employment level of income, which is, say, OY_f, then at full employment the balance of payments will be in deficit Nor is this all. As real income increases there is a tendency for imports to increase faster, so that the imports curve curves upwards. And as output (income) approaches full employment there is a tendency for exports to be diverted to home consumption so that

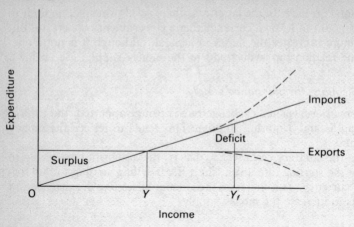

Fig. 14.2

the exports line curves downwards. These tendencies are shown by dotted lines.

The intractability of the British problem becomes clear. If the propensity to import is firmly established, and if exports are to a significant extent governed by external conditions beyond our control, then the position of the two curves is difficult to shift. Policy therefore, is thrown back on moving *income* between Y and Y_f. This is known as demand management, or 'stop-go'.

The only way out of this dilemma is to operate on the two 'ifs', the propensity to import, and exports. The propensity to import may be hard to shift, partly because there are many things that we *have* to import simply because we cannot produce them ourselves, partly because there are things that we can produce ourselves but where the foreign product is demonstrably and probably unalterably superior (wine, for example), partly because some foreign products carry a fashionable cachet. The element of 'foreign preference' that we can work on is that stemming from the superiority of foreign design, price and functional excellence in products that we *can* and do produce ourselves; the range of goods, that is, where the foreign product is preferred for no other reason than that it is better value. So something can be done to shift the propensity to import.

Similar arguments, looked at the other way round, apply to exports: if we are to export more we have to produce for the foreign customer goods and services that for one or other of the reasons suggested above, he will buy more of.

Only by operating on imports and exports in this way can we, or, for that matter, any country, escape from the contradictions of an economy that cannot sustain both full employment *and* a zero balance of payments. Professor Lord Kaldor puts it thus[5]:

The main shortcoming of post-war 'full employment' policies (in the British context) was that they regarded the problem of insufficient demand as if it had been mainly due to insufficient investment in relation to the amount of savings forthcoming at full employment, rather than of insufficient exports in relation to imports associated with full-employment income. Hence the policy instruments were designed to generate 'consumption-led' growth rather than 'export-led' growth which, by its very nature, militated against a fast growth of productivity and involved policy-generated instabilities in reaction to periodic balance-of-payments crises.

To return to our diagram, it may be noted that even if a current account deficit can be sustained Y_f is not by itself an equilibrium position because the *leakages* through imports (payment for which goes to swell foreign incomes) exceed the *injections* through exports. Left to itself the economy would run down to income Y, through the downward operation of the multiplier. If the economy is to be in equilibrium at Y_f then somewhere in the system there has to be an excess of domestic expenditure over receipts.

The New Cambridge School argues that this excess occurs in the public sector, so that the deficit on current account is the mirror image of the deficit on government account. But the New Cambridge result is arrived at by a certain amount of Procrustean manipulation of the statistics and it is not generally accepted.

All the Keynesian model tells us for certain is that if there is a deficit on the current account of the balance of payments then there is excess domestic demand somewhere in the system. The limitation of the Keynesian model for balance of payments analysis is that it is concerned only with goods and services and thus only with the current account of the balance of payments. It tells us nothing about capital flows.

Notes

1. *United Kingdom Balance of Payments*, 1980 Edition, HMSO.
2. In a closed economy income (Y) = consumption (C) plus investment (I). In equilibrium planned savings (S) equals planned investment (I). In an open economy income (Y) = consumption (C) plus investment (I) plus exports (E) minus imports (M). If exports do *not* equal imports then planned savings cannot equal planned investment.
   If we add a government sector then it will be here that part of the compensating imbalance is found if governemnt expenditure does not equal government revenue.

3. The exchange rate is something of a political football, and the public's reaction characteristically illogical. When, under Labour Governments and a fixed exchange rate, the rate was under pressure and (twice) devalued, the Opposition made political capital out of it. When, under a Labour Government and a floating exchange rate, the pound fell, again the Opposition got political mileage out of it. When, however, under a Conservative Government, North Sea Oil and a floating exchange rate, the pound rose, no one was happy: exporters complained, imports flowed in, and the Government gave every indication of wishing the rate would come down, while apologising that it could not do anything about a rate that the market determined. Eventually, in June 1981, and again in November 1982, the market did bring the rate down, very quickly.

    Funny old thing, the exchange rate. What the British would really like, one suspects, is a fixed but floating exchange rate, with different values for exporters and importers.

4. Deflationary and inflationary are not, however, opposites: deflationary means 'contractionary'and the opposite is 'expansionary'; and the opposite of inflationary is disinflationary.

5. Memorandum to the Treasury and Civil Service Committee, Published in 'Memoranda on Monetary Policy', H of C 720 July 1980.

6. The Exchange Equalisation Account (EEA) was established on 24 June 1932 by Section 24(1) of Finance Act, 1932. It is under the control of HM Treasury, with the Bank of England authorised to act as agents. The transactions of the EEA are confidential and the accounts are not published, although since 1937 they have been shown to the Public Accounts Committee.

7. This is the scenario at the heart of the recommendations of the Cambridge Economic Policy Group.

Part four

Chapter fifteen

Maps of the moon

We have all of us become used to finding ourselves sometimes on the one side of the moon and sometimes on the other, without knowing what route or journey connects them . . . .

Keynes[1]

In our journey towards an understanding of economic controversies we have looked at a number of economic models. We began with an outline of the classical system, and followed with a summary of Keynes's new model. We saw how the Keynesian model was modified in practice. We drew up a list of the component parts of the monetarist system and we described how that system might work, but we did not specify the system as precisely as we specified the Keynesian, partly because it is a system that does not lend itself easily to specification, partly because there is no one monetarist system. Indeed, it is almost part of the monetarist philosophy that the economic system is so complex and sophisticated and involves, and should involve, so much individual choice, that we had better not try to say too precisely how it works. Monetarists place a good deal of faith in 'natural forces' – 'natural' rates of employment and of interest.

The time has come to lay out these and other models in a rather more systematic way so as to display their basic beliefs and attitudes to policy options and economic instruments.

We identify nine different 'schools' – eight if one disregards the 'Monetarist General' school on the grounds that it is subsumed under one or other of the monetarist sub-schools. The first three schools are mainly of historical interest; only the remainder are current contenders. Table 15.1 summarises the results under standardised headings.

1. Classical

A 'natural law' system of economics in which prices are flexible and all markets clear, given certain (unrealistic) assumptions about auctions and re-contract. Excess supply, including excess supply of labour, can always be eliminated by a fall in prices.

Say's law (supply creates its own demand) ensures that there is no shortage of effective demand. The price level is determined by the quantity of money which, in turn, depends upon flows of bullion. As bullion flows out in response to higher prices this provides a partial built-in stabiliser against inflation. Fiscal policy and incomes policy are not policy instruments.

2. Keynes

The forces maintaining the economy at or returning it to full employment may not be powerful enough, especially if the economy falls into deep and prolonged recession. Because makers of consumer goods do not spend on consumption the whole of their incomes, it follows that producers of consumer goods can never recoup the whole of what they pay out in incomes unless incomes generated by production for consumption are augmented by incomes generated by investment expenditure. Hence, total investment expenditure must equal what consumers save (do not spend). If private investment is inadequate for this purpose, the government must make good the shortfall.

Money is a liquid asset and its price is the rate of interest, determined by the demand for liquidity and the supply of money.

Prices rise as the economy nears full-capacity working, and at full capacity further additions to demand produce true inflation. Because of output bottlenecks and immobile resources, problems probably begin to emerge at above 95 per cent capacity utilisation. If, with full employment, unions press for higher wages, this is a political, not an economic problem.

In the basic theory, the exchange rate was not an issue, because the analysis was of a closed economy. But Keynes's views on the exchange rate were pragmatic: the rate should be whatever was consistent with full capacity working, i.e. the rate should adjust to output, not the other way round.

3. 'Keynesians'

Use the basic Keynesian model, but interpret it to mean that the economy can be 'fine tuned'by fiscal action. Moreover it can be run

Table 15.1

School	Basic beliefs	Attitude to: Money supply and interest rates	Fiscal policy
1. Classical	Prices are flexible and natural economic laws always tend to move the economy to equilibrium	Money supply dependent on flows of bullion into and out of the economy. Interest rate determined by supply of and demand for savings. Changes in money supply affect prices and activity.	Not considered as an economic instrument. Budgets should be balanced.
2. Keynes	Same as classics except that the forces tending to move the economy to full employment are too weak to be relied upon. Supreme importance of individual choice and liberty, which 'the market' helped to provide.	Money supply controlled by authorities. In conjunction with the community's liquidity preference schedule, it determines the r. of i. The r. of i. should be kept low because, together with the marginal efficiency of capital schedule, it determines the volume of private investment.	'Public works' can be used to make good any shortfall in private investment expenditure and maintain an adequate level of effective demand. Regard should be paid to the distribution of demand as well as to its total.

Attitude to: Output and employment	Prices and inflation	Exchange rate	Incomes policy
Supply created its own demand (Say's law) so economies always tended to full employment, disturbed only by 'the trade cycle'. No explicit theory of aggregate demand. Employment determined by supply of and demand for labour.	Individual prices determined by supply and demand. Price level determined by quantity of money.	Determined by price of gold (Gold Standard).	Unheard of.
The economy may tend to full employment but it is the responsibility of government to ensure that total demand is adequate. Employment depends upon aggregate demand and the real wage.	Bottlenecks will cause the price level to rise as the economy nears full capacity. At full capacity further additions to demand generate true inflation.	Not at issue in the GT, which assumed a closed economy. Fixed rate preferred. The rate should adjust to the needs of the economy, not the other way round.	Not considered. Probably in favour, because union power seen as a political, not economic, problem, requiring a political solution.

Table 15.1 *contd.*

School	Basic beliefs	Attitude to: Money supply and interest rates	Fiscal policy
3. Keynesians	In the desirability and possibility of economic management using the Keynesian model.	As Keynes. Interest rates, not the money supply, to be the object of regulation.	To be the primary instrument of economic regulation. High levels of both expenditure and taxation.
4. Monetarists; General	Same as classics. 'The market' to be supreme and the private sector to be as large (public sector as small) as possible.	Money supply is main determinant of the price level. Should be closely controlled, probably by setting a constant, low, rate of growth. In a manner similar to Keynes interest rate determined by supply of and demand for money. Must accept whatever rate thrown up. R. of i. not a policy objective.	Ineffective as a policy instrument. Deficit cannot permanently raise output and employment. 'Fine tuning' impossible, unnecessary and harmful.
Monetarists; Rational expectations (or New Classical)	Prices are flexible. Economic agents form rational expectations and act accordingly.		

Attitude to: Output and employment	Prices and inflation	Exchange rate	Incomes policy
Economy can be run very close to its capacity limits. Full employment an overriding policy objective.	Moderate inflation can be tolerated as the price of full employment	As Keynes.	In favour. Main instrument of inflation control.
Economy will settle at a 'natural' rate of output and employment determined by 'real' forces.	Similar to classics, but with more sophisticated monetary theory. Control of inflation the primary policy objective.	Flexible. Not a policy objective. (No intervention). Is part of the transmission mechanism from money to prices (except that Professor Friedman is adamant that it is *not* part of the transmission mechanism).	Not needed, because price level determined by money supply, not costs. Not wanted because distorts markets and misallocates resources. But some monetarists would tolerate, to speed and smooth the adjustment process.
Quick response, little loss.	Prices, including wages, adjust quickly.	Flexible. Part of the transmission mechanism but not the major part.	Wholly against.

School	Basic beliefs	Attitude to: Money supply and interest rates	Fiscal policy
	Expectations respond to announcements about monetary policy.		
Monetarists; Gradualists	Prices are flexible but not as flexible as the rational expectationists believe. Expectations are formed by experience and are therefore adaptive rather than rational.		
Monetarists; Pragmatists	Sympathetic to control of money supply but believe costs would be high because of sluggish response of wages.	The whole weight of policy should *not* be put on setting and achieving monetary targets.	Failing an incomes policy, would (as a poor second best) run a relaxed fiscal policy with a tight monetary policy.
5. Reconstructed Keynesians	Use the Keynesian analytical framework with the addition of monetary targets. Only modified faith in market forces	Money supply is one element in total liquidity and should not be ignored. But the achievement of monetary targets should not be the main objective.	To be used as a policy instrument but consistently with money supply targets.

Attitude to: Output and employment	Prices and inflation	Exchange rate	Incomes policy
Because of slow response the main burden of adjustment (to a tight monetary policy), falls in the first place on output and employment.	Prices and wages adjust slowly.	Flexible. Important, but not the principle transmission mechanism.	Against.
A high exchange rate places the main burden on exporting and import-competing industries. This causes recession in manufacturing industry.	Wage behaviour responds sluggishly. The recession puts pressure on wages and prices.	A high exchange rate is a major part of the transmission mechanism. (See preceeding two columns).	In favour, to supplement monetary policy.
A high level of output and employment is a policy objective, and *can* be achieved through fiscal and monetary action.	Control of inflation is a policy objective, but not overriding.	Floating, with intervention to limit the range of float.	Strongly in favour. Main instrument of inflation control.

Table 15.1 *contd.*

School	Basic beliefs	Attitude to: Money supply and interest rates	Fiscal policy
	Industry needs to be planned, supported, subsidised.		
6. Anti-monetarist.	Deny the three basic tenets of monetarism that	It is liquidity that has to be controlled, with interest rates.	With money supply discounted, this is the main policy instrument for influencing output and employment.
	1. there is a measure of money that is significant	See previous column.	
	2. that it can be controlled with existing methods		
	3. that prices respond flexibly to market conditions.		

very close to its capacity frontier; if this generates inflation it can be controlled by incomes policy. It is 'liquidity' that should be controlled, not the quantity of money, and the instrument of control is the rate of interest – which implies that the quantity of money cannot also be controlled. Because the interest rate influences private investment it should be as low as possible. Since the primary policy objective is to maintain a high level of employment the exchange rate can be allowed to decline to stimulate exports.

4. Monetarists

General

Basic conception of the economy similar to the classics: prices are

Attitude to: Output and employment	Prices and inflation	Exchange rate	Incomes policy
Same as Reconstructed Keynesians, except leave out 'and monetary'	Same as R.K.	Floating. Since the money supply does not matter, they are not in principle against intervention but recognise risks of triggering destabilising capital flows.	Same as R.K.

flexible and the market allocates resources in accordance with relative prices. With the demand for money stable, with respect to income, output and prices respond to people's attempts to adjust their demand for money to the supply. In the long run the price level depends on the quantity of money; and output and employment settle at a 'natural' level that cannot be permanently changed by fiscal action. Since the price level is determined by the quantity of money and not by costs, inflation must be countered by monetary measures and not by incomes policies, which are unnecessary, ineffective and damaging. The exchange rate is just another price, to be determined by supply and demand. Monetarists differ among themselves mainly on three things – the degree of flexibility of prices; the transmission mechanism from money to output and prices; and the nature of expectations.

Rational expectations

The extreme monetarist school, otherwise known as New Classical because of its belief in fully flexible prices and the efficiency of markets. Economic agents act rationally and will react quickly to the economic situation as they see it and, because prices, including wages, are highly flexible, output and prices will adjust rapidly to announced monetary targets. Adjustment costs in terms of lost output will therefore be small. Incomes policies are unnecessary because unions are one set of economic agents that respond rationally to monetary signals. A flexible exchange rate is part of the transmission mechanism, but not the major part.

Gradualists

The Gradualists, perhaps the 'central' monetarist school, differ from the Rational Expectationalists on two points: the flexibility of prices, and expectations. Because they do not believe that prices are as flexible as the Rational Expectationalists do, they recognise that much more of the burden of adjustment will be thrown upon interest rates, output and employment. The effect on prices comes through later, after a lag of perhaps two years. Because of this sluggish adjustment to changes in the money supply, the gradualists prefer a slow, steady, rather than rapid, reduction in the rate of growth of the money supply. (This is the course adopted by the United Kingdom Government). They concede that a case *can* be made for the complementary use of incomes policy to ease the unemployment problem, but in the end reject such policy. Gradualists are open to the criticism that if, as they suppose, adjustment is slow, all the more reason to proceed quickly – otherwise the painful process will drag on for years. In contradistinction to the New Classical school, Gradualists believe that expectations are formed by experience; that economic agents expect prices to fall in response to a reduction in the money supply only *after* they have seen them fall. Expectations are, therefore, *adaptive* rather than rational.

A flexible exchange rate is an essential part of the Gradualist scheme but they concede that, because of slow adjustment, the burden of a high exchange rate induced by monetary constraint will fall upon exporting and import-competing industries, reducing output and employment. The exchange rate is not, however, regarded as the principal transmission mechanism from money to prices.

Pragmatists

Are sympathetic to the idea that the money supply should be controlled but they believe that, largely because of the inertia of wage behaviour, the costs are likely to be high and they do not, therefore, favour putting the whole weight on setting and achieving monetary targets. They fully understand the argument that if Governments are seen to pursue their monetary targets unrelentingly, then this might modify union behaviour, and reduce inflation. But, as a matter of judgement, they do not think this likely.

They argue that the main effect of monetary policy is through the foreign sector, i.e. through a high exchange rate and the pressure this puts on exporting industries and on import-competing industries. It is the recession that follows from this that slows down the rate of wage inflation.

Thus, in the Pragmatists' view, the costs of reducing inflation by monetary policy fall upon manufacturing industry. To reduce this cost they would supplement monetary policies with incomes policies. As a poor second best, they would run a tight monetary policy with a relaxed fiscal policy.

5. Reconstructed Keynesians

Cling to the Keynesian analytical framework as having more explanatory power than the monetarist, but acknowledge that it is right to give some importance to the control of the money supply if for no better reason than that it makes foreigners (who hold, or might hold, sterling) and the International Monetary Fund, happy. Fiscal policy would be the primary instrument for controlling the level of demand; and incomes policy the main instrument for controlling inflation which, as a policy objective, would have high but not absolute priority. It remains to be seen – or not seen, if monetarist policies are successful and carry the day – how far Reconstructed Keynesians have reconstructed their views on how finely the economy can be tuned and how close to capacity it can be run.

6. Anti-monetarists

Reject the three basic tenets of monetarism: that any measure of money has any particular significance in measuring the tightness or otherwise of credit conditions; that the authorities can, with existing methods, control that measure; and that prices respond flexibly to market conditions. Their analytical framework is therefore Keynesian.

Whereas monetarists begin by assuming that there is some supply of money that can be independently determined as the 'right' supply, or quantity, Anti-Monetarists believe that, under present methods of monetary control in the United Kingdom, it is the *demand* for money that determines the supply. It is therefore only by depressing the demand for money, by deflation, that the supply can be reduced.

Monetarism, they argue, reduces the *demand* for money by reducing the money value of output. But since *prices* and wages are not flexible, the lower *value* of output is achieved only by a lower *volume* of output and, hence, lower employment.

Even if, by different instruments, the money supply as measured could be controlled, this would be only partially effective because economic agents could escape this control by extending their use of the various forms of credit that are not reflected in the money supply figures. (e.g. inter-firm credit). It is liquidity, or general credit conditions that the Anti-monetarists would control; and since such control would be by interest rates no independent targets could be set for the money supply (since both cannot be controlled).

The absence of monetary targets would tend (other things being equal) to depress the exchange rate. This need be no bad thing, as it stimulates exports and import-competing industries. But with large amounts of foot-loose capital sloshing around the world it could be dangerous to try to instigate a fall in the rate.

Summary

The classical system is no longer a runner, so we need spend no time over it except, perhaps, to recall Keynes' dictum that it embodied some permanent truths that we neglect at our peril. Nor need we linger over Keynes because we know what his teaching is but we cannot say how he would have applied it to present problems.

The Keynesians clearly have much in common with the Anti-monetarists; but they are presented here as a historical school that antedated monetarism and is now defunct, in the sense that all its followers must have embraced or rejected the monetarist teaching and now be members of one or other of the modern schools.

All the monetarist schools share a similar vision of the way the economy works and, among policy options, give a high, sometimes absolute, priority to the defeat of inflation. The New Classical or Rational Expectationalists are the most extreme, differing from the Gradualists both in their assessment of how flexible prices are and in the way expectations are formed. These differences lead to differing views on the speed with which monetarist policies take effect.

The Pragmatists have much common ground with the Gradualists and differ mainly in that Pragmatists would not place the whole weight of adjustment on the money supply but would, in particular, allow some form of incomes policy. Gradualists, Pragmatists and Anti-monetarists all share a scepticism about the flexibility of prices.

In terms of *policies* there does not appear to be much to choose between Pragmatists and Reconstructed Keynesians; it is a matter of the differing emphasis given to incomes policy, fiscal policy and monetary control. Reconstructed Keynesians accept the need for some monetary control, but not the monetary analysis.

Thus, moving down from extreme monetarists to Reconstructed Keynesians, we find an overlap of opinion, sometimes a significant overlap, between contiguous schools. There is little overlap, however, with the Anti-Monetarists. With them, we have moved to the other side of the moon.

There are those who hold that the lively contemporary debate demonstrates that economics is not dead but alive and well, and probably living on the Committee Room floor at the House of Commons.[2] Others would say that it is all rather sad, and only goes to show what they had said all along, that if you laid all the economists end to end it would be a very good idea but they still would not reach a conclusion. If the debate goes on it is not easy to say whether the schismatic tendency will continue or whether some consensus might eventually form, around, say, the Anti-Reconstructed Monetarist faction.

Appendix

Models compared

It may be useful to lay out for inspection the bare bones of our three main models:

The Classical system

In the Classical system the rate of interest (i) is determined by the demand for investment funds (I) and the supply of savings (S). The real wage (W_R) is determined by the demand for labour (L_D) and the supply of labour (L_S). The amount of employment (E) depends upon the real wage. Aggregate supply (A_S) calls forth aggregate demand (A_D). The absolute price level (P) is determined by the quantity of money (M). All markets are cleared by changes in relative prices.

The symbols $\rightarrow$ means 'depends on' or 'influenced by'.

The symbol $\leftrightarrow$ means that the dependence works in both directions.

A bar $\overline{}$ over a symbol signifies that it is fixed, i.e. unchanging.

$I \rightarrow i$

$S \rightarrow i$

$i \leftrightarrow I, S$

$L_D \rightarrow W_R$

$L_S \rightarrow W_R$

$W_R \leftrightarrow L_D, L_S$

$E \rightarrow W_R$

$A_S = A_D$

$P \rightarrow M$

Putting this system together we shall arrive at a rate of interest, a real wage, and a level of output and employment. There is an implicit assumption that aggregate supply is also maximum supply, calling forth maximum demand. The demand for labour, therefore, is a full-employment demand. If there is, nevertheless, unemployment it is because the real wage is too high and it can, therefore, be eliminated by lowering the real wage.

The Keynesian system

In this system we have a liquidity preference function (L), related to income, which in conjunction with the money supply (M) determines the rate of interest (i). There is an investment demand schedule which in conjunction with the rate of interest determines the amount of investment. (I). We have our familiar set of identities, $Y = C + S$, $S = I$, $Y = C + I$. Consumption depends upon income. Employment (E) is related to income.

$L \rightarrow Y, i$

$M = \overline{M}$

$i \rightarrow L, M$

$I \rightarrow i$

$S = I$

$Y = C + I$

$C \rightarrow Y$

$E \rightarrow Y$

If we solve this system we find that, like the classical system, it does not necessarily produce a full employment level of income. Nor does it say what the price level will be, for the sole purpose of the money supply is to determine, in conjunction with the liquidity preference schedule, the interest rate. Nor will it throw up any real wage, for there are no supply and demand functions for labour. To change (increase) employment we must change (increase) income, which we can do by operating on consumption or, preferably, investment.

The monetarist system

Here we begin with the demand for money (D), which is related to income, and the (fixed) supply of money $(\bar{M})$. People's attempts to adjust their demand for money to the supply affect real output (Y). Employment (E) is determined by the real wage (W_R) (which, as in the classical system, we may assume depends on the supply of and the demand for labour). The absolute price level (P) depends on the quantity of money. Relative prices are flexible.

$$D \rightarrow Y$$
$$M = \bar{M}$$
$$Y \longleftrightarrow D,M$$
$$E \rightarrow W_R$$
$$P \rightarrow M$$

There is no employment solution unless we assume a relationship between the real wage and the money supply.

$$W_R \longleftrightarrow \bar{M}$$

This does not ensure full employment and, since the money supply is fixed, full employment can be induced only by changing (lowering) the real wage.

An eclectic system

Elements of the monetarist and Keynesian systems may be brought together as follows. There is a demand for money (D) that depends on real incomes; and a fixed supply of money $(\bar{M})$. Together these determine rates of interest (i). As in the monetarist system, people's attempts to adjust their demand for money to the supply generate changes in income (Y). Employment (E) depends on the real wage (W_R).

$$D \rightarrow Y$$
$$M = \bar{M}$$
$$i \rightarrow D,\bar{M}$$
$$Y \leftrightarrow D,\bar{M}$$
$$E \rightarrow W_R$$

So far this is the monetarist scenario with the explicit inclusion of rates of interest, but without a price level. Again, it will not yield an employment solution. To complete it we have either to add the monetarist condition that real wages are related to the money supply

$$W_R \to \overline{M}$$

or the Keynesian condition that employment is related to income

$$E \to Y$$

Now income (Y) depends partly on the money supply (M) so instead of $E \to Y$ we can write

$$E \to M$$

which says that employment can be changed (increased) by changing (increasing) the money supply. But we already have $E \to W_R$. If we substitute $E \to M$ for $E \to W_R$ then W_R goes out of the system, $W_R \to M$ has to go and we are left with a semi-Keynesian system in which employment depends on output and output depends on the money supply, with no mention of the real wage.

A better formulation is to relax the assumption that the money supply is fixed (remove the bar from over M) and write

$$W_R \leftrightarrow M$$

We can then produce full employment *either* by adjusting the real wage to the money supply (the monetarist solution); or by adjusting the money supply to the real wage (the Keynesian solution). Or we may adjust both to some intermediate position.

We can if we like add $P \to M$ to the system. Then with $P \to \overline{M}$ prices are stable and with $P \to M$ they may not be.

Notes

1. GT, p.292.
2. See the following publications of the Treasury and Civil Service Committee.
   Session 1980–81
   > Monetary Policy
   > Vol I Report H of C 163 – I
   > Vol II Minutes of Evidence H of C 163 – II
   > Vol III Appendices H of C 163 – III
   Session 1979–80
   > Memoranda on Monetary Policy
   > Vol I H of C 720
   > Vol II H of C720–II

Chapter sixteen

Summing up

Sir Roger told them, with the air of a man who would not give his judgement rashly, that much might be said on both sides.

Joseph Addison

The distinguishing feature of the classical system of economics that Keynes inherited was that it was self-equilibrating, a 'natural' system, in some sense of that word. There was a balance, and if that balance was disturbed, for whatever reason, an in-built economic gyroscope would restore equilibrium. It was natural that all men should work, and so the system would ensure that they did or at least could. If they did not, it must be because they chose not to; and one way they could choose not to would be by demanding too high a price for their labour. There was too, a certain natural justice in the system; a man was paid the product of his labour, or at least the marginal product which, admittedly, was not quite the same thing, and so the harder and better he worked, the more he would produce and the more he would receive. In their own self-interest, men, collectively and individually, would seek to provide those things which other men needed or wanted; and these wants would be signalled by what they were prepared to pay.

It was a voting system in which the votes were pounds, shillings and pence. Since prices were flexible, the votes would direct the resources of production and distribution to the production and distribution of what was required. The system would also ensure that the price of the product or service was divided among the factors which contributed to its production in proportion to what each factor had contributed. It was true that the mere possession of land might attract a disproportionate reward but that was because it was fixed in supply, and since ownership had been decided long ago and sanctified by law, that was an issue that could not be reopened.

The ownership of money, or capital, attracted rewards, apparently without excessive labour. But capital was 'stored up' labour; a store of value acquired by working and earning but not spending. The earnings of capital were the reward from abstinence. And as the Church enjoined abstinence from almost everything that was pleasurable, the pursuit of abstinence could ensure rewards in both this world and the next. In the material world, abstinence was embodied in savings, and the more savings there were, the lower would be the rate of interest, and the lower the rate of interest the more investment there would be and the more wealth for the future.

This world of equilibrium economics, the sanctity of savings, and unending unemployment, Keynes found wanting: the facts, there for all to see, did not fit the theory. For Keynes, it was not sufficient just to change the facts, even if that could be done. It was profoundly unsatisfactory to have a corpus of economic theory, universally taught and believed, that could not accommodate the world as it was.

What was needed was a new theory, but one which preserved the best of the old. As is apparent from the GT, Keynes had a deep respect for the truths embodied in the classical teaching. And in an article he wrote just before his death,[1] he said:

I find myself moved, not for the first time, to remind contemporary economists that the classical teaching embodied some permanent truths of great significance . . .

There are in these matters deep undercurrents at work, natural forces, one can call them, or even the invisible hand, which are operating towards equilibrium . . . If we reject the medicine from our system altogether, we may just drift on from expedient to expedient and never really get fit again.

Thus Keynes did not deny, as the modern monetarists certainly would not deny, that the economy has a *tendency* to return to equilibrium; and under equilibrium in this context, we must include something approaching full employment. But in the 1930s, the forces returning the economy to full employment were too weak. It was as if the economy had strayed too far outside the corridor within which the natural forces could operate.

Keynes identified the problem as a lack of effective demand. Deeply embedded in the classical teaching was Say's law that supply creates its own demand. This was necessarily true in a barter economy and it was taken for granted that it would hold true also in a monetary economy, because money was only a veil, beneath which the real forces of the economy operated.

The key that opened the door to the theory of effective demand was the propensity to consume, together with the concept of production's being dichotomised into two sectors: production for consumption and production for investment. If people spent less than they earned in the production of consumption goods on the consumption of consumption goods, then the producers of consumption goods could never recoup their expenditure. The difference – what people saved (did not spend) must be made good by expenditure on investment goods. Investment must equal savings. Keynes could find in the classical teaching no laws that ensured that the required level of investment would take place. There was no natural force within the economy strong enough to ensure that the level of aggregate demand was adequate.

Since the natural forces were lacking, unnatural forces, in the shape of the Government, had to take responsibility for the level of demand. The major policy implication was that the Government must make good any shortfall in private investment. But that was not all. The extent of the shortfall was at least partly attributable to saving (not spending). Saving could be anti-social behaviour. In maintaining full employment, it was better to spend than to save. Thus, Keynesian analysis affronted both the belief in a natural, and possibly divinely, ordered economy, and the belief in saving as both an earthly and a spiritual virtue. It was not a prescription likely to endear him to conservatives. He was, moreover, an intellectual with a devotion to the arts, married to a ballerina – and a foreign one at that.

For the success of his teaching Keynes enjoyed one piece of very good luck, and one piece of very bad luck. The good luck was that shortly after the publication of the GT, Britain began to rearm and then went to war. The expenditure by the Government on these two events quickly eliminated unemployment, demonstrating beyond argument the validity of Keynes's central proposition. Contrary to the Treasury view, Government spending could and did raise output and employment. We had 'learned a trick or two'.

The bad luck was that he timed his death very badly, so that he was unable to influence economic policy in the post-war years. The field was left to others who, in his name, espoused policies with which it is extremely unlikely he would have had anything to do. Already, in 1946, just before his death, he was deploring how much 'modernist stuff, gone wrong and turned sour and silly, is circulating'.

The conservative backlash against Keynes began to surface in the United States in the 1950s and by the early 1970s had spread to the United Kingdom, much nourished by the inflationary excesses of policies passing under the name of 'Keynesianism'.

The focal point of the new conservative economics was the money supply. This had a number of attractions. The new theory could be presented as having respectable roots in antiquity, although in its professional, as distinct from its popular, form, it owed much more to Keynes than to the classics. At the popular level, the slogan that 'too much money causes inflation' was easy to believe; while at the academic level, the sheer mystery of the processes involved was a challenge to the ingenuity of economists. And no ambitious economomist wants to let pass a bandwagon which appears to be nicely rolling. This dual life of which the new quantity theory was capable, greatly helped the spread of the gospel and the conversion of the heathen. There was something for everyone: simplicity and certainty for the faithful and some new mysteries upon which the high priests could exercise their theological muscle.

Politically, the appeal of the new theory to the right wing was that it proved that Government intervention in the economy was, in the long run, and possibly in the short run, ineffective. To the conservative politician, as to the man in the street, the new doctrine had the supreme virtue of simplicity. In place of all the tiresome business of economic management, using different policy instruments, balancing one objective against another, there was just one lever to pull: the money supply. Control the money supply and everything else fell into place.

In particular, there was no need for incomes policies and hence no need to negotiate with the trade unions. If trades unions chose to bargain for unrealistic wages then all they would achieve would be unemployment, the responsibility for which could be laid at their door, not that of the Government. The level of unemployment had nothing to do with the level of demand but everything to do with the level of wages.

The chosen instrument had the virtue of anonymity. The control of the money supply had something of the authority of a natural law, and if unpleasant consequences followed from its application, well that was no more than could be expected from going against natural law, or, at least, against the laws of economics which, as everyone knows, are always pretty dismal.

Monetarism restored the authority of the market. Once the monetary rule was established, the market could safely be left to do the rest. And because the market was efficient, as much as possible must be left to it. This was a further justification for reducing the size of a public sector already diminished in importance by the absence of any need for Government intervention in the manipulation of the level of demand.

In the longer run, the disciplines of the market would create an efficient economy, eliminate the inefficient and do away with subsidies, thus further reducing public expenditure.

Thus, from a right-wing political standpoint, the new monetarism appeared to have a great deal to offer. Its attractions, however, concealed some fairly fundamental practical difficulties. The first is that people's ability to spend depends not only upon the amount of money they have, but also upon their access to credit. To take one simple example: if one firm has spare cash it can lend it to other firms, either directly or in the form of trade credit. The money supply is not increased, but people have more money to spend. The money supply is only a part of the total liquidity available.

Secondly, there is the difficulty, some would say the impossibility, of defining money. If a theory and a policy depends *entirely* upon controlling the money supply, it is a considerable weakness if the money supply cannot be defined.

There is, thirdly, the difficulty that even if the money supply can be identified, in some arbitrary way, control of it may not be possible. In the United Kingdom the relevant money supply was identified as Sterling M3, but its control proved impossible.

It is surprising that, despite its superficial political attractions, a theory with such manifest weaknesses should have been fashioned into the main plank of a Government's programme, the one thing on which it stood or fell. Perhaps everybody, and not only conservative politicians, was ready to try anything that seemed remotely plausible. As Keynes put it:[2]

At the present moment people are unusually expectant of a more fundamental diagnosis; more particularly ready to receive it; eager to try it out, if it should be even plausible. But apart from this contemporary mood, the ideas of economists and political philosophers, both when they are right and when they are wrong, are more powerful than is commonly understood. Indeed the world is ruled by little else. Practical men, who believe themselves to be quite exempt from any intellectual influences, are usually the slaves of some defunct economist. Madmen in authority, who hear voices in the air, are distilling their frenzy from some academic scribbler of a few years back.

It might be thought that monetarism carried with it such inherent weaknesses that there would be difficulties enough. But the Government succeeded in introducing several more of its own making.

Its prime objective was to bring down the rate of inflation. But one of its early acts was almost to doubt the rate of Value Added Tax, from 8 to 15 per cent. And the Value Added Tax, of course, feeds straight through into the retail price index. The cost of living, as conventionally measured, was raised at a stroke. It does appear that at this stage, although they modified their views later, Ministers were so taken with the simple idea that it was the money supply which determined the rate of inflation that they overlooked the fact that inflation is affected by anything that puts up prices.

To try and restrict the money supply, the Government was compelled to impose very high rates of interest. Yet, for its chosen money supply, the target money supply, it chose a measure, Sterling M3, which includes those bank accounts on which interest is paid, instead of a narrower measure, M1, which excludes such balances. The high rates of interest may have attracted money *into* the monetary measure which it was their purpose to reduce, or at least to control. And when the high rates of interest did impose some stringency on the banks, the Bank of England stood ready to be a lender of first resort and relieve that stringency. Even if the Bank of England had not been prepared, some would say eager, to act in this way, it is doubtful whether the money supply could have been properly controlled with existing techniques. In short, the Government entered upon a policy which rested almost entirely on the control of the money supply by choosing a probably inappropriate measure of the money supply and without first ensuring that it had the technical means to control it. After two disastrous years it modified both its monetary target and its methods of control.

The monetarist experiment in the United Kingdom is likely to stand or fall by its success in defeating inflation, for inflation is the wagon to which the monetarists have hitched their star.

Analysis of the nature of inflation shows that it is essentially a reactive process, sustained, in the United Kingdom, by a demand for an unrealistic real wage. The defeat, or control, of inflation, depends, therefore on a successful intervention in the reactive process, and, in particular, on finding a way to restrain the demands for a real wage higher than the economy can bear. One such way would be an incomes policy. But a careful examination of the nature of wage bargaining leads to the conclusion that for perfectly legitimate and understandable reasons, trade unions' attitudes make an incomes policy difficult to achieve and sustain.

The combination of full employment and a powerful trade union movement makes it extremely hard to achieve stable prices. Indeed, it has long been recognised that the coexistence of these three – full employment, union power and stable prices – forms a sort of Bermuda triangle into which economists disappear without trace. Keynes labelled the problem political rather than economic. What monetarists have sought to do is to reclaim it for economists, by offering a monetary solution. And it is perfectly understandable that they should do so, for whatever else is obscure about inflation, it is evident that political solutions to it, by which I mean incomes policies, imposed on or negotiated with the unions, have failed to halt it for very long.

The difficulty with the monetarist solution is, as our analysis shows, that some measure of co-operation from the unions is a *necessary* condition for its success. And since a fully efficient incomes policy would be a *sufficient* instrument to control inflation, monetary policy is a second best solution. To put it another way, if we have no incomes policy and no (or a weak) monetary policy, we are in trouble. If we have a strong monetary policy and no incomes policy we are also in trouble because we may defeat inflation but at considerable cost. If we have a strong monetary policy *and* an incomes policy, we shall succeed. But if we have a really effective incomes policy we do not need a strong monetary policy.

Monetary policy works by attacking two corners of the inflationary triangle: full employment and union power. Since I shall almost certainly be misunderstood at this point let me make it as clear as I can that I am not saying that monetarism, or this Conservative Government, sets out to create unemployment. Unemployment follows as a consequence of a tight monetary policy and an uncooperative trade union movement. It is important to distinguish between the *intentions* of the Government and the *consequences* of monetarism. Unemployment is a consequence, not a policy objective.

Unemployment reduces pressure simultaneously on prices and on costs by lowering the pressure of demand for both goods and services. It therefore reduces *de facto* the power of the unions (*de jure* methods of reducing union power are something else, and beyond the scope of this book).

By modifying the behaviour of firms in passing on price increases and the behaviour of labour in demanding wage increases, monetarism effectively interrupts the reactive process of inflation.

Thus monetarism does not so much solve the problem of reconciling full employment, union power and stable prices, as abolish it. If full employment does not exist and union power is weakened then the problem of non-stable prices *from those causes* goes away.

While British monetarism may be judged on its success against inflation its deeper purpose is to arrest the decline of British industry and to regenerate the economy. Yet the monetary squeeze, whose severity appears to have been masked because it was measured by the wrong monetary aggregate, bit most fiercely on the private sector, while the public sector was hardly affected. The Public Sector Borrowing Requirement for 1980–81 which had been put at not more than £8½ billion in the Budget of March 1980 turned out at over £13 billion. To fund this borrowing as far as possible by sales of debt to the non-bank public very high rates of interest had to be maintained, perpetuating the squeeze on the private sector. Moreover, the high interest rates attracted considerable inflows of capital from abroad, forcing up the rate of exchange, making exports more difficult, imports easier and reducing output in the export and import competing industries. The high rate of exchange did, however, help to reduce the rate of inflation. Both effects will be reversed by a fall in the exchange rate.

To the committed monetarist the high rates of interest and the high exchange rate are part of the monetarist discipline, at least in the transitional phase, and are to be welcomed in so far as, as good disciplines should, they induce better behaviour in the shape of tougher and more cost-conscious management, better working methods, more realistic trade union attitudes, and so. While this sort of effect has been apparent in some of our exporting industries, the British monetarists have nevertheless emasculated the discipline by continuing to pour quite vast amounts of money into uncompetitive industries. By Friedmanian standards we are not monetarists at all. Nor have the British monetarists had much success in reducing the size of the public sector; a few quangos have been killed off, a few public enterprises sold off, some at bargain prices. But the great monolith of the public sector remains largely untouched, and probably untouchable.

The verdict on monetarism is not yet in nor, so far as its success in the regeneration of British industry is concerned, can it be for some years. What it has done so far is to confirm monetarist theory in so far as that theory predicts that strict control of the money supply will first reduce output and then, after a lag, prices. But this result has come about despite the fact that the monetary aggregate chosen by the Government has not in fact been controlled. That would appear to be irrelevant to the result achieved. But what is undeniable is that, for one reason or another, the country has experienced a very severe recession. And there must be few economists, of whatever label, who would not expect a severe recession to have precisely these results. The argument is not about whether an inflation can be halted by depressing an economy and creating unemployment but about whether that is the most sensible way to do it. You do not need to be a monetarist to create a recession: even a

Keynesian could do it. The trouble, some would say, is that he wouldn't.

The monetarist church has much in common with the religions that have haunted man. A prophet appears, offering salvation in return for faith: there are mysteries, into which it is wise not to enquire too deeply; no one has ever returned from the other side. There is a sophisticated doctrine for the theologians and a simpler credo for the priests. The subtle teachings of the prophet solidify into dogma. There are schisms. Whether God exists or not is of no consequence: it is enough to believe that he exists. It is faith that comforts the faithful; and rational expectations that cure inflation.

If, being apparently incapable of defeating inflation by rational means, we require a faith, then monetarism is as good as any and, if it works, will have served a useful purpose. Whether it works or not, we shall have learned something. Sir Dennis Robertson observed that 'Highbrow opinion is like a hunted hare; if you stand still long enough it will come back to the place it started from.' I would prefer to regard the process as helical: we may return to the same point on the circle, but higher up.

Notes

1. 'The Balance of Payments of the United States'. Published posthumously, *Economic Journal*, Vol. LVI, No. 222 June 1946, pp.172–87.
2. GT, concluding paragraph.

Bibliography

'A man' said Dr Johnson, 'will turn over half a library to make one book.' And that, in the sense that I have picked the brains of other authors, is how this book has been made. In another sense it is not true at all; for the library of economics is vast, and I have read only a tiny part of it. What books, then, should I list? I could list those books that I have read and that have helped my understanding; or I could make a probably longer list of those books that I ought to have read and have not, but that *you* ought to read. In the end the only sensible thing to do seemed to be to list only those books, articles and publications quoted or referred to in the text and notes. To that rule there must be one exception: the indispensable study by Leijonhufvud which, strangely, gets no specific mention in the text.

Ball R. J. and Doyle, Peter (eds), *Inflation*, Penguin 1969.

Bank of England, *Quarterly Bulletin*, (BEQB) various issues; 'Methods of monetary control', 24 Nov. 1980, republished in BEQB, Dec. 1980.

— and HM Treasury, *Monetary Control*, Cmnd. 7858, 20 Mar. 1980.

Barclays Bank Ltd, *Barclays Review*, various issues.

Blackaby, Frank, 'Incomes and inflation', in J. Robinson (ed.), *After Keynes*, Oxford: Blackwell 1973.

Burton, John, 'Positively Milton Friedman'. A discussion paper prepared for J. R. Shackleton and G. Locksley (eds), *Twelve Contemporary Economists*, Macmillan 1981.

Central Statistical Office, *United Kingdom Balance of Payments*, HMSO, *Financial Statistics*, various issues; *Economic Trends*, various issues.

Congdon, Tim, *Monetarism: An Essay in Definition*, Centre for Policy Studies 1978.

Croome, David R., and Johnson, Harry G. (eds), *Money in Britain 1959–1969*, Oxford University Press 1970.

Day, Prof. A.C.L., *Outline of Monetary Economics*, Clarendon Press 1957.

Doyle, Peter, *see* Ball and Doyle.

Friedman, Prof. Milton, *The Quantity Theory of Money – A Re-Statement*; (ed.) *Studies in the Quantity Theory of Money*; 'Statement on monetary theory and policy', in *Employment Growth and Price Levels*, US Govt Printing Office; 'Memorandum' submitted to the Treasury and Civil Service Committee, June 1980. H of C 720 Aug. 1980.

— and Rose Friedman, *Free to Choose*, Secker and Warburg 1980.

Galbraith, Prof. J. K., Article (no title) in *Observer Business*, 31 Aug. 1980, p. 15.

Harrod, Sir R. F., *The Life of John Maynard Keynes*, Macmillan 1951.

Heilbroner, Robert L., *The Great Economists*, Eyre and Spottiswoode 1955

Hicks, Prof. Sir J., *The Crisis in Keynesian Economics*, Oxford: Blackwell 1974; 'The formation of an economist', *Banca Nazionale del Lavoro*, Sept. 1979.

Hume, David, (1711–1776) Essay, 'Of Money'

Hutchison, Prof. T. W., *Economics and Economic Policy in Britain 1946–66*, George Allen and Unwin 1968; *Keynes v. the 'Keynesians'* . . .?, The Institute of Economic Affairs 1977.

Johnson, Prof. Harry G., *On Economics and Society*, The University of Chicago Press 1975 (includes 'The Keynesian Revolution and the Monetarist Counterrevolution'); *see also* Croome and Johnson.

Kahn, R. F., 'The relation of home investment to unemployment', *Economic Journal* 1937; 'On re-reading Keynes', *Proceedings of the British Academy*, Vol. LX, 1974.

Kaldor, Prof. Lord, 'Memorandum' submitted to the Treasury and Civil Service Committee, July 1980, H of C 720, Aug. 1980.

Keynes, J. M., *The Collected Writings of John Maynard Keynes*, edited for the Royal Economic Society by Elizabeth Johnson and Donald Moggridge, Macmillan and St Martins Press; *General Theory of Employment, Interest and Money*, Macmillan 1936; *Essays in Persuasion*, Macmillan 1931; 'After the General Theory', *Quarterly Journal of Economics*, Feb. 1937; 'The balance of payments of the United States', *Economic Journal*, Vol. LVI, 222, June 1946; 'How to Avoid a Slump', three articles in *The Times* 12, 13, 14 Jan. 1937; 'Borrowing for defence: is it inflation?; *The Times* 11 Mar. 1937.

Keynes, Milo (ed.), *Essays on John Maynard Keynes*, Cambridge University Press 1975.

Lipsey, Prof. Richard G., *An Introduction to Positive Economics*, (3rd edn), Weidenfeld and Nicolson, 1971.

Leijonhufvud, A., *On Keynesian Economics and the Economics of Keynes: A Study in Monetary Theory*, Oxford University Press 1968.

Moggridge, Prof. Donald E., 'Keynes: The Economist', in *Keynes: Aspects of the man and his work*, Macmillan 1974; *Keynes*, Fontana/Collins 1976 (contains useful 'Notes on Further Reading').

Morton, W. A., 'Trade Unionism, Full Employment and Inflation; *American Economic Review* Vol. 40 (1950). In Ball and Doyle.

O'Brien, D. P., *The Classical Economists*, Clarendon Press, Oxford 1975.

Patinkin, Prof. Don, 'The Chicago tradition, the Quantity Theory, and Friedman', *Journal of Money and Credit* 1, Feb. 1969.

Peden, G. C., 'Keynes, the Treasury and Unemployment in the later nineteen-thirties', *Oxford Economic Papers*, Vol. 32, No. 1 Mar. 1980.

Radcliffe, The Rt. Hon., the Lord, GBE, [Chairman of the] *Committee on the Working of the Monetary System Report*, Cmnd. 827, Aug. 1959, HMSO.

Robinson, Prof. Austen, 'A personal view' in Milo Keynes, op. cit.

Robinson, Joan (ed.), *After Keynes*, Oxford: Blackwell 1973.

Rose, Prof. Harold, *Barclays Review*, May 1981 and other issues.

Shackle, Prof. G.L.S., *The Years of High Theory*, Cambridge University Press 1967; 'Evolution of thought in economics', in *Banca Nationale del Lavoro*, No. 132, 1980.

Skidelsky, Prof. Robert, 'The Reception of the Keynesian Revolution', in Milo Keynes, op. cit.

Smith, Adam, *An Inquiry into the Nature and Causes of the Wealth of Nations*, Henry Frowde, Oxford University Press 1904.

HM Treasury, *Financial Statement and Budget Reports*, 1980, 81, 82; *Economic Progress Report*, No. 123, Jul. 1980; Press Notices, various.

Treasury and Bank of England, *Monetary Control*, Command 7858, 20 Mar. 1980, HMSO.

Treasury and Civil Service Committee of The House of Commons *Memorandum on Monetary Policy*, Vol. I, H of C 720; Vol. II, H. of C 720–II; *Monetary Policy*, Vol. I, H of C 163–I; Vol. II, H of C 163–II; Vol. III H of C 163–III.

Index

vii Keynes & ... & expands on ...

2-4 Mankiw & Keynes

13-4 Wages & economic theory & Say's law

15-6 The Real System of Marketing — national ... no ...

32-5 the Multiplier

38-9 income & saving

41-2 Money is what you define money to be

43-5 liquidity preference

46-8 The general theory

48-50 Effective demand

43,51 Currency

55-6 Hoard the money 5 years

57-8 Keynes on War & ballot ...

59 Keynes & ...in a boom

68 ...on elasticity

69 A misguided welfare in forces

71-3 Mankiw 85-7, 123

80-2 Keynes on supply, ...& the common

90,110 Diggers about desiring money

92-3 the Radclyffe Commith . 106

73-6 Sterling M3

94-6 The money supply

96-8 Govt...with the PSBR & getting it wrong 100-1

100-1 The Bank on the effects of high interest rates & recession

104-5 the forecasting trying to control liabilities rather than assets

106 A good summary

111 The burden of public debt

112,135 galloon

112-6 ...the monetary targets 117-9, 124, 128-30

117 ...on english

117-22 ...& wages

120-1 gold ...

123 The ... & the Bank of England

124-31 the MTFS

135-4 ...

146-7 Purchasing power of the pound since 1920

155-6-7 Conclusion on ...policy

15860 ...involuntary unemployment & the real wage 163-5

178-9 The exchange rate & the money supply

188-202 The Keynes school

196,199-201 the anti-monetarist

205-6 the classical self-equilibrating system

208-9 Mankiw, how ... & it might ...

209 ...& monetarism ,& supply ... & govt chose

209-10, 211 the government's ... 212

213 the monetarist theory